P9-CET-535

Privilege

Privilege

A Reader

SECOND EDITION

Michael S. Kimmel and Abby L. Ferber,
EDITORS

WESTVIEW PRESS

A Member of the Perseus Books Group

Copyright © 2010 by Westview Press
Published by Westview Press,
A Member of the Perseus Books Group

All rights reserved. Printed in the United States of America. No part of this book
may be reproduced in any manner whatsoever without written permission
except in the case of brief quotations embodied in critical articles and reviews.
For information, address Westview Press, 2465 Central Avenue, Boulder,
Colorado 80301.

Find us on the World Wide Web at www.westviewpress.com.

Westview Press books are available at special discounts for bulk purchases in the
United States by corporations, institutions, and other organizations. For more
information, please contact the Special Markets Department at the Perseus
Books Group, 2300 Chestnut Street, Suite 200, Philadelphia, PA 19103, or call
(800) 810-4145, ext. 5000, or e-mail special.markets@perseusbooks.com.

Library of Congress Cataloging-in-Publication Data

Privilege a reader / Michael S. Kimmel and Abby L. Ferber, editors. — 2nd ed.
    p. cm.
Includes index.
ISBN 978-0-8133-4426-3 (alk. paper)
1. Social classes—United States. 2. United States—Social conditions—1980–
I. Kimmel, Michael S. II. Ferber, Abby L., 1966–
HN90.S6P75 2010
305.0973—dc22
                                                              2009038768

10 9 8 7 6 5 4 3 2

*For Eddie Moore Jr., founder and director
of the White Privilege Conference, visionary leader,
and relationship builder.*
—A. L. F.

*And for Harry Brod, who has been a mentor
in understanding the intersectional position
of the superordinate.*
—M. S. K.

Contents

III. Examining Intersections

IV. Moving Forward

Credit Lines

CHAPTER 1
"White Privilege and Male Privilege," by Peggy McIntosh. Copyright © 1988 by Peggy McIntosh, Working Paper 189, Wellesley College. Center for Research on Women, Wellesley College, Wellesley, MA 02481.

CHAPTER 2
"The Black Male Privileges Checklist," by Jewel Woods. Copyright © 2008 by Renaissance Male Project. Updated and revised version reprinted by permission of the author.

CHAPTER 3
"Why Are Droves of Unqualified, Unprepared Kids Getting into Our Top Colleges? Because Their Dads Are Alumni," by John Larew. Reprinted with permission from the *Washington Monthly*. Copyright © by Washington Monthly Publishing, LLC, 1200 18th Street, Suite 330, Washington, DC 20036; (202) 955-9010. www.washingtonmonthly.com.

CHAPTER 4
"On Being Okie," by Roxanne Dunbar-Ortiz. Adapted from *Red Dirt: Growing Up Okie,* 2nd Edition. University of Oklahoma Press, 2006. Copyright Roxanne Dunbar-Ortiz. Reprinted by permission of the author.

CHAPTER 5

"Becoming 100 Percent Straight," by Michael A. Messner. Reprinted by permission of the author.

CHAPTER 6

"The Heterosexual Questionnaire," by M. Rochlin. Reprinted by permission of the author.

CHAPTER 7

"Privilege, Power, Difference, and Us," in *Privilege, Power and Difference,* by Allan Johnson. Copyright © 2001 by McGraw-Hill. Reprinted with permission from the McGraw-Hill Companies.

CHAPTER 8

"How Jews Became White," by Karen Brodkin Sacks. This is a revised and expanded version of a paper published in *Jewish Currents* in June 1992 and delivered at the 1992 meetings of the American Anthropological Association in the session "Blacks and Jews, 1992: Reaching Across the Cultural Boundaries," organized by Angela Gilliam. Copyright Karen Brodkin Sacks. Reprinted by permission of the author.

CHAPTER 9

"Masculinity as Homophobia," by Michael S. Kimmel. Reprinted from *Theorizing Masculinities* by Harry Brod. Copyright © 1994 by Sage Publications.

CHAPTER 10

"On White Pride, Reverse Racism, and Other Delusions," by Tim Wise. Copyright © 2009 by Tim Wise. Reprinted by permission of the author.

CHAPTER 11

"Class: Still Alive and Reproducing in the United States." Adapted from "Class in the United States: Not Only Alive but Reproducing" by Diana Kendall, originally published in *Research in Social Stratification and Mobility,* Vol. 24, Issue 1, 2006, pp. 89–104. Reprinted by permission of the author.

CHAPTER 12

"Invisibility/Hypervisibility: The Paradox of Normative Whiteness," by Maureen T. Redding. Adapted from an article originally published in *Transformations* 9, no. 2 (Fall 1998): 55–64. Copyright New Jersey Project, September 30, 1998. Provided by ProQuest LLC. Reprinted by permission of the author.

CHAPTER 13

"Class and Race: The New Black Elite." Copyright © 1999 by bell hooks. From *Where We Stand: Class Matters* by bell hooks. Reprinted by permission of Routledge, Inc., The Taylor & Francis Group.

CHAPTER 14

"How Gay Stays White and What Kind of White It Stays," by Allan Bérubé, from *The Making and Unmaking of Whiteness,* Brander Rasmussen et al., eds., pp. 234–265. Copyright © 2001, Duke University Press. All rights reserved. Reprinted by permission of the publisher.

CHAPTER 15

"Subverting Racism from Within," by Becky Thompson, from *Becoming and Unbecoming White: Owning and Disowning a Racial Identity,* Christine Clark and James O'Donnell, eds. Copyright © 1999, Bergin & Garvey. Reprinted by permission of the publisher.

CHAPTER 16

"Toward a New Vision: Race, Class, and Gender as Categories of Analysis and Connection," by Patricia Hill Collins. Adapted from an article originally published in *Race, Sex, and Class 1,* no. 1, Fall 1993. Reprinted by permission of the author.

CHAPTER 17

"Dismantling Privilege and Becoming an Activist." Copyright © 2009 by Abby L. Ferber. Printed by permission of the author.

Preface

Confronting privilege makes one extremely uncomfortable—a productive and healthy discomfort, to be sure, but discomfort just the same. And, once the process of confrontation has begun, it's difficult to resist what a colleague once called "premature self-congratulation," the often earnest, if insufferable proclamations of the newly converted. "Thanks so much for bringing this privilege thing to our attention," we might be tempted to say, "we'll take it from here."

The ability to live with that discomfort and without that preachy self-congratulatory tone is the hallmark of the works we have collected here. It is a struggle, both political and stylistic, and we hope that these essays will prove to be as unsettling and as comforting as they have been for the editors.

After all, we have found our way to these essays, and to editing this book together, because we have been so unsettled and challenged by the process of confronting our own unearned privilege. Many of the essays in this volume have actually helped us as we first began to think our ways through these issues.

They've challenged us, but they've also supported and sustained our own inquiries. They've reminded us that we have a lot of company in this project. We are grateful to the authors in this volume for their courage and wisdom.

The process of producing a book like this is as much form as it is content, as much practical concerns as it is political engagement, as much technical as theoretical. And we have been ably assisted by Aprie Wells, Abby's student work-study assistant, and Shari Patterson, her departmental program assistant who helped tremendously with the logistics of the book's assembly.

We've also had a dedicated staff at Westview Press. At its inception Jill Rothenberg embraced the project, and our editor, Alex Masulis, guided it through two editions with care and grace. Sandra Beris and Erica Lawrence oversaw production and promotion respectively, with one eye on the keenest of detail and the other on the big picture. We're grateful to them all.

In addition, Abby thanks: Sandi Morgen and The Center for the Study of Women in Society at the University of Oregon, and Elizabeth Higginbotham and the Transforming the Curriculum summer program at the University of Memphis, both of which were instrumental in providing support and crucial networks as I began to discover and research privilege, including my own. I also want to thank Andrea Herrera, my friend and colleague, the Department of Sociology at the University of Colorado at Colorado Springs, and the many other truly outstanding faculty who make my work there so gratifying. Of course, I also must recognize the never-ending love, encouragement, and accommodation of Joel and Sydney, who keep me grounded and sane. And finally, I want to thank my mentor, Michael Kimmel, whose work has been truly inspirational for me, and whose friendship, support, and collaboration I value more than he can possibly know.

Michael thanks: a group of friends (Lillian Rubin, Troy Duster, Martin Sanchez-Jankowski, Angela Harris, Jerry Karabel, and the late and dearly missed Michael Rogin) who began discussing whiteness a decade ago in a little study group; my long-time friends Harry Brod, Marty Duberman, Michael Kaufman, Mike Messner, and Don Sabo, who have sustained the endless conversation; my European colleagues and friends, notably Harry Ferguson, Jeff Hearn, Oystein Holter, Lars Jalmert, Jorgen Lorentzen; and my friend and co-editor Abby Ferber, for her inspiring work and deeply ethical vision. I'm also grateful to my colleagues and students at SUNY Stony Brook, my intellectual home for more than a decade, and to Amy and Zachary, my home forever.

We live in a nation where—despite all ideological assertions about meritocracy, about how individuals are free to rise as high as they can, based solely on their individual achievements—race, class, and gender are the best predictors of what we social scientists call "life chances"—your level of wealth, your occupation, health, even marital happiness. Ours is a nation where characteristics of your birth are the best predictors of where you will end up at your death. On the other hand, we actually do want to live in a nation in which those ideals of individual achievement are actually realized, where talent, motivation, ambition, and hard work actually do pay off, where race, class, sexuality and gender predict very little about your economic and social life.

Together, we dedicate the book to all the people who have influenced us in our work to make the unseen visible, teaching the privileged about privilege, and to those who virtually had no choice but to examine race, class, gender, and sexuality as they daily confront the effects of inequality based on those experiences.

In dedicating this book to them, we, the editors, also rededicate ourselves to the task of continuing to explore and challenge privilege—personally, politically, and pedagogically.

Introduction
Toward a Pedagogy of the Oppressor

Michael S. Kimmel

This Breeze at My Back

To run or walk into a strong headwind is to understand the power of nature. You set your jaw in a squared grimace, your eyes are slits against the wind, and you breathe with a fierce determination. And still you make so little progress.

To walk or run with that same wind at your back is to float, to sail effortlessly, expending virtually no energy. You do not feel the wind; it feels you. You do not feel how it pushes you along; you feel only the effortlessness of your movements. You feel like you could go on forever. Only when you turn around and face that wind do you realize its strength.

Being white, or male, or heterosexual in the United States is like running with the wind at your back. It feels like just plain running, and we rarely, if ever, get a chance to see how we are sustained, supported, and even propelled by that wind.

This book tries to make the wind visible.

In recent years, the study of discrimination based on gender, race, class, and sexuality has mushroomed, creating a large body of literature and a growing number of courses addressing these issues. Of course, the overwhelming majority of the research has explored the experiences of the victims of racism, sexism, homophobia, and class inequality. It is the "victims," the "others," who have begun to make these issues visible to contemporary scholars and lay people alike. This is, of course, politically as it should be: The marginalized always understand first the mechanisms of their marginalization; it remains for them to convince the center that the processes of marginalization are in fact both real and remediable.

When presented with evidence of systematic discrimination, majority students are often indifferent, and sometimes defensive and resistant. "What does this have to do with me?" they ask. The more defensive among them immediately mention several facts that they believe will absolve them of inclusion into the superordinate category. "My family never owned slaves," "I have a gay friend," and "I never raped anyone" are fairly typical responses. Virtually none seems able to discuss white people as a group. Some will assert that white people differ dramatically from one another, that ethnicity and religion are more important than race. Others maintain that white people, as a group, are not at all privileged. And virtually all agree that racism is a problem of individual attitudes, prejudiced people, and not a social problem.

Such statements are as revealing as they are irrelevant. They tell us far more about the way we tend to individualize and personalize processes that are social and structural. They also tell us that majority students resist discussing inequality because it would require that they feel guilty for crimes someone else committed.

Even those students who are willing to engage with these questions tend to personalize and individualize them. They may grudgingly grant the systematic nature of inequality, but to them, racism, sexism, heterosexism are bad attitudes held by bad people. They are eager to help those bad people see the error of their ways and change their attitudes to good attitudes. This usually will come about through better education.

Students who are white, heterosexual, male, or middle class need to go further. We need to see how we are stakeholders in the understanding of structural inequality, how the dynamics that create inequality for some also benefit others. Privilege needs to be made visible.

Exciting new research in a variety of disciplines, including sociology, literature, and cultural studies, is examining what previously passed as invisible, neutral, and universal. We now can see how the experience of "privilege" also shapes the lives of men, white people, and heterosexuals. Such an inquiry, long overdue, will enable us to more fully understand the social dynamics of race, class, gender, and sexuality and how they operate in all our lives.

Making Privilege Visible

To be white, or straight, or male, or middle class is to be simultaneously ubiquitous and invisible. You're everywhere you look, you're the standard against which everyone else is measured. You're like water, like air. People will tell you they went to see a "woman doctor," or they will say they went to see "the doctor." People will tell you they have a "gay colleague," or they'll tell you about a "colleague." A white person will be happy to tell you about a "black friend," but when that same person simply mentions a "friend," everyone will assume the person is white. Any college course that doesn't have the word "woman" or "gay" or "minority" in its title is a course about men, heterosexuals, and white people. But we call those courses "literature," "history," or "political science."

This invisibility is political. I first confronted this invisibility in the early 1980s, when I participated in a small discussion group on feminism. In one meeting, a white woman and a black woman were discussing whether all women were, by definition, "sisters" because they all had essentially the same experiences and because all women faced a common oppression by men. The white woman asserted that the fact that they were both women bonded them, in spite of racial differences. The black woman disagreed.

"When you wake up in the morning and look in the mirror, what do you see?" she asked.

"I see a woman," replied the white woman.

"That's precisely the problem," responded the black woman. "I see a *black* woman. To me, race is visible every day, because race is how I am *not* privileged in our culture. Race is invisible to you, because it's how you are privileged. It's why there will always be differences in our experience."

As I witnessed this exchange, I was startled, and groaned—more audibly, perhaps, than I had intended. Someone asked what my response had meant.

"Well," I said, "when I look in the mirror, I see a human being. I'm universally generalizable. As a middle-class white man, I have no class, no race, and no gender. I'm the generic person!"

Sometimes I like to think that it was on that day that I *became* a middle-class white man. Sure, I had been all those before, but they had not meant much to me. Since then, I've begun to understand that race, class, and gender didn't refer only to other people, who were marginalized by race, class, or gender privilege. Those terms also described me. I enjoyed the privilege of invisibility. The very processes that confer privilege to one group and not another group are often invisible to those on whom that privilege is conferred. What makes us marginal or powerless are the processes we see, partly because others keep reminding us of them. Invisibility is a privilege in a double sense—describing both the power relations that are kept in place by the very dynamics of invisibility, and in the sense of privilege as luxury. It is a luxury that only white people have in our society not to think about race every day of their lives. It is a luxury that only men have in our society to pretend that gender does not matter.

That discussion took place over twenty years ago, but I was reminded of it recently when I went to give a guest lecture for a female colleague at my university. We teach the same course on alternate semesters, and she always gives a guest lecture for me, and I give one for her. As I walked in to the auditorium, one student looked up at me and said "Oh, finally, an objective opinion!"

All that semester, whenever my colleague opened her mouth, what this student saw was "a woman"—biased. But when I walked in, I was, in this student's eyes, *unbiased,* an objective opinion—disembodied Western rationality, standing right in front of the class! This notion that middle-class white men are "objective" and everyone else is "biased" is the way that inequalities are reproduced.

Let me give you another example of how power is so often invisible to those who have it. Most of you have e-mail addresses, and you write e-mail messages to people all over the world. You've probably noticed that there is one big difference between e-mail addresses in the United States and e-mail addresses of people in other countries: their addresses have "country codes" at the end of the address. So, for example, if you were writing to someone in South Africa, you'd put "za" at the end, or "jp" for Japan, or "uk" for England (United Kingdom), or "de" for Germany (Deutschland).

Even if you write to someone at a university in another country, you have to use the country code; for example, it would be "ac.uk" for an academic institution in Britain, or "edu.au" for an educational institution in Australia. But when you write to people in the United States, the e-mail address ends with "edu" for an educational institution, "org" for an organization, "gov" for a federal government office, or "com" or "net" for commercial Internet service providers. Why is it that the United States doesn't have a country code?

It is because when you are the dominant power in the world, everyone else needs to be named. When you are "in power," you needn't draw attention to yourself as a specific entity; rather, you can pretend to be the generic, the universal, the generalizable. From the point of view of the United States, all other countries are "other" and thus need to be named, marked, noted. Once again, privilege is invisible. In the world of the Internet, as Michael Jackson sang, "we are the world."

There are consequences to this invisibility: Privilege remains invisible, and it is hard to generate a politics of inclusion from invisibility. The invisibility of privilege means that many men, like many white people, become defensive and angry when confronted with the statistical realities or the human consequences of racism or sexism. Since our privilege is invisible, we may become defensive. Indeed, we may even feel like victims ourselves.

In his recent book *The Envy of the World,* *Newsweek* writer Ellis Cose underscores this issue when he counsels other black people in this way:

> Given such psychologically complex phenomena as racial guilt and racial pain, you are not likely to find much empathy or understanding when you bring racial complaints to whites. The best you can generally hope for is an awkward silence accompanied by the suspicion that you are crying wolf (excerpted in *Newsweek,* January 28, 2002, p. 52).

I was reminded of this reaction from the privileged recently when I appeared on a television talk show opposite three "angry white males"—three men who felt that they had been the victims of workplace discrimination. The show's title, no doubt to entice a large potential audience, was "A Black Woman Took My Job." In my comments to these angry men, I invited them to consider what the word "my" meant in that title, that they felt that the jobs were originally "theirs," that they were entitled to them, and that when some "other" person—black, female—got the job, that person was really taking "their" job. But by what right is that his job? The answer is by convention, by a historical legacy of such profound levels of discrimination that we have needed decades of affirmative action policies to even begin to make slightly more level a playing field that has tilted so decidedly in one direction.

Our task is to begin to make visible the privilege that accompanies and conceals that invisibility.

The Invisible Knapsack

One way to understand how privilege works—and how it is kept invisible—is to look at the way we think about inequality. We always think about inequality from the perspective of the one who is hurt by the inequality, not the one who is helped. Take, for example, wage inequality based on gender. We're used to hearing that women make about 71 cents for every dollar a man makes. In that statistic women's wages are calculated as a function of men's wages; men's wages are the standard (the $1) against which women's wages are calculated. In this way, the discrimination against women is visible—doing the same job, they earn less, just because they are women.

But what if we changed the statistics? What if we expressed men's wages as a function of women's wages? What if we said that for every dollar earned by a woman, men make $1.34? Then it wouldn't be the discrimination that was visible—it would be the privilege. Just for being a male, a male worker received an additional 34 cents. This is what sociologist R. W. Connell calls the "masculinity dividend"—the unearned benefits that accrue to men, just for being men.

One could easily apply this model to race, class, and sexuality. Several of the authors in this volume probe their own experiences as a way to enable others to see what had earlier been invisible. Perhaps no one has done that more successfully than Peggy McIntosh, in her celebrated essay on what she calls the "invisible knapsack." The invisible knapsack contains all the little benefits that come to us simply because we are white, or straight, or middle class, or male. We have to open up that knapsack, dump its contents out and take a look at all the very different ways that these ascribed characteristics (those we were born with) have become so obscured that we have come to believe that the events of our lives are the results of achieved characteristics.

Making gender, race, class, and sexuality visible—both as the foundations of individual identity and as the social dynamics of inequality—means that we pay some attention to the differences among them as well. Often students argue that gender is different from race, because, as one of my students put it, "you have to live every day with a person of the opposite sex, but you don't have to live so intimately with people of another race." Leaving aside the potential racism or heterosexism of such a statement—one might, after all, live intimately with someone of a different race, or one might not live with someone of the opposite sex—this student does point to an important issue: *Just as forms of inequality are not all the same, forms of privilege are not all the same.*

For example, two of the four dimensions we discuss in this book—race and gender—appear, at least on the surface, to be based on characteristics that are present at birth: one's sex or race. That means that they are always visible to an observer. (Well, at least nearly always. There are, of course, people who change their biological sex, or who dress differently from established norms, and those who try and pass as members of another race, and even those, like Michael Jackson, who seemed to be using aggressive surgical techniques to be taken for the other.) Thus the privileges based on gender or race may feel even more invisible, because those who are privileged by race and gender did nothing to earn their privilege.

The other two dimensions—sexuality and class—are not immediately visible to the public. One can more easily pass as a member of a privileged group. But sexual minorities also may feel that their identity is not a social construction but the fulfillment of an inner essence—that is, it is more like race and gender than it is like class. While race and biological sex may be evidently inborn, biologically based, or "God-given," sexuality also feels like that, to both heterosexuals and homosexuals.

Class, however, does not. In fact, class seems to feel exactly the opposite—as a status that one was not born with but that one has earned. Class is less visible than the other dimensions because while our objective position in an economic order depends on empirically measurable criteria (income, occupation, education), class as an everyday experience rests on other people's evaluation of our presentation of self. It is far easier to pass as something we are not—both for people of modest means to affect the lifestyle of the rich and famous and for very wealthy people to affect the styles of the poor. While most of us would like to have everyone think we are wealthier than we actually are, it is often the case that the truly wealthy want everyone to think they are *less* wealthy than they are. We may dress "up" while they dress "down."

Often we will associate ourselves with the trappings of the class to which we aspire as opposed to the class from which we actually come. Take, for example, fashion. I am reasonably certain that most of the readers of this essay have at some point in their lives gone bowling. And I am equally certain that very few readers, if any, have ever played polo. And yet I would bet that many of you would be very happy to shell out a lot of money for a garment that identified you as a polo player (for example, a Ralph Lauren "Polo" shirt with a little polo player on it) than for an equally well-made garment with a little bowler on it. In fact, you would be eager to pay a premium on that Polo shirt precisely because the brand has become associated with a class position to which you can only aspire.

Class can be concealed and class feels like something we have earned all by ourselves. Therefore, class privilege may be the one set of privileges we are least interested in examining because they feel like they are ours by right, not by birth. All the more reason to take a look at class.

The Souls of White (and Straight and Middle-Class and Male) Folk

This is a difficult thing to do, and there is no question that it will make us feel uncomfortable. It's unpleasant to acknowledge that all the good things that have happened to you are not simply the result of your hard work and talent and motivation but the result of something that you had no power over. Sometimes it will make us feel guilty, other times defensive. Sometimes we just feel powerless. "What can I possibly do to change this massive system of inequality?"

In a culture such as ours, all problems are thought to be individual problems, based on bad attitudes, wrong choices, or our own frailties and addictions. When confronted with structural or social problems, we think either that the solutions are either aggregated individual solutions—*everyone* needs to change their attitudes—or that there are no solutions. A single, lone individual has no chance, we think, to change the system. "You can't fight City Hall."

We feel powerless, impotent. We can become mired in guilt. Some people argue that guilt is a negative emotion, and that we shouldn't have to feel guilty for the things that happened generations—even centuries—ago.

Occasionally, someone is moved by that guilt to attempt to renounce his or her privilege. Some books now counsel us to become "race traitors" or to "refuse" to be a man.

And sometimes a posture of self-negation feels moral and self-righteous. Guilt isn't always a "bad" emotion after all. Consider how you might feel about a German student who said that he or she really didn't want to feel guilty about genocide in World War II. "After all, I personally never sent a Jew to the gas chambers." Or a white South African who proclaimed that he or she never actually benefited from apartheid, since they got their job and their wealth by virtue of their own hard work and determination.

Guilt may be appropriate, even a necessary feeling—for a while. It does not freeze us in abjection but can motivate us to transform the circumstances that made us feel guilty in the first place, to make connections between our experiences and others' and to become and remain accountable to the struggles for equality and justice around the world. Guilt can politicize us. (Perhaps that's one reason why we often resist it.)

While noble in intention, however, this posture of guilty self-negation cannot be our final destination as we come to understand how we are privileged by race, class, gender, and sexuality. Refusing to be men, white, or straight does neither the privileged nor the unprivileged much good. One can no more renounce privilege than one can stop breathing. It's in the air we breathe.

And it is embedded in the social architecture that surrounds us. Renouncing privilege ultimately substitutes an individual solution for a structural and social problem. Inequality is structural and systematic as well as individual and attitudinal. Eliminating inequalities involves more than changing everyone's attitudes.

Trying to rid oneself of bad attitudes, renouncing one's unearned privilege also brings us no further than the feelings of impotent despair that we often feel in the face of such overwhelming systemic problems. We feel lonely. We feel isolated from our friends, our families, or our classmates. It's the loneliness of the long-distance runner against the wind.

The struggles against inequality are collective struggles, enormous social movements that unite people across geography, race, religion, class, sexuality, and gender. Participating in these struggles to end inequality brings one into the long history of those who have stood alongside the victims of oppression, those who have added their voices to the voices of those who had earlier been silenced. Examining our privilege may be uncomfortable at first, but it can also be energizing, motivating, and engaging.

A Method of Analysis

In this book, we try to use an "intersectional approach" to explore the ways in which race, class, gender, and sexuality intersect and interact. This theory was first developed by women of color who argued that the variables of race, class, gender, and sexuality could not be separated in understanding their experiences. This approach was a response to the traditional studies of race, which focused on race alone, and usually ended up focused narrowly on men of color, and women's studies, which often focused only on the experiences of white women. But some of these theorists asked different questions: Where does the black person stop and the woman begin? How can one analyze the totality of one's experience without examining the ways in which all these categories coincide, collide, contradict?

This volume uses an intersectional analysis to explore the ways in which race, gender, class, and sexuality interact in the lives of those who are privileged by one or more of these identities. We bring together leading thinkers and writers on all of these dimensions, to examine both the parallels and the ruptures among these different but connected relationships. Written both personally and analytically, these essays can bring the reader inside the experiences and enable us all to begin to theorize our own lives as well as to explore the ways in which these systems intersect in people's lives.

Ultimately, we believe that examining the arenas in which we are privileged as well as those in which we are not privileged will enable us to understand our society more fully and engage us in the long historical process of change.

PART ONE

Making Privilege Visible

1
White Privilege and Male Privilege

*A Personal Account of
Coming to See Correspondences
Through Work in Women's Studies*

Peggy McIntosh

Through work to bring materials and perspectives from Women's Studies into the rest of the curriculum, I have often noticed men's unwillingness to grant that they are over-privileged in the curriculum, even though they may grant that women are disadvantaged. Denials which amount to taboos surround the subject of advantages which men gain from women's disadvantages. These denials protect male privilege from being fully recognized, acknowledged, lessened, or ended.

Thinking through unacknowledged male privilege as a phenomenon with a life of its own, I realized that since hierarchies in our society are interlocking, there was most likely a phenomenon of white privilege which was similarly denied and protected, but alive and real in its effects. As a white person, I realized I had been taught about racism as something which puts others at a disadvantage, but had been taught not to see one of its corollary aspects, white privilege, which puts me at an advantage.

I think whites are carefully taught not to recognize white privilege, as males are taught not to recognize male privilege. So I have begun in an untutored way to ask what it is like to have white privilege. This paper is a partial record of my personal observations, and not a scholarly analysis. It is based on my daily experiences within my particular circumstances.

I have come to see white privilege as an invisible package of unearned assets which I can count on cashing in each day, but about which I was "meant" to remain oblivious. White privilege is like an invisible weightless knapsack of special provisions, assurances, tools, maps, guides, codebooks, passports, visas, clothes, compass, emergency gear, and blank checks.

Since I have had trouble facing white privilege, and describing its results in my life, I saw parallels here with men's reluctance to acknowledge male privilege. Only rarely will a man go beyond acknowledging that women are [dis]advantaged to acknowledging that men have unearned advantage, or that unearned privilege has not been good for men's development as human beings, or for society's development, or that privilege systems might ever be challenged and *changed.*

I will review here several types or layers of denial which I see at work protecting, and preventing awareness about, entrenched male privilege. Then I will draw parallels, from my own experience, with the denials which veil the facts of white privilege. Finally, I will list 46 ordinary and daily ways in which I experience having white privilege, within my life situation and its particular social and political frameworks.

Writing this paper has been difficult, despite warm receptions for the talks on which it is based.[1] For describing white privilege makes one newly accountable. As we in Women's Studies work to reveal male privilege and ask men to give up some of their power, so one who writes about having white privilege must ask, "Having described it, what will I do to lessen or end it?"

The denial of men's overprivileged state takes many forms in discussions of curriculum change work. Some claim that men must be central in the curriculum because they have done most of what is important or distinctive in life or in civilization. Some recognize sexism in the curriculum but deny that it makes male students seem unduly important in life. Others agree that certain *individual* thinkers are blindly male-oriented but deny that there is any systemic tendency in disciplinary frameworks or epistemology to over-empower men as a group. Those men who do grant that male privilege takes institutionalized and embedded forms are still likely to deny that male hegemony has opened doors for them personally. Virtually all men deny that male overreward alone can explain men's centrality in all the inner sanctums of our most powerful institutions. Moreover, those few who will acknowledge that male privilege systems have over-empowered them usually end up doubting that we could dismantle these privilege systems. They may say they will work to improve women's status, in the society or in the university, but they can't or won't support the idea of lessening men's. In curricular terms, this is the point at which they say that they regret they cannot use any of the interesting new scholarship on women because the syllabus is full. When the talk turns to giving men less cultural room, even the most thoughtful and fair-minded of the men I know well tend to reflect, or fall back on, conservative assumptions about the inevitability of present gender relations and distributions of power, calling on precedent or sociobiology and psychobiology to demonstrate that male domination is natural and follows inevitably from evolutionary pressures. Others resort to arguments from "experience" or religion or social responsibility or wishing and dreaming.

After I realized, through faculty development work in Women's Studies, the extent to which men work from a base of unacknowledged privilege, I understood that much of their oppressiveness was unconscious. Then I remembered the frequent charges from women of color that white women whom they encounter are oppressive. I began to understand why we are justly seen as oppressive, even when we don't see ourselves that way. At the very least, obliviousness of one's privileged state can make a person or group irritating to be with. I began to count the ways in which I enjoy unearned skin privilege and have been conditioned into oblivion about its existence, unable to see that it put me "ahead" in any way, or put my people ahead, overrewarding us and yet also paradoxically damaging us, or that it could or should be changed.

My schooling gave me no training in seeing myself as an oppressor, as an unfairly advantaged person, or as a participant in a damaged culture. I was taught to see myself as an individual whose moral state depended on her individual moral will. At school, we were not taught about slavery in any depth; we were not taught to see slaveholders as damaged people.

Slaves were seen as the only group at risk of being dehumanized. My schooling followed the pattern which Elizabeth Minnich has pointed out: whites are taught to think of their lives as morally neutral, normative, and average, and also ideal, so that when we work to benefit others, this is seen as work which will allow "them" to be more like "us." I think many of us know how obnoxious this attitude can be in men.

After frustration with men who would not recognize male privilege, I decided to try to work on myself at least by identifying some of the daily effects of white privilege in my life. It is crude work, at this stage, but I will give here a list of special circumstances and conditions I experience which I did not earn but which I have been made to feel are mine by birth, by citizenship, and by virtue of being a conscientious law-abiding "normal" person of good will. I have chosen those conditions which I think in my case *attach somewhat more to skin-color privilege* than to class, religion, ethnic status, or geographical location, though of course all these other factors are intricately intertwined. As far as I can see, my Afro-American co-workers, friends, and acquaintances with whom I come into daily or frequent contact in this particular time, place, and line of work cannot count on most of these conditions.

1. I can if I wish arrange to be in the company of people of my race most of the time.
2. I can avoid spending time with people whom I was trained to mistrust and who have learned to mistrust my kind or me.
3. If I should need to move, I can be pretty sure of renting or purchasing housing in an area which I can afford and in which I would want to live.
4. I can be pretty sure that my neighbors in such a location will be neutral or pleasant to me.
5. I can go shopping alone most of the time, pretty well assured that I will not be followed or harassed.
6. I can turn on the television or open to the front page of the paper and see people of my race widely represented.
7. When I am told about our national heritage or about "civilization," I am shown that people of my color made it what it is.

8. I can be sure that my children will be given curricular materials that testify to the existence of their race.

9. If I want to, I can be pretty sure of finding a publisher for this piece on white privilege.

10. I can be pretty sure of having my voice heard in a group in which I am the only member of my race.

11. I can be casual about whether or not to listen to another woman's voice in a group in which she is the only member of her race.

12. I can go into a music shop and count on finding the music of my race represented, into a supermarket and find the staple foods which fit with my cultural traditions, into a hairdresser's shop and find someone who can cut my hair.

13. Whether I use checks, credit cards, or cash, I can count on my skin color not to work against the appearance of financial reliability.

14. I can arrange to protect my children most of the time from people who might not like them.

15. I do not have to educate my children to be aware of systemic racism for their own daily physical protection.

16. I can be pretty sure that my children's teachers and employers will tolerate them if they fit school and workplace norms; my chief worries about them do not concern others' attitudes toward their race.

17. I can talk with my mouth full and not have people put this down to my color.

18. I can swear, or dress in second hand clothes, or not answer letters, without having people attribute these choices to the bad morals, the poverty, or the illiteracy of my race.

19. I can speak in public to a powerful male group without putting my race on trial.

20. I can do well in a challenging situation without being called a credit to my race.

21. I am never asked to speak for all the people of my racial group.

22. I can remain oblivious of the language and customs of persons of color who constitute the world's majority without feeling in my culture any penalty for such oblivion.

23. I can criticize our government and talk about how much I fear its policies and behavior without being seen as a cultural outsider.

24. I can be pretty sure that if I ask to talk to "the person in charge," I will be facing a person of my race.

25. If a traffic cop pulls me over or if the IRS audits my tax return, I can be sure I haven't been singled out because of my race.

26. I can easily buy posters, post-cards, picture books, greeting cards, dolls, toys, and children's magazines featuring people of my race.

27. I can go home from most meetings of organizations I belong to, feeling somewhat tied in rather than isolated, out-of-place, outnumbered, unheard, held at a distance, or feared.

28. I can be pretty sure that an argument with a colleague of another race is more likely to jeopardize her chances for advancement than to jeopardize mine.

29. I can be pretty sure that if I argue for the promotion of a person of another race, or a program centering on race, this is not likely to cost me heavily within my present setting, even if my colleagues disagree with me.

30. If I declare there is a racial issue at hand, or there isn't a racial issue at hand, my race will lend me more credibility for either position than a person of color will have.

31. I can choose to ignore developments in minority writing and minority activist programs, or disparage them, or learn from them, but in any case, I can find ways to be more or less protected from negative consequences of any of these choices.

32. My culture gives me little fear about ignoring the perspectives and powers of people of other races.

33. I am not made acutely aware that my shape, bearing, or body odor will be taken as a reflection on my race.

34. I can worry about racism without being seen as self-interested or self-seeking.

35. I can take a job with an affirmative action employer without having my co-workers on the job suspect that I got it because of my race.

36. If my day, week, or year is going badly, I need not ask of each negative episode or situation whether it has racial overtones.

37. I can be pretty sure of finding people who would be willing to talk to me and advise me about my next steps, professionally.

38. I can think over many options, social, political, imaginative, or professional, without asking whether a person of my race would be accepted or allowed to do what I want to do.

39. I can be late to a meeting without having the lateness reflect on my race.

40. I can choose public accommodation without fearing that people of my race cannot get in or will be mistreated in the places I have chosen.

41. I can be sure that if I need legal or medical help, my race will not work against me.

42. I can arrange my activities so that I will never have to experience feelings of rejection owing to my race.

43. If I have low credibility as a leader I can be sure that my race is not the problem.

44. I can easily find academic courses and institutions which give attention only to people of my race.

45. I can expect figurative language and imagery in all of the arts to testify to experiences of my race.

46. I can choose blemish cover or bandages in "flesh" color and have them more or less match my skin.

I repeatedly forgot each of the realizations on this list until I wrote it down. For me, white privilege has turned out to be an elusive and fugitive subject. The pressure to avoid it is great, for in facing it I must give up the myth of meritocracy. If these things are true, this is not such a free country; one's life is not what one makes it; many doors open for certain people through no virtues of their own. These perceptions mean also that my moral condition is not what I had been led to believe. The appearance of being a good citizen rather than a troublemaker comes in large part from having all sorts of doors open automatically because of my color.

A further paralysis of nerve comes from literary silence protecting privilege. My clearest memories of finding such analysis are in Lillian Smith's unparalleled *Killers of the Dream* and Margaret Andersen's review of Karen and Mamie Fields' *Lemon Swamp.* Smith, for example, wrote about walking toward black children on the street and knowing they would step into the gutter; Andersen contrasted the pleasure which she, as a white child, took on summer driving trips to the South with Karen Fields' memories of driving in a closed car stocked with all necessities lest, in stopping, her black family should suffer "insult, or worse." Adrienne Rich also recognizes and writes about daily experiences of privilege, but in my observation, white women's writing in this area is far more often on systemic racism than on our daily lives as light-skinned women.[2]

In unpacking this invisible knapsack of white privilege, I have listed conditions of daily experience which I once took for granted, as neutral, normal, and universally available to everybody, just as I once thought of a male-focused curriculum as the neutral or accurate account which can speak for all. Nor did I think of any of these perquisites as bad for the holder. I now think that we need a more finely differentiated taxonomy of privilege, for some of these varieties are only what one would want for everyone in a just society, and others give license to be ignorant, oblivious, arrogant, and destructive. Before proposing some more finely tuned categorization, I will make some observations about the general effects of these conditions on my life and expectations.

In this potpourri of examples, some privileges make me feel at home in the world. Others allow me to escape penalties or dangers which others suffer. Through some, I escape fear, anxiety, or a sense of not being welcome or not being real. Some keep me from having to hide, to be in disguise, to feel sick or crazy, to negotiate each transaction from the position of being an outsider or, within my group, a person who is suspected of having too close links with a dominant culture. Most keep me from having to be angry.

I see a pattern running through the matrix of white privilege, a pattern of assumptions which were passed on to me as a white person. There was one main piece of cultural turf; it was my own turf, and I was among those who could control the turf. I could measure up to the cultural standards and take advantage of the many options I saw around me to make what the culture would call a success of my life. *My skin color was an asset for any move I was educated to want to make,* I could think of myself as "belonging" in major ways, and of making social systems work for me. I could freely disparage, fear, neglect, or be oblivious to anything outside of the dominant cultural forms. Being of the main culture, I could also criticize it fairly freely. My life was reflected back to me frequently enough so that I felt, with regard to my race, if not to my sex, like one of the real people.

Whether through the curriculum or in the newspaper, the television, the economic system, or the general look of people in the streets, we received daily signals and indications that my people counted, and that others *either didn't exist or must be trying, not very successfully, to be like people of my race.* We were given cultural permission not to hear voices of people of other races, or a tepid cultural tolerance for hearing or acting on such voices. I was also raised not to suffer seriously from anything which darker-skinned people might say about my group, "protected," though perhaps I should more accurately say *prohibited,* through the habits of my economic class and social group, from living in racially mixed groups or being reflective about interactions between people of differing races.

In proportion as my racial group was being made confident, comfortable, and oblivious, other groups were likely being made inconfident, uncomfortable, and alienated. Whiteness protected me from many kinds of hostility, distress, and violence, which I was being subtly trained to visit in turn upon people of color.

For this reason, the word "privilege" now seems to me misleading. Its connotations are too positive to fit the conditions and behaviors which "privilege systems" produce. We usually think of privilege as being a favored state, whether earned or conferred by birth or luck. School graduates are reminded they are privileged and urged to use their (enviable) assets well. The word "privilege" carries the connotation of being something everyone must want. Yet some of the conditions I have described here work to systematically overempower certain groups. Such privilege simply *confers dominance,* gives permission to control, because of one's race or sex. The kind of privilege which gives license to some people to be, at best, thoughtless, and at worst, murderous should not continue to be referred to as a desirable attribute. Such "privilege" may be widely desired without being in any way beneficial to the whole society.

Moreover, though "privilege" may confer power, it does not confer moral strength. Those who do not depend on conferred dominance have traits and qualities which may never develop in those who do. Just as

Women's Studies courses indicate that women survive their political circumstances to lead lives which hold the human race together, so "underprivileged" people of color who are the world's majority have survived their oppression and lived survivors' lives from which the white global minority can and must learn. In some groups, those dominated have actually become strong through *not* having all of these unearned advantages, and this gives them a great deal to teach the others. Members of so-called privileged groups can seem foolish, ridiculous, infantile, or dangerous by contrast.

I want, then, to distinguish between earned strength and unearned power conferred systemically. Power from unearned privilege can look like strength when it is in fact permission to escape or to dominate. But not all of the privileges on my list are inevitably damaging. Some, like the expectation that neighbors will be decent to you, or that your race will not count against you in court, should be the norm in a just society and should be considered as the entitlement of everyone. Others, like the privilege not to listen to less powerful people, distort the humanity of the holders as well as the ignored groups. Still others, like finding one's staple foods everywhere, may be a function of being a member of a numerical majority in the population. Others have to do with not having to labor under pervasive negative stereotyping and mythology.

We might at least start by distinguishing between positive advantages which we can work to spread, to the point where they are not advantages at all but simply part of the normal civic and social fabric, and negative types of advantage which unless rejected will always reinforce our present hierarchies. For example, the positive "privilege" of belonging, the feeling that one belongs within the human circle, as Native Americans say, fosters development and should not be seen as privilege for a few. It is, let us say, an entitlement which none of us should have to earn; ideally it is an *unearned entitlement*. At present, since only a few have it, it is an *unearned advantage* for them. The negative "privilege" which gave me cultural permission not to take darker-skinned Others seriously can be seen as arbitrarily conferred dominance and should not be desirable for anyone. This paper results from a process of coming to see that some of the power which I originally saw as attendant on being a human being in the United States. consisted in *unearned advantage* and *conferred dominance,* as well as other special circumstances not universally taken for granted.

In writing this paper I have also realized that white identity and status (as well as class identity and status) give me considerable power to choose whether to broach this subject and its trouble. I can pretty well decide whether to disappear and avoid and not listen and escape the dislike I may engender in other people through this essay, or interrupt, take over, dominate, preach, direct, criticize, or control to some extent what goes on in reaction to it. Being white, I am given considerable power to escape many kinds of danger or penalty as well as to choose which risks I want to take.

There is an analogy here, once again, with Women's Studies. Our male colleagues do not have a great deal to lose in supporting Women's Studies, but they do not have a great deal to lose if they oppose it either. They simply have the power to decide whether to commit themselves to more equitable distributions of power. They will probably feel few penalties, whatever choice they make; they do not seem, in any obvious short-term sense, the ones at risk, though they and we are all at risk because of the behaviors which have been rewarded in them.

Through Women's Studies work I have met very few men who are truly distressed about systemic, unearned male advantage and conferred dominance. And so one question for me and others like me is whether we will be like them, or whether we will get truly distressed, even outraged, about unearned race advantage and conferred dominance, and if so, what we will do to lessen them. In any case, we need to do more work in identifying how they actually affect our daily lives. We need more down-to-earth writing by people about these taboo subjects. We need more understanding of the ways in which white "privilege" damages white people, for these are not the same ways in which it damages the victimized. Skewed white psyches are an inseparable part of the picture, though I do not want to confuse the kinds of damage done to the holders of special assets and to those who suffer the deficits. Many, perhaps most, of our white students in the United States. think that racism doesn't affect them because they are not people of color; they do not see "whiteness" as a racial identity. Many men likewise think that Women's Studies does not bear on their own existences because they are not female; they do not see themselves as having gendered identities. Insisting on the universal *effects* of "privilege" systems, then, becomes one of our chief tasks, and being more explicit about the *particular* effects in particular contexts is another. Men need to join us in this work.

In addition, since race and sex are not the only advantaging systems at work, we need to similarly examine the daily experience of having age advantage, or ethnic advantage, or physical ability or advantage related to nationality, religion, or sexual orientation. Prof. Marnie Evans suggested to me that in many ways the list I made also applies directly to heterosexual privilege. This is a still more taboo subject than race privilege: the daily ways in which heterosexual privilege makes married persons comfortable or powerful, providing supports, assets, approvals, and rewards to those who live or expect to live in heterosexual pairs. Unpacking that content is still more difficult, owing to the deeper imbeddedness of heterosexual advantage and dominance, and stricter taboos surrounding these.

But to start such an analysis I would put this observation from my own experience: The fact that I live under the same roof with a man triggers all kinds of societal assumptions about my worth, politics, life, and values, and triggers a host of unearned advantages and powers. After recasting many elements from the original list, I would add further observations like these:

1. My children do not have to answer questions about why I live with my partner (my husband).
2. I have no difficulty finding neighborhoods where people approve of our household.
3. My children are given texts and classes which implicitly support our kind of family unit, and do not turn them against my choice of domestic partnership.
4. I can travel alone or with my husband without expecting embarrassment or hostility in those who deal with us.
5. Most people I meet will see my marital arrangements as an asset to my life or as a favorable comment on my likability, my competence, or my mental health.
6. I can talk about the social events of a weekend without fearing most listeners' reactions.
7. I will feel welcomed and "normal" in the usual walks of public life, institutional and social.
8. In many contexts, I am seen as "all right" in daily work on women because I do not live chiefly with women.

Difficulties and dangers surrounding the task of finding parallels are many. Since racism, sexism, and heterosexism are not the same, the advantaging associated with them should not be seen as the same. In addition, it is hard to disentangle aspects of unearned advantage which rest more on social class, economic class, race, religion, sex, and ethnic identity than on other factors. Still, all of the oppressions are interlocking, as the Combahee River Collective statement of 1977 continues to remind us eloquently.[3]

One fact seems clear about all of the interlocking oppressions. They take both active forms which we can see and embedded forms which, as a member of the dominant group, one is taught not to see. In my class and place, I did not see myself as racist because I was taught to recognize racism only in individual acts of meanness by members of my group, never in invisible systems conferring unsought racial dominance on my group from birth. Likewise, we are taught to think that sexism or heterosexism is carried on only through individual acts of discrimination, meanness, or cruelty toward women, gays, and lesbians, rather than in invisible systems conferring unsought dominance on certain groups. Disapproving of the systems won't be enough to change them. I was taught to think that racism could end if white individuals changed their attitudes; many men think sexism can be ended by individual changes in daily behavior toward women. But a man's sex provides advantage for him whether or not he approves of the way in which dominance has been conferred on his group. A "white" skin in the United States opens many doors for whites whether or not we approve of the way dominance has been conferred on us. Individual acts can palliate, but cannot end, these problems. To redesign social systems, we need first to acknowledge their colossal unseen dimensions. The silences and denials surrounding privilege are the key political tool here. They keep the thinking about equality or equity incomplete, protecting unearned advantage and conferred dominance by making these subjects taboo. Most talk by whites about equal opportunity seems to me now to be about equal opportunity to try to get into a position of dominance while denying that *systems* of dominance exist.

It seems to me that obliviousness about white advantage, like obliviousness about male advantage, is kept strongly inculturated in the United States so as to maintain the myth of meritocracy, the myth that

democratic choice is equally available to all. Keeping most people unaware that freedom of confident action is there for just a small number
of people props up those in power and serves to keep power in the hands
of the same groups that have most of it already. Though systemic change
takes many decades, there are pressing questions for me and, I imagine,
for some others like me, if we raise our daily consciousness on the
perquisites of being light-skinned. What will we do with such knowledge? As we know from watching men, it is an open question whether we
will choose to use unearned advantage to weaken hidden systems of advantage, and whether we will use any of our arbitrarily awarded power
to try to reconstruct power systems on a broader base.

Notes

This paper was funded by the Anna Wilder Phelps Fund through the generosity of
Anna Emery Hanson. I have appreciated commentary on this paper from the
Working Papers Committee of the Wellesley College Center for Research on
Women, from members of the Dodge seminar, and from many individuals, in-
cluding Margaret Andersen, Sorel Berman, Joanne Braxton, Johnnella Butler, San-
dra Dickerson, Marnie Evans, Beverly Guy-Sheftall, Sandra Harding, Eleanor
Hinton Hoytt, Pauline Houston, Paul Lauter, Joyce Miller, Mary Norris, Gloria
Oden, Beverly Smith, and John Walter.

1. This paper was presented at the Virginia Women's Studies Association conference in Richmond in April 1986 and the American Educational Research Association conference in Boston in October 1986 and discussed with two groups of
participants in the Dodge Seminars for Secondary School Teachers in New York
and Boston in the spring of 1987.

2. Andersen, Margaret, "Race and the Social Science Curriculum: A Teaching
and Learning Discussion," *Radical Teacher,* November 1984, pp. 17–20. Smith, Lillian, *Killers of the Dream,* New York, 1949.

3. "A Black Feminist Statement," The Combahee River Collective, pp. 13–22 in
Hull, Scott, Smith, eds., *All the Women Are White, All the Blacks Are Men but Some
of Us Are Brave: Black Women's Studies,* The Feminist Press, 1982.

2

The Black Male Privileges Checklist

Jewel Woods

What does "privilege" have to do with Black men?[1] We understand some kinds of privilege. The twentieth-century white privilege to call a black man "boy" even if that black man happened to be sixty years old or older. The white privilege to drive a car and never have to worry about racial profiling. These are privileges that have nothing to do with what a person has earned but rather are based entirely on race. As African Americans, we have the ability to critique and condemn these types of "unearned assets" because we recognize that these privileges come largely at our expense. We have also learned from social and political movements that have sought to redress these privileges and academic disciplines that have provided us with the tools to critically examine and explore them.

However, there is another type of privilege that has caused untold harm to both black men and women, but our community has not had the benefit of that privilege being challenged by a social and political movement from within, nor has it been given adequate attention within our academic community. The privilege that I am referring to is male privilege. Just as white privilege comes at the expense of African Americans and other people of color, black male privilege comes at the expense of women in general, and black women in particular.

Given the devastating history of racism in this country, it is understandable that getting black men to identify with the concept of male privilege isn't easy! For many of us, the phrase "black male privilege" seems like an oxymoron—three words that simply do not go together. Although it is understandable that some black men are hesitant or reluctant to examine the concept of male privilege, the African American community will never be able to overcome the serious issues we face if we as black men do not confront our role in promoting and sustaining male supremacist attitudes and actions.

Inviting black men and boys into a conversation about male privilege does not deny centuries of discrimination or the burden of racism that we continue to suffer today. As long as a black man can be tasered nine times in fourteen minutes,[2] arrested in his own home for "disorderly conduct,"[3] or receive fewer callbacks for a job than a white man with a felony record,[4] we know that racism that targets black men is alive and kicking.

But race is not the only factor. Examining black male privileges offers black men and boys an opportunity to go beyond old arguments of "personal responsibility" or "blaming the man" to gain a deeper level of insight into how issues of class and race are shaped by gender. *Often times the focus on our experiences of racial oppression removes gender-based domination from the analytical—and the political—eye.*

The items presented on the Black Male Privileges Checklist reflect aspects of black men's lives we take for granted. I offer this checklist based on years of experience working with men and the profound influence of black woman activists and intellectuals such as bell hooks, Angela Davis, Patricia Hill-Collins, Kimberly Crenshaw, and numerous others. I have faith that we as African American men have far more to gain than we have to lose by challenging our male privileges.

I also believe there are more similarities between men than there are differences. Therefore, many items on the Black Male Privileges Checklist apply to men generally, and others might apply to all men of color. However, because of the specific privileges black men possess in relationship to black women, certain items apply only to black men. *I will leave it up to the reader to determine which items apply only to black men and which items apply to all men of color or men in general.*

The Black Male Privileges Checklist

LEADERSHIP AND POLITICS

1. I don't have to choose my race over my sex in political matters.
2. When I read African American history textbooks, I will learn mainly about black men.
3. When I learn about the Civil Rights and Black Power movements, most of the leaders that I will learn about will be black men.
4. I can rely on the fact that in the nearly one-hundred-year history of national civil rights organizations such as the NAACP and the Urban League, virtually all of the executive directors have been men.
5. I will be taken more seriously as a political leader than black women.
6. I can be pretty sure that all of the "race leaders" I see featured in the media will be men like me.
7. I can live my life without ever having read black feminist authors or knowing about black women's history or black women's issues.
8. I could be a member or an admirer of a black liberation organization such as the Black Panther Party, where an "out" rapist like Eldridge Cleaver could assume a leadership position, without feeling threatened or demeaned because of my sex.
9. I will make more money than black women at equal levels of education and occupation.
10. I know that most of the national "opinion framers" in black America, including talk show hosts and politicians, are men.

BEAUTY

11. I have the ability to define black women's beauty by European standards in terms of skin tone, hair, and body size. In comparison, black women rarely define me by European standards of beauty in terms of skin tone, hair, or body size.
12. I do not have to worry about the daily hassles of having my hair conform to some standard image of beauty the way black women do.

13. I do not have to worry about the daily hassles of being terrorized by the fear of gaining weight. In fact, in many instances bigger is better for my sex.

14. My looks will not be the central standard by which my worth is valued by members of the opposite sex.

SEX AND SEXUALITY

15. I can purchase pornography that typically shows men defiling women by the common practice of the "money shot."

16. I can believe that causing pain during sex is connected with a woman's pleasure without ever asking her.

17. When it comes to sex, if I say "No," chances are that it will not be mistaken for "Yes."

18. If I am raped, no one will assume that "I should have known better" or suggest that my being raped had something to do with how I was dressed.

19. I can use sexist language like bonin', laying the pipe, hittin' it, and banging that convey images of sexual acts based on dominance and performance.

20. I live in a world where polygamy is still an option for men in some countries.

21. I can be involved with younger women socially and sexually and it will be considered normal.

22. In general, the more sexual partners that I have the more stature I receive among my peers.

23. I have easy access to pornography that involves virtually any category of sex where men degrade women, often young women.

24. When I consume pornography, I can gain pleasure from images and sounds of men causing women pain.

POPULAR CULTURE

25. I have the privilege of coming from a tradition of humor based largely on insulting and disrespecting women; especially mothers.

26. I have the privilege of not having black women dress up and play funny characters—often overweight—that are supposed to look like me, for the entire nation to laugh at.

27. When I go to the movies, I know that most of the leads in black films will be men. I can also be confident that all of the action heroes in black films will be men.
28. I can easily assume that most of the artists in hip-hop are members of my sex.
29. I can rest assured that most of the women that appear in hip-hop videos are there solely to please men
30. Most of lyrics I listen to in popular hip-hop perpetuate the ideas of men dominating women, sexually and socially.
31. I can consume and popularize the word pimp, which is based on the exploitation of women, with virtually no opposition from other men.
32. I can hear and use language that refers to women as bitches and ho's, that demeans women, with virtually no opposition from men.
33. I can wear a shirt that others and I commonly refer to as a "wife beater" and never have the language challenged.
34. Many of my favorite movies include images of strength that do not include women and often are based on violence.
35. Many of my favorite genres of films, such as martial arts, are based on male violence.

ATTITUDES/IDEOLOGY
36. I have the privilege to define black women as having "an attitude" without referencing the range of attitudes that black women have.
37. I have the privilege of defining black women's attitudes without defining my attitudes as a black man.
38. I can believe that the success of the black family is dependent on men serving as the head of the family rather than in promoting policies that strengthen black women's independence or that provide social benefits to black children.
39. I have the privilege of believing that a black woman cannot raise a black son to be a man.
40. I have the privilege of believing that a woman must submit to her man.
41. I have the privilege of believing that before slavery, gender relationships between black men and women were perfect.

42. I have the privilege to define ideas such as feminism as being anti-black.

43. I have the privilege of believing that the failure of the black family is due in part to black women not allowing black men to be men.

44. I have the privilege of defining gender roles within the household.

45. I have the privilege of believing that black women are different sexually from other women and judging them negatively based on this belief.

SPORTS

46. I will make significantly more money as a professional athlete than women will.

47. My financial success or popularity as a professional athlete will not be associated with my looks.

48. I can talk about sports or spend large portions of the day playing video games while women are most likely tending to household chores or child care duties.

49. I have the privilege to restrict my displays of emotion to certain spheres, such as sports.

50. If I am a coach, I can motivate, punish, or embarrass a player by saying that the player plays like a girl.

51. Most sports talk show hosts that are members of my race are men.

52. I can rest assured that most of the coaches—even in predominantly female sports within my race—are male.

53. I am able to play sports outside without my shirt on and not worry it will be considered a problem.

54. I am essentially able to do anything inside or outside without my shirt on, whereas women are always required to cover up.

DIASPORA/GLOBAL

55. I have the privilege of not being concerned that I am a member of a sex subjected to mutilation and disfigurement to deny our sexual sensations or to protect our virginity for males.

56. I have the privilege of not having rape be used as a primary tactic or tool to terrorize my sex during war and times of conflict.

57. I have the privilege of not being able to name one female leader in Africa or Asia, past or present, that I pay homage to the way I do male leaders in Africa and/or Asia.
58. I have the ability to travel around the world and have access to women in developing countries both sexually and socially.
59. I have the privilege of being a part of the sex that starts wars and that wields control of almost all the existing weapons of war and mass destruction.

COLLEGE

60. In college, I will have the opportunity to date outside of the race at a much higher rate than black women will.
61. I have the privilege of having the phrase "sowing my wild oats" apply to my sex as if it were natural.
62. I know that the further I go in education the more success I will have with women.
63. By the time I enter college, and even through college, I have the privilege of not having to worry whether I will be able to marry a black woman.
64. In college, I will experience a level of status and prestige that is not offered to black women even though black women may outnumber me and outperform me academically.

COMMUNICATION/LANGUAGE

65. What is defined as "news" in black America is defined by men.
66. I can choose to be emotionally withdrawn and not communicate in a relationship and it may be considered unfortunate, yet normal.
67. I have the privilege of not knowing what words and concepts like patriarchy, misogyny, phallocentric, complicity, colluding, and obfuscation mean.

RELATIONSHIPS

68. I have the privilege of marrying outside my race at a much higher rate than black women.
69. My "strength" as a man is never connected with the failure of the black family, whereas the strength of black women is routinely associated with the failure of the black family.

70. If I am considering a divorce, I know that I have substantially more marriage and cohabitation options than my spouse.

71. Chances are I will be defined as a "good man" by things I do not do as much as what I do. If I don't beat, cheat, or lie, then I am a considered a "good man." In comparison, women are rarely defined as "good women" based on what they do not do.

72. I have the privilege of not having to assume most of the household or child care responsibilities.

CHURCH AND RELIGIOUS TRADITIONS

73. In the black church, the majority of the pastoral leadership is male.

74. In the black church tradition, most of the theology has a male point of view. For example, most will assume that the man is the head of household.

PHYSICAL SAFETY

75. I do not have to worry about being considered a traitor to my race if I call the police on a member of the opposite sex.

76. I have the privilege of knowing men who are physically or sexually abusive to women and yet I still call them friends.

77. I can videotape women in public—often without their consent—with male complicity.

78. I can be courteous to a person of the opposite sex that I do not know and say "hello" or "hi" and not fear that it will be taken as a come-on or fear being stalked because of it.

79. I can use physical violence or the threat of physical violence to get what I want when other tactics fail in a relationship.

80. If I get into a physical altercation with a person of the opposite sex, I will most likely be able to impose my will physically on that person.

81. I can go to parades or other public events and not worry about being physically and sexually molested by persons of the opposite sex.

82. I can touch and physically grope women's bodies in public—often without their consent—with male complicity.

83. In general, I have the freedom to travel in the night without fear of rape or sexual assault.
84. I am able to be out in public without fear of being sexually harassed by individuals or groups of the opposite sex.

Background

The Black Male Privileges Checklist was born out of years of organizing men's groups and the numerous—often heated—conversations I have had with men while using Barry Deutsch's Male Privilege Checklist.[5] In my experience, most men raise objections to at least some items on the Male Privilege Checklist. However, "men of color," especially African American men, often have the sharpest criticisms of the Male Privilege Checklist and the greatest difficulty connecting to the idea of male privilege.

There are many reasons black men are reluctant to identify with the concept of male privilege. One of the most important reasons is that our experience with privilege has largely focused specifically on race, based on a history of political, economic, and military power whites have historically exercised over black life. This conceptualization of privilege has not allowed us to see ourselves as privileged because the focus has been placed largely on white domination. Our inability to have a more expansive understanding of privilege and power has foreclosed important insights into virtually every aspect of black men's lives as well as the lives of other men of color. As black men, we have also been skeptical of profeminist males, most of whom were (and still are) white and middle class. Black men who fought for freedom during the Civil Rights and the Black Power movements were suspicious—to say the least—of the motives of white men requesting that black men give up the privileges they never felt they had. Given the timing of the profeminist male movement and the demographics of these men, it has not been easy to separate the message from the messenger. Black men had a similar reaction to the voices of black feminists, whom we viewed as being influenced by white middle-class feminism. In addition, many of the items on the Male Privilege Checklist simply did not apply to black men and other men of color. As a result, many black men argued that the list should have been called the White Male Privilege Checklist. In light of these considerations, the Black Male Privileges Checklist differs from the Male Privilege Checklist in several respects.

First, it departs from an "either/or" view of privilege that suggests that an individual or a group can only be placed into one category, isolating race or gender and ignoring the ways in which these traits interact in shaping our lives. Therefore, the focus is on privilege*s* and not privilege. It also highlights belief systems that often serve as the basis for justifications and rationalizations of exploitation and discrimination. Second, the Black Male Privileges Checklist takes a life-course perspective, acknowledging the fact that privilege takes on different forms at various points in men's lives. Third, it takes a global perspective to highlight the privilege that black males have as Americans, and the privileges black men share with other men of color worldwide. African American men rarely acknowledge the privilege we have in relationship to people in developing countries—especially women. Too often, our conception of privilege is limited to white men and does not lead us to reflect on the power that men of color in Africa, Asia, and Latin America exercise over women. Finally, it calls for action, not just awareness. We need men of color to be actively involved in social welfare and social justice movements.

As men of color, we have a responsibility to acknowledge that we participate in this sex/gender system even though it offers us little reward. Most African Americans, for example, take for granted the system of capitalism that we all participate in, even though we know that it does not offer us the same rewards that it offers whites. The sex/gender system, which privileges men over women, operates in similar ways for all men. However, black men and other men of color participate in the sex/gender system without receiving the same material and nonmaterial rewards white men do. More importantly, the participation of black men and other men of color in the sex/gender system further weakens communities of color, which already suffer under the weight of racial and class oppression.

Finally, the Black Male Privileges Checklist is a tool that can be used by any individual, group, organization, family, or community interested in black males having greater insight into their individual lives and the collective lives of black women and girls. It is also a living tool that will grow and be amended as more discussion and dialogue occurs. This is the first edition of the Black Male Privileges Checklist, and it will be updated regularly. This checklist was created with black men in mind and does not necessarily capture the experiences and cultural references of other ethnic minority males. I would welcome dialogue with others who are concerned about these constituencies as well.

Notes

1. Please visit our website, http://renaissancemaleproject.com, to view our Teen and Male Youth Privileges Checklist, a historic tool for all young males, schools, community organizations, youth groups, sports teams, and families, that can be used to assist our young males in becoming the type of adult men we want them to be.

2. This case refers to twenty-one-year-old African American male Baron Pikes, who, according to the officer's report, died in police custody after being tasered while lying on the ground in handcuffs. http://www.chicagotribune.com/news/chi-taser_witt-web-jul19,0,2201847.story (retrieved August 1, 2009).

3. Henry Louis Gates Jr., a distinguished African American scholar at Harvard University and editor in chief of the widely read and highly influential online African American news journal TheRoot.com, was arrested at his home for disorderly conduct. http://www.theroot.com/views/roots-editor-chief-arrested (retrieved August 1, 2009).

4. According to research conducted by Princeton University sociologist Devah Pager, white males with criminal felony records received more callbacks for jobs than similarly qualified black males without criminal felony records (Devah Pager, "The Mark of a Criminal Record," *American Journal of Sociology* 108, no. 5 (2003): 937–975.

5. Barry Deutsch, http://www.amptoons.com/blog/the-male-privilege-check list, September 15, 2004 (retrieved May 29, 2009). Barry Deutsch's list was inspired by Peggy McIntosh's 1988 article "White Privilege and Male Privilege: A Personal Account of Coming to See Correspondences through Work in Women's Studies" (Working Paper 189, Wellesley Center for Women, Wellesley, MA), available at mmcintosh@wellesley.edu.

3

Why Are Droves of Unqualified, Unprepared Kids Getting into Our Top Colleges?

Because Their Dads Are Alumni

John Larew

Growing up, she heard a hundred Harvard stories. In high school, she put the college squarely in her sights. But when judgment day came in the winter of 1988, the Harvard admissions guys were frankly unimpressed. Her academic record was solid—not special. Extracurriculars, interview, recommendations? Above average, but not by much. "Nothing really stands out," one admissions officer scribbled on her application folder. Wrote another, "Harvard not really the right place."

At the hyperselective Harvard, where high school valedictorians, National Merit Scholarship finalists, musical prodigies—11,000 ambitious kids in all—are rejected annually, this young woman didn't seem to have much of a chance. Thanks to Harvard's largest affirmative action program, she got in anyway. No, she wasn't poor, black, disabled, Hispanic, native American, or even Aleutian. She got in because her mom went to Harvard.

Folk wisdom at Harvard holds that "Mother Harvard does not coddle her young." She sure treats her grandkids right, though. For more than 40 years, an astounding one-fifth of Harvard's students have received admissions preference because their parents attended the school. Today, these overwhelmingly affluent, white children of alumni—"legacies"—are three times more likely to be accepted to Harvard than high school kids who lack that handsome lineage.

Yalies, don't feel smug: Offspring of the Old Blue are two-and-a-half times more likely to be accepted than their unconnected peers. Dartmouth this year admitted 57 percent of its legacy applicants, compared to 27 percent of nonlegacies. At the University of Pennsylvania, 66 percent of legacies were admitted last year—thanks in part to an autonomous "office of alumni admissions" that actively lobbies for alumni children before the admissions committee. "One can argue that it's an accident, but it sure doesn't look like an accident," admits Yale Dean of Admissions Worth David.

If the legacies' big edge seems unfair to the tens of thousands who get turned away every year, Ivy League administrators have long defended the innocence of the legacy stat. Children of alumni are just smarter; they come from privileged backgrounds and tend to grow up in homes where parents encourage learning. That's what Harvard Dean of Admissions William Fitzsimmons told the campus newspaper, the *Harvard Crimson,* when it first reported on the legacy preference last year. Departing Harvard President Derek Bok patiently explained that the legacy preference worked only as a "tie-breaking factor" between otherwise equally qualified candidates.

Since Ivy League admissions data is a notoriously classified commodity, when Harvard officials said in previous years that alumni kids were just better, you had to take them at their word. But then federal investigators came along and pried open those top-secret files. The Harvard guys were lying.

This past fall, after two years of study, the U.S. Department of Education's Office for Civil Rights (OCR) found that, far from being more qualified or even equally qualified, the average admitted legacy at Harvard between 1981 and 1988 was significantly *less* qualified than the average admitted nonlegacy. Examining admissions office ratings on academics, extracurriculars, personal qualities, recommendations, and other categories, the OCR concluded that "with the exception of the athletic rating, [admitted] nonlegacies scored better than legacies in *all* areas of comparison."

Exceptionally high admit rates, lowered academic standards, preferential treatment . . . hmmm. These sound like the cries heard in the growing fury over affirmative action for racial minorities in America's elite universities. Only no one is outraged about legacies.

- In his recent book, *Preferential Policies,* Thomas Sowell argues that doling out special treatment encourages lackluster performance by the favored and resentment from the spurned. His far-ranging study flits from Malaysia to South Africa to American college campuses. Legacies don't merit a word.
- Dinesh D'Souza, in his celebrated jeremiad *Illiberal Education,* blames affirmative action in college admissions for declining academic standards and increasing racial tensions. Lowered standards for minority applicants, he hints, may soon destroy the university as we know it. Lowered standards for legacies? The subject doesn't come up.
- For all his polysyllabic complaints against preferential admissions, William F. Buckley Jr. (Yale '50) has never bothered to note that son Chris (Yale '75) got the benefit of a policy that more than doubled his chance of admission.

With so much silence on the subject, you'd be excused for thinking that in these enlightened times hereditary preferences are few and far between. But you'd be wrong. At most elite universities during the eighties, the legacy was by far the biggest piece of the preferential pie. At Harvard, a legacy is about twice as likely to be admitted as a black or Hispanic student. As sociologists Jerome Karabel and David Karen point out, if alumni children were admitted to Harvard at the same rate as other applicants, their numbers in the class of 1992 would have been reduced by about 200. Instead, those 200 marginally qualified legacies outnumbered all black, Mexican-American, native American, and Puerto Rican enrollees put together. If a few marginally qualified minorities are undermining Harvard's academic standards as much as conservatives charge, think about the damage all those legacies must be doing.

Mind you, colleges have the right to give the occasional preference—to bend the rules for the brilliant oboist or the world-class curler or the guy whose remarkable decency can't be measured by the SAT. (I happened to benefit from a geographical edge: It's easier to get into Harvard from West Virginia than from New England.) And until standardized tests and grade point average perfectly reflect the character, judgment, and drive of a student, tips like these aren't just nice, they're fair. Unfortunately, the extent of the legacy privilege in elite American colleges suggests something more than the occasional tie-breaking tip. Forget meritocracy. When 20 percent of Harvard's student body gets a legacy preference, aristocracy is the word that comes to mind.

A Caste of Thousands

If complaining about minority preferences is fashionable in the world of competitive colleges, bitching about legacies is just plain gauche, suggesting an unhealthy resentment of the privileged. But the effects of the legacy trickle down. For every legacy that wins, someone—usually someone less privileged—loses. And higher education is a high-stakes game.

High school graduates earn 59 percent of the income of four-year college graduates. Between high school graduates and alumni of prestigious colleges, the disparity is far greater. A *Fortune* study of American CEOs shows the usual suspects—graduates of Yale, Princeton, and Harvard—leading the list. A recent survey of the Harvard Class of 1940 found that 43 percent were worth more than $1 million. With some understatement, the report concludes, "A picture of highly advantageous circumstances emerges here, does it not, compared with American society as a whole?"

An Ivy League diploma doesn't necessarily mean a fine education. Nor does it guarantee future success. What it *does* represent is a big head start in the rat race—a fact Harvard will be the first to tell you. When I was a freshman, a counselor at the Office of Career Services instructed a group of us to make the Harvard name stand out on our resumes: "Underline it, boldface it, put it in capital letters."

Of course, the existence of the legacy preference in this fierce career competition isn't exactly news. According to historians, it was a direct result of the influx of Jews into the Ivy League during the twenties. Until then, Harvard, Princeton, and Yale had admitted anyone who could pass their entrance exams, but suddenly Jewish kids were outscoring the

WASPs. So the schools began to use nonacademic criteria—"character," "solidity," and, eventually, lineage—to justify accepting low-scoring blue bloods over their peers. Yale implemented its legacy preference first, in 1925—spelling it out in a memo four years later: The school would admit "Yale sons of good character and reasonably good record . . . regardless of the number of applicants and the superiority of outside competitors." Harvard and Princeton followed shortly thereafter.

Despite its ignoble origins, the legacy preference has only sporadically come under fire, most notably in 1978's affirmative action decision, *University of California Board of Regents v. Bakke.* In his concurrence, Justice Harry Blackmun observed, "It is somewhat ironic to have us so deeply disturbed over a program where race is an element of consciousness, and yet to be aware of the fact, as we are, that institutions of higher learning . . . have given conceded preferences to the children of alumni."

If people are, in fact, aware of the legacy preference, why has it been spared the scrutiny given other preferential policies? One reason is public ignorance of the scope and scale of those preferences—an ignorance carefully cultivated by America's elite institutions. It's easy to maintain the fiction that your legacies get in strictly on merit as long as your admissions bureaucracy controls all access to student data. Information on Harvard's legacies became publicly available not because of any fit of disclosure by the university, but because a few civil rights types noted that the school had a suspiciously low rate of admission for Asian-Americans, who are statistically stronger than other racial groups in academics.

While the ensuing OCR inquiry found no evidence of illegal racial discrimination by Harvard, it did turn up some embarrassing information about how much weight the "legacy" label gives an otherwise flimsy file. Take these comments scrawled by admissions officers on applicant folders:

- "Double lineage who chose the right parents."
- "Dad's [deleted] connections signify lineage of more than usual weight. That counted into the equation makes this a case which (assuming positive TRs [teacher recommendations] and Alum IV [alumnus interview]) is well worth doing."
- "Lineage is main thing."
- "Not quite strong enough to get the clean tip."

- "Classical case that would be hard to explain to dad."
- "Double lineage but lots of problems."
- "Not a great profile, but just strong enough #'s and grades to get the tip from lineage."
- "Without lineage, there would be little case. With it, we'll keep looking."

In every one of these cases, the applicant was admitted.

Of course, Harvard's not doing anything other schools aren't. The practice of playing favorites with alumni children is nearly universal among private colleges and isn't unheard of at public institutions, either. The rate of admission for Stanford's alumni children is "almost twice the general population," according to a spokesman for the admissions office. Notre Dame reserves 25 percent of each freshman class for legacies. At the University of Virginia, where native Virginians make up two-thirds of each class, alumni children are automatically treated as Virginians even if they live out of state—giving them a whopping competitive edge. The same is true of the University of California at Berkeley. At many schools, Harvard included, all legacy applications are guaranteed a read by the dean of admissions himself—a privilege nonlegacies don't get.

Little White Elis

Like the Harvard deans, officials at other universities dismiss the statistical disparities by pointing to the superior environmental influences found in the homes of their alums. "I bet that, statistically, [legacy qualifications are] a little above average, but not by much," says Paul Killebrew, associate director of admissions at Dartmouth. "The admitted group [of legacies] would look exactly like the profile of the class."

James Wickenden, a former dean of admissions at Princeton who now runs a college consulting firm, suspects otherwise. Wickenden wrote of "one Ivy League university" where the average combined SAT score of the freshman class was 1,350 out of a possible 1,600, compared to 1,280 for legacies. "At most selective schools, [legacy status] doubles, even trebles the chances of admission," he says. Many colleges even place admitted legacies in a special "Not in Profile" file (along with recruited athletes and some minority students), so that when the school's SAT scores are published, alumni kids won't pull down the average.

How do those kids fare once they're enrolled? No one's telling. Harvard, for one, refuses to keep any records of how alumni children stack up academically against their nonlegacy classmates—perhaps because the last such study, in 1956, showed Harvard sons hogging the bottom of the grade curve.

If the test scores of admitted legacies are a mystery, the reason colleges accept so many is not. They're afraid the alumni parents of rejected children will stop giving to the colleges' unending fundraising campaigns. "Our survival as an institution depends on having support from alumni," says Richard Steele, director of undergraduate admissions at Duke University, "so according advantages to alumni kids is just a given."

In fact, the OCR exonerated Harvard's legacy preference precisely because legacies bring in money. (OCR cited a federal district court ruling that a state university could favor the children of out-of-state alumni because "defendants showed that the alumni provide monetary support for the university.") And there's no question that alumni provide significant support to Harvard: Last year, they raised $20 million for the scholarship fund alone.

In a letter to OCR defending his legacies, Harvard's Fitzsimmons painted a grim picture of a school where the preference did not exist—a place peeved alumni turned their backs on when their kids failed to make the cut. "Without the fundraising activities of alumni," Fitzsimmons warned darkly, "Harvard could not maintain many of its programs, including needs-blind admissions."

Ignoring, for the moment, the question of how "needs-blind" a system is that admits one-fifth of each class on the assumption that, hey, their parents might give us money, Fitzsimmons's defense doesn't quite ring true. The "Save the Scholarship Fund" line is a variation on the principle of "Firemen First," whereby bureaucrats threatened with a budget cut insist that essential programs rather than executive perks and junkets will be the first to be slashed. Truth be told, there is just about nothing that Harvard, the richest university in the world, could do to jeopardize needs-blind admissions, provided that it placed a high enough priority on them.

But even more unclear is how closely alumni giving is related to the acceptance of alumni kids. "People whose children are denied admission are initially upset," says Wickenden, "and maybe for a year or two their interest in the university wanes. But typically they come back around when they see that what happened was best for the kids." Wickenden has put his money where his mouth is: He rejected two sons of a Princeton trustee involved in a $420 million fundraising project, not to mention the child of a board member who managed the school's $2 billion endowment, all with no apparent ill effect.

Most university administrators would be loathe to take such a chance, despite a surprising lack of evidence of the legacy/largess connection. Fitzsimmons admits Harvard knows of no empirical research to support the claim that diminishing legacies would decrease alumni contributions, relying instead on "hundreds, perhaps thousands of conversations with alumni whose sons and daughters applied."

No doubt some of Fitzsimmons's anxiety is founded: It's only natural for alumni to want their kids to have the same privileges they did. But the historical record suggests that alumni are far more tolerant than administrators realize. Admit women and blacks? *Well, we would,* said administrators earlier this century—*but the alumni just won't have it.* Fortunately for American universities, the bulk of those alumni turned out to be less craven than administrators thought they'd be. As more blacks and women enrolled over the past two decades, the funds kept pouring in, reaching an all-time high in the eighties.

Another significant historical lesson can be drawn from the late fifties, when Harvard's selectiveness increased dramatically. As the number of applications soared, the rate of admission for legacies began declining from about 90 percent to its current 43 percent. Administration anxiety rose inversely, but Harvard's fundraising machine has somehow survived. That doesn't mean there's *no* correlation between alumni giving and the legacy preference, obviously; rather, it means that the people who would withhold their money at the loss of the legacy privilege were far outnumbered by other givers. "It takes time to get the message out," explains Fitzsimmons, "but eventually people start responding. We've had to make the case [for democratization] to alumni, and I think that they generally feel good about that."

Heir Cut

When justice dictates that ordinary kids should have as fair a shot as the children of America's elite, couldn't Harvard and its sister institutions trouble themselves to "get the message out" again? Of course they could. But virtually no one—liberal or conservative—is pushing them to do so.

"There must be no goals or quotas for any special group or category of applicants," reads an advertisement in the right-wing *Dartmouth Review*. "Equal opportunity must be the guiding policy. Males, females, blacks, whites, Native Americans, Hispanics . . . can all be given equal chance to matriculate, survive, and prosper based solely on individual performance."

Noble sentiments from the Ernest Martin Hopkins Institute, an organization of conservative Dartmouth alumni. Reading on, though, we find these "concerned alumni" aren't sacrificing *their* young to the cause. "Alumni sons and daughters," notes the ad further down, "should receive some special consideration."

Similarly, Harvard's conservative *Salient* has twice in recent years decried the treatment of Asian-Americans in admissions, but it attributes their misfortune to favoritism for blacks and Hispanics. What about legacy university favoritism—a much bigger factor? *Salient* writers have twice endorsed it.

What's most surprising is the indifference of minority activists. With the notable exception of a few vocal Asian-Americans, most have made peace with the preference for well-off whites.

Mecca Nelson, the president of Harvard's Black Students Association, leads rallies for the hiring of more minority faculty. She participated in an illegal sit-in at an administration building in support of Afro-American studies. But when it comes to the policy that Asian-American activist Arthur Hu calls "a 20-percent-white quota," Nelson says, "I don't have any really strong opinions about it. I'm not very clear on the whole legacy issue at all."

Joshua Li, former co-chair of Harvard's Asian-American Association, explains his complacency differently: "We understand that in the future Asian-American students will receive these tips as well."

At America's elite universities, you'd expect a somewhat higher standard of fairness than that—especially when money is the driving force behind the concept. And many Ivy League types *do* advocate for more just and lofty ideals. One of them, as it happens, is Derek Bok. In one of Harvard's annual reports, he warned that the modern university is slowly turning from a truth-seeking enterprise into a money-grubbing corporation—at the expense of the loyalty of its alums. "Such an institution may still evoke pride and respect because of its intellectual achievements," he said rightly. "But the feelings it engenders will not be quite the same as those produced by an institution that is prepared to forgo income, if need be, to preserve values of a nobler kind."

Forgo income to preserve values of a nobler kind—it's an excellent idea. Embrace the preferences for the poor and disadvantaged. Wean alumni from the idea of the legacy edge. And above all, stop the hypocrisy that begrudges the great unwashed a place at Harvard while happily making room for the less qualified sons and daughters of alums.

After 70 years, it won't be easy to wrest the legacy preference away from the alums. But the long-term payoff is as much a matter of message as money. When the sons and daughters of today's college kids fill out *their* applications, the legacy preference should seem not a birthright, but a long-gone relic from the Ivy League's inequitable past.

4
On Being Okie

Roxanne Dunbar-Ortiz

White trash: I believe the first time I heard that term was when I saw *Gone with the Wind,* referring to some pretty creepy people, dirt poor, sneaking, conniving, violent tenant farmers, or perhaps migrant cotton pickers. At the time I saw the movie my father was alternately a tenant farmer, migrant cotton picker, and ranch hand, but I did not for one minute identify with those whom the planters and the enslaved Africans called "white trash."

I identified with Scarlet, with the O'Hara family, the original Scots-Irish settlers. The fact that my father's ancestors were original Scots-Irish old settlers was what made me feel superior. And those characterized as "white trash" in *Gone with the Wind* were surely also descendants of Scots-Irish old settlers. Their sons would die fighting to defend the very slave-owning ruling class that kept them poor. Their greatest heroes had been Confederate irregulars during the war and afterwards mythologized outlaws like Jesse James.

Often I asked my mother why my father's family name, Dunbar, was shared by a black person. In English class we read the poems of African-American poet Paul Laurence Dunbar. I hoped my mother would say he was a relative of ours because I loved his poetry. But she said that my

Dunbar ancestors were "Scotch-Irish" and had once owned huge planta-
tions and many slaves and that slaves took the names of the masters.

"How do we know we're related to the masters and not the slaves?" I
would ask.

"Because you are white," my part-Indian mother would answer.

I grew up in rural Oklahoma. We Okies are those tough, land-poor los-
ers whose last great hope in the American dream was born and died with
the "opening" of Oklahoma and Indian territories. Our great shame, like
all "white trash" and colonial dregs around the world, is poverty, that is,
"failure" within a system that purports to favor us. The dregs of colonialism, those who did not and do not "make it," being the majority in some
places, like most of the United States, represent evidence of the lie of the
American dream.

According to historian James Gregory in his definitive study, *American
Exodus: The Dust Bowl Migration and Okie Culture in California,* by 1950
four million people or nearly a quarter of all persons born in Oklahoma,
Texas, Arkansas, or Missouri lived outside that region. A third of them settled in California while most of the others moved to Arizona, New Mexico,
Oregon, and Washington. The best-known period of this trek westward is
the period of the Dust Bowl, the 1930s, when the majority of the migrants
first camped, and then settled mainly in the agricultural valleys of California, but Oklahoma settlers had already been moving west ever since they began homesteading in Oklahoma in the 1890s. During World War II many of
the Central Valley Dust Bowl migrants moved nearer the defense plants, particularly around Los Angeles while a half-million more Southwestern migrants, dubbed "defense Okies," arrived to take wartime jobs. The great
majority of them maintained ties back home.

The core group of those designated as "Okies" are descendants of Ulster-
Scots—"Scotch-Irish"—colonial settlers.[1] Usually the Ulster-Scots descendants say their ancestors came to North America from Ireland, but their trek
was more complicated than that. The Ulster-Scots were a people born and
bred of empire. They were Protestant Scottish settlers in the English "plantation" of Ulster in Northern Ireland in the early 1600s. A bitter war with the
indigenous Irish of Ulster in the last years of the reign of Elizabeth I had
ended in an English victory. A half-million acres of land in Northern Ireland
were settled ("planted") under English protection; these settlers who con-
tracted with the devil of early colonialism came from western Scotland.

By 1630, the English and Scots population settled in Ulster was larger than British settlement in all North America—21,000 English and 150,000 Lowland Scots. In 1641, the indigenous Irish rebelled and killed ten thousand settlers. The response of the Puritan English revolutionary government of Cromwell was fierce. The Puritan policy of exterminating Indians in North America was similar, Richard Slotkin argues, to Puritan policy in Ireland, "where systematic assaults were made on Celtic tribalism, native bardic myth-historians were forbidden to sing, isolated clans were exterminated, and the rest of the population was ravaged. Cromwell even attempted to establish a wild Irish reservation in western Ireland."

So the Ulster-Scots were already seasoned colonialists before they filled the ranks of the British settlers to North America. Before ever meeting American Indians, these Ulster-Scots had perfected scalping for bounty on the Irish. Later, during the early nineteenth century, after the United States was independent of Britain, Irish Catholics would immigrate in the millions, but the Ulster-Scots were another breed—they were the foot soldiers of empire; the Ulster-Scots and their progeny formed the shock troops of the "westward movement," that is, empire.

Ulster-Scot immigration to North America represented a mass movement between 1720 and the War of Independence. Most of them headed for the western borders of the colonies and built communities on the frontier, where they predominated. During the French and Indian War of 1754–1763 the English armies and colonial militias were largely made up of Ulster-Scots. By the time of US independence, Scots, mainly Ulster-Scots, made up around one-sixth of the population of the thirteen colonies, and, in some states like Pennsylvania, a third. During the Revolution most Scottish settlers—Lowlander and Highlander, older settlers and newcomers—remained loyal to the English Crown. The Ulster-Scots, however, were in the forefront of the struggle for independence and formed the backbone of Washington's fighting forces. Most of the names at Valley Forge were Scots-Irish, my ancestors. They saw themselves, and their descendants see themselves, as the true and authentic patriots, the ones who spilled blood for independence and spilled rivers of blood to acquire Indian land, who won the land by "blood-right," leaving "bloody footprints" across the continent. The books written about the frontier settlers fill libraries, but none fulfill the dream of Oscar Ameringer, immigrant from Bavaria and US Socialist Party leader during my grandfather's Wobbly days:

> I wish someone would look up the names on the roster of Washington's army at Valley Forge and trace the bloody footprints of their descendants across the North American continent until they were washed up and washed out on the shore of the Pacific. What an all-American Odyssey it would make! What a great history of the Rise and Fall of American Civilization.

During the last two decades of the eighteenth century, first- and second-generation Ulster-Scots continued to move westward into the Ohio Valley, West Virginia, Kentucky, and Tennessee. They were the predominant element in the westward population movement, maintaining many of the Scots ways, with non-Scots settlers tending to be absorbed (like Daniel Boone, whose heritage was English and Welsh). Ulster-Scots were overwhelmingly frontier settlers rather than scouts, explorers, or fur traders. They cleared forests, built log cabins, and killed Indians, forming a wall of protection for the new US and during times of war employing their fighting skills effectively. They restlessly moved three or four times before settling at least semi-permanently.

The majority of Ulster-Scot settlers were cash-poor and had to indenture themselves to pay for their passage to North America. But once settled they came to predominate, not only as soldier-settlers, but also as contributors in the fields of medicine, religion and education. Perhaps most important, by the end of the eighteenth century the Scottish Presbyterian Church was the largest, strongest and most influential church next to New England's Congregationalist Church. Ulster-Scot membership in the Presbyterian Church waned on the frontier, but the new evangelical sects retained some Calvinist doctrines, particularly the notion of the people of the covenant, commanded by God to go into the wilderness to build the new Israel.

Many descendants of the frontier trekkers moved on from Kentucky and Tennessee to Missouri and Arkansas (including Daniel Boone himself in his old age) and then moved on to Oklahoma during the late nineteenth and early twentieth centuries. This was the trek of my ancestors. Breaking every treaty with the Indians, the federal government allowed the settlers to overrun Oklahoma and Indian territories. Millions of landless farmers made the Run to stake their claims, but only a fraction acquired land, or held on to it. In 1898, the Oklahoma settlers showed their appreciation—a third of Teddy Roosevelt's "Rough Riders" who invaded Cuba were recruited from Oklahoma Territory.

But Oklahoma was where the American dream had come to a halt. For nearly three hundred years, the English Crown and then the United States had offered free or cheap land to British and Ulster-Scot settlers, then to Germans and Scandinavians, then to Polish and Czech peasants. If a farming family fell on hard times or wanted greater opportunity, they picked up and moved on, homesteading newly "opened" territory. By 1880 all the arable land of the continent was owned—much of it by larger operators—and millions were landless. While many of those pushed off the land poured into the cities to work, most stayed in rural areas as tenants, sharecroppers, migrant farm workers, cowpunchers, and miners, and later as roughnecks and roustabouts in the oil fields.

Okies and other descendants of the trekker culture do not think of ourselves as foot soldiers of empire, nor is that the image of us that dominates the popular imagination. We consider ourselves to be the true native-born Americans, the personification of what America is supposed to be, and we know that means being Scots-Irish original settlers, those who fought for and won the continent.

Okies are thus the latter-day carriers of America's national origin myth, a matrix of stories that attempts to justify conquest and settlement, transforming the white frontier settler into an "indigenous people," believing that they are the true natives of the continent, much as those other Calvinist settlers, the South African Boers, regard themselves as the "true" children of Israel, established by a God-given Covenant.

However, self-blame, a sprinkling of the white-skin privilege of scapegoating with license to violence against people of color, and serving as cops and in the military conspire to neutralize or redirect our anger. But above all it's that dream and the ideology, the "sacred" origin myth—the religion of "Americanism"—which keeps us doped and harmless, that and alcohol and drugs and cheap consumer items, especially sex and violence. But without the dream/ideology, none of the other tricks would work.

I consider myself fortunate to have been thrown into the volatile 1960s civil rights, anti–Vietnam War, and women's liberation movements in which I experienced the non-benign nature of Americanism. Yet through it all I have tried to figure out the role that working class whites play. On the night of the assassination of Martin Luther King, Jr., alienation from my own past and from everything about the United States and its history ravaged my mind. Of course my vitriolic negation of my people was a negation of myself and was by no means the final word. My ambivalence to my heritage remains alive and well—maddening as ever—today in my middle age.

The poor whites I come from, Okies and their descendants, were those who formed the popular base for the post–World War II rise of the hard right in Orange County, California. Richard Nixon the anti-Communist was their man. They were the "little people" and "silent majority" addressed by Nixon as President, then by Ronald Reagan. They were among the bigots, including my father, who supported George Wallace. During the 1980s, they helped swell the ranks of the Christian Coalition, promoting anti-abortion and anti-gay initiatives. They fall in and out of the owning and working class, unreliable in union struggles. Depending on economic times they may be self-employed or reluctantly working for a boss, but their dream is always to acquire land or property. We are descendants of peasants and cling to that world view mixed with a common history of fighting to acquire land, blood for land, to seize the promised land, implement the Covenant. We are the true Chosen People.

A populist tradition is associated with poor whites, yet often they hate the rich only out of envy. Hostile to "big government," they are in the vanguard of defending their country, claiming to want to "save" it, or to "restore" it. As Okie country artist Merle Haggard sings: "When you're runnin' down my country, hoss, you're walkin' on the fightin' side of me." Many have been eager cannon fodder as well as officers in US foreign wars, believing they are the designated beneficiaries of the theft of land from Indians and to the booty of empire, the whole world their stage.

The only tangible advantage for most has been the color of their skin and the white supremacy, particularly toward African Americans, that pervades the culture; what they are *not*—black, Asian, foreign born—is as important as what they are—white, "true" Americans—in their sense of propriety and self-esteem. These are not insignificant rewards.

Survival dynamics are acknowledged and well-known about communities of color in the United States but are hardly known to exist with poor whites. That hasn't always been so; during the three periods of leftist surges in the twentieth century (the first two decades, the 1930s, and the 1960s), great attention and tribute were paid to the internal dynamics of poor white families and communities, to the point of romanticization. Because social and economic status are so shaky for poor whites and self-blame or scapegoating so prevalent, class consciousness is damaged. The false consciousness of poor whites in the US is an example, in Marxian terms, of "superstructure" (ideology) overriding "economic base," or economic self-interest.

Despite fantasies of and occasional success in becoming a movie or sports star and other get-rich-quick schemes, the two most successful means of class-climbing for poor whites, like other poor groups in the US, are marrying up and out and/or education. Marrying up and out is probably more possible for women than men, and is certainly something my mother preached to my sister and me. Indeed, marriage was my way out of my class and into the middle class. It was during those six years of marriage and that transformation that I slowly comprehended the class question, and realized, as in Merle Haggard's lyric, ". . . another class of people put us somewhere just below . . . "

I was eighteen and Jimmy was nineteen when we married. Jimmy had grown up on the family estate outside Oklahoma City. The house, which his father had built himself, was to me a fantasy world, the kind of place I could only imagine from reading Jane Austen novels—a rambling five-bedroom, two-bath, native-stone structure with a stone fireplace, thick carpets, fine antiques, chandeliers, and cut-glass crystal and bone china displayed in mahogany "breakfronts," as they called the glass-front display cabinets. The place was surrounded by a stream and woods and gardens. At the end of a long stone path was a huge stone patio and barbecue pit. Unlike in a Victorian novel, there were even two working oil wells on the property.

As Jimmy showed me around the first time he took me to meet his family, he was suddenly a stranger to me. I could not even comprehend growing up like he had, and, of course, he could not even imagine how I'd grown up. The land had been homesteaded by his mother's Scots-Irish family, who farmed it. When his mother married his father, who was descended from Dutch Calvinists, they lived there, and then inherited it. They were simple farming people, potentially poor whites, but during the Depression and World War II the construction company Jimmy's father worked for grew huge and rich off New Deal and war contracts, and he climbed from journeyman carpenter to an executive as chief superintendent. After the war he sold some of the land to the state to build the Tulsa Turnpike, invested in real estate, then built the new house. Jimmy grew up rich, no doubt about it. I suppressed a tiny warning signal that I now interpret as the fear that I was repeating what my mother had done—marrying

into a better family and never being able to be as "good" as the mother/
matriarch; because she was dead, Jimmy's mother shone all the brighter,
her angelic and righteous presence never absent. She was the model I was
supposed to imitate.

Jimmy's father fit my image of a patriarch or an English country gentleman out of one of my favorite novels at the time, Galsworthy's *The
Forsyte Saga*—a man of property. He wore a fine cashmere overcoat and a
fur cap. I had never seen anyone with a fur cap. He greeted me by shaking
my hand, a gesture I had never before experienced. A strange thought
passed through my mind as I walked down the aisle holding my father's
arm. It occurred to me that my father might have had my new father-in-
law for a boss when he worked for the WPA during the thirties. The
thought made me feel like a traitor and haunted me during the marriage.

At my wedding, if my father had asked me if I really wanted to go
through with it, maybe I would have said, "No, Daddy, oh no, please save
me from this fate." I knew I was not getting married for anything but protection and class-climbing. But Daddy did not ask, and instead of taking
me away, he gave me away. Years later he would tell me that indeed he
came close to objecting.

One reason I married Jimmy was so I could continue at the university
where we had met. His father offered to pay our tuition and provide a free
place for us to live and a car. Yet within a week after the wedding Jimmy
announced that he wanted us to be self-supporting and persuaded me to
work, saying that otherwise his sisters would regard me as trying to get a
free ride off the family. What Jimmy's older sisters thought of me mattered
a great deal, to him and to me. I agreed to work. So began the pattern that
would doom our marriage.

Jimmy and I lived in the three-room garage apartment—near the "big
house"—that had once been servants' quarters; now they hired day laborers
and housekeepers to maintain the house and the grounds. I idolized Jimmy's
family and adopted them as my own, especially his sister Helen, who lived
with her husband in a cottage they had built nearby on the family property.
She called me "a diamond in the rough." I accepted the role and submitted to
being polished. Helen said that I was from good peasant stock like Tolstoy's
characters and embodied the nobility of the peasantry, enriched by being
part Indian. I shivered with pleasure when she told me those things.

They were New Deal liberals, my new family, not very common in Oklahoma during the 1950s, when integration and trade unions were considered the twin pillars of communism. Jimmy's father had hired black laborers on projects and invited his workers and their families, including blacks, to his famous barbecues. And they weren't strict church-goers, belonging to the most liberal Christian denomination. I left the racial bigotry and Southern Baptist Bible-thumping far behind.

I began to wonder about the price I had to pay for my new status when one really hot summer Saturday afternoon Jimmy and I with his sister and her husband went to drink beer in a joint we hadn't been to before, attracted by the air-conditioning sign. The barmaid turned out to be a woman from my rural community whom I hadn't seen for nearly two years. I was surprised by my joy in seeing her. She wore a tight-fitting red sundress and looked different, not so much older but somehow hard, her skin rough. She remained strikingly beautiful with her mane of thick black hair and smoky skin. She hesitated, and I thought she didn't remember me, but she was studying my companions. I introduced her. Suddenly I was aware that Jimmy didn't approve of her. He glared at me as if I were a stranger. After she had served us, he said, "You got some outstanding old friends." Later he berated me for associating with a prostitute: "You associate with lowlife like that and you will become like them."

Other warning signals alerted me to the class chasm between Jimmy and his family and me. On a driving trip to Colorado, all along the highways were broken-down cars and pickups with women and children and old people sitting in the shade while a man worked under the hoods. They beckoned for us to stop and help. Jimmy passed them by. No one in my family would ever have passed up a stranded motorist, but then we never strayed far from home.

When I asked Jimmy why we didn't stop, he said, "They're hustlers, rob you blind, highway bandits." I asked how he knew that, and he said, "I just know. They use the kids and old people for bait to get you to stop, then rob you. They're transients, fruit pickers, white trash." I stared into the sad faces as we passed by and tried to see the con artists and criminals behind the masks. But they merely looked familiar, like my own relatives.

Yet we got plenty of help on the highway. Each time we had a flat tire or the radiator overheated, someone stopped to help us or gave Jimmy a ride to the next station and brought him back. The cars that stopped were old and the people looked much like those who tried to get us to stop. New cars whizzed on by. I asked Jimmy why they weren't afraid of us, and he explained that they could tell.

Then one autumn day in the third year of marriage I was home sick and found myself the only person on the grounds. I had never been alone there before. The place was so serene and lovely, the oak leaves bright yellow, a maple tree flaming red, the blackjacks burnished copper. The huge lawn that sloped down to the creek was still a carpet of green thanks to the sprinkler system. I sat down on the stone bench in the patio that was halfway between the creek and the big house. Although I was only thirty-five miles east from where I grew up, it was so different, rolling hills with trees rather than flat and barren, no cannibalized old cars and junk around.

"How lucky I am," I said aloud and felt like yelling it since no one would hear. I could never have dreamed of being a part of that kind of life three years earlier. Jimmy's family had taken me in as one of their own. Forever and ever I would be safe and secure and loved. I loved my sisters-in-law and father-in-law as if they were my own flesh. I would never be poor or want for anything again. I tingled with happiness, tears of joy streaming down my face.

The sound of a car startled me out of my reverie. The mail carrier: he always brought everyone's mail to the big house and put it on the back porch where we could each fish out our own. I strolled up the hill to check. There was a letter to Jimmy's sister Helen from another sister who had recently moved to California. The envelope was barely sealed. I slipped the letter out of the envelope and unfolded the two pages. My eyes fell on the middle of the first page, and the words hit me like a blast of icy wind: *I think you are right that it remains to be seen if Roxie will drag Jimmy down to her level or if he can pull her up to his. Coming from her background she may be beyond rescue. I wish Jimmy would leave her.*

I had to sit down to keep from falling. I could not believe what I was reading, and that there had been other letters and conversations, letters about me ruining Jimmy. The letter was almost entirely about me, mostly a discussion of the condition of "white trash," whether it was genetic or social, and the "complication" that I was part Indian. I read the letter a second time, telling myself they were concerned about me because they loved me and wanted to help me. But it wasn't there; only concern for Jimmy and the wish that I would disappear or had never appeared. The letter ended by saying that Jimmy had met me at a vulnerable time in his life, just after their mother's death, and I, being a gold-digger and devious, had entrapped him and pressured him for a quick marriage.

■   ■   ■

I have made my home in California nearly all of the past four decades. Until recently, California had felt to me like a foreign country, a place of exile, which was exactly what I wanted of it.

When my husband and I moved to San Francisco in 1960, our Oklahoma license tags provoked angry honking, obscene gestures, and hisses of "Go home, Okies" and "Dumb Okies" from some other drivers. We changed the tags and I began working on getting rid of my Okie accent and usages. I called the elm tree "ellum," an aerial "errol," an inch and a fish "eench" and "feesh." While I said "prolly" they said "probably," and I "renched" rather than rinsed. I knew how to spell almost faultlessly, and although I thought I spelled phonetically, my ear heard differently than San Franciscans'. I stumbled through what I thought was my own language, trying to find my bearings, saying "shadder" meaning shadow, "small" meaning smile, and "chimley," which they called chimney. I called a female sheep a "yo."

I was aware that out there just over the Coastal Range lay a vast valley, stretching from Redding in the north to Bakersfield in the south, populated by people like me, or like I didn't want to be—"Dust Bowl Okies." And I was aware that in the Santa Clara Valley in northern California and in the San Bernardino Valley and in Orange County in southern California were dense pockets of people like me, or like I did not want to be—"defense Okies"—those who came during World War II to work in the war industry. And although I supported the United Farm Workers movement, I did so from a distance and did not venture into that valley where Mexican farm workers and descendants of Okie farm workers lived at odds. I must have traveled Highway 99, and later I-5 when it was built parallel to 99, up and down California's Central Valley a thousand times, passing through, headed for L.A. or Portland, Mexico or Canada, New Mexico or Oklahoma. But I stopped in the Central Valley only if necessary. I did not want to talk to the people I knew were there, people I didn't want to be like.

When I was at UCLA in the mid-sixties, I was well aware that most of the cops in the Los Angeles Police Department were people like me, or like I did not want to be. And I was embarrassed and secretive about that knowledge, particularly during the Watts uprising in the summer of 1965, after white LAPD cops shot a black man in cold blood.

In 1967, during the height of the anti–Vietnam war and counterculture youth movements, a friend and I were walking away from a movie theater in West Los Angeles around midnight when an LAPD patrol car skidded to a stop beside us, red lights flashing. There was a 9 P.M. curfew for anyone under twenty-one since the Sunset Boulevard police riot against celebrating street youth the year before. We were over twenty-one but never got a chance to prove it. My friend, a foreign student, was clearly terrified; he had a student visa but was from a country where being stopped by the police or army meant pain and suffering if not death, especially if a bribe wasn't offered, and he had little money on him. He reached inside his jacket, he told me later, to calm his pounding heart. In a flash, the two cops drew their weapons and crouched into firing positions. My friend had the good sense to raise his arms, palms open, way above his head, and I followed suit. However, the cops remained in firing position, apparently unimpressed by our disarmed helplessness. They finally stood up, rammed their revolvers into their holsters, stomped around us, kicked at the trunk of a palm tree, all the while calling us "hippies," "communists," "peaceniks," and they tried to scare us with threats while discussing between themselves what to do with us.

But they gave themselves away: I recognized the way they moved, the way they talked, not just their Okie accents but as if they moved and talked in slow motion, compared with most Californians I knew, managing to appear humble and arrogant, graceful as cats and dangerous all at the same time. I was no longer scared. I said, "Where y'all from? I'm from near El Reno." The effect was immediate. Suddenly the two cops, probably a decade older than me, became friendly Okies. We chatted, mostly letting them talk because my Oklahoma accent did not come back easily to me, about our origins and family ties—their parents had been Dust Bowl Okies from Choctaw and from Prague in southeastern Oklahoma—then about the weather, and they apologized for the trouble, and asked if they could give us a ride—"No thanks!" I said—and then they drove away. They never even checked our identification.

It was hard to explain to my foreign friend what magic I had performed. I can't say that I really understood it myself at the time. But that was a moment of necessity, of survival; it wasn't often that I revealed my roots, and other rootless Californians like myself rarely asked, "Where are you from?" or if they did, they really meant, Where do you live? not Where do you come from originally? or Who are you really?

Even when I began working on [my] book I still had no desire for any relationship or interchange with those people like me out there beyond California's cities. I was interested in Oklahoma history, in the radicalism my grandfather was part of, that legacy. I identified myself as working class, part poor white, part Indian, anything but "Okie."

Then I met Wilma Elizabeth McDaniel, the poet known throughout the California Central Valley as the "Okie bard" and "Okie poet laureate," and found myself at home among California Okies for the first time. Wilma's poems and stories made me realize that I could not write a memoir about growing up in Oklahoma without acknowledging my ties to those who had left and who have, through their struggles, their music and their stories, preserved and reinvented our history as a people.

Soon after meeting, Wilma and I decided to visit Weed Patch, the migrant labor camp set up by Roosevelt for the Okie migrants, where Steinbeck's Joad family lived, and where Dorothea Lange took so many of her classic photographs. The hundred-mile trip down Highway 99 from Wilma's home in Tulare to Weed Patch, which is south of Bakersfield, took about two hours. As we drove that stretch, Wilma told me stories about the people, the hardships, the courage, the tragedies, about her own family and the many stories she had heard from others. Every place had a story— Tipton, Pixley, Earlimart, Delano and McFarland (whose history I had known only through the UFW movement), Rosedale, Oildale, Lamont. Then we arrived at Weed Patch.

To our surprise, we found that it's still a functioning farm worker camp, nearly deserted in the middle of a weekday with the workers in the fields. Signs were in Spanish and English. The weather-stripped wooden buildings at the camp entrance must have been the original ones, no longer in use, but there were no markers or museum to explain anything. Most of the small cabins had been built since the thirties but were fairly shabby. The camp was bounded by a tall chain-link fence and I could almost imagine a guard tower with armed security officers, like a low-security

California prison. As Wilma and I poked around, the camp manager approached us, alert with suspicion. The sign at the entrance clearly stated: *This center is for residents and visitors of residents only. Others are trespassers and will be prosecuted.* Another sign read *No Credit.* I tried to explain why we were there; the manager was Mexican, so I tried in Spanish, too, but the suspicion in his face only melded into bewilderment. He told us to go ahead and look around and went back inside the building.

There was not much to see, just a barren, run-down labor camp in the middle of plowed-up cotton fields on a chilly and windy December day. Yet Wilma and I stood there in awe, as if at a sacred site. Later we confided in each other that we each thought we had heard voices, Okie voices, and we were each overwhelmed by a sense that that place was profoundly connected to who we've been and who we've become.

Later, Wilma wrote a poem about that visit:

> *I went there*
> *and walked on the years*
> *ever so carefully*
> *as if on broken glass*
> *yet my feet bled*
> *through my shoes*
> *seeping from my heart*
>
> *And my hands blistered*
> *from imaginary hoes*
> *thrust into them*
> *from the rawness of the past*
>
> *And there was no mistake*
> *I felt hunger*
> *it started from a sign*
> *that read No Credit*
> *and increased the length*
> *of Weedpatch Highway.*

Back in San Francisco, I called my father in Oklahoma and told him about the Weed Patch camp—he'd read *The Grapes of Wrath* several times.

He said, "Yeah, them poor folks sure did suffer, couldn't even grow their own food. Least you kids never went hungry like them."

For the first time in my life I felt unashamed, and even proud, that the bottom line of my life is that I never had to go hungry.

Note

1. See Carl Degler, *Out of Our Past* (New York: Harper, 1959); Francis Jennings, *The Invasion of America: Indians, Colonialism, and the Cant of Conquest* (New York: W. W. Norton, 1975); William C. MacLeod, "Celt and Indian: Britain's Old World Frontier in Relation to the New," in *Beyond the Frontier,* ed. Paul Bohannan and Fred Plog (New York: Natural History Press), 1967; Richard Slotkin, *Regeneration Through Violence: The Mythology of the American Frontier, 1600–1860* (Middletown, CT: Wesleyan University Press, 1973).

5

Becoming
100 Percent Straight

Michael A. Messner

Many years ago I read some psychological studies that argued that even for self-identified heterosexuals it is a natural part of their development to have gone through "bisexual" or even "homosexual" stages of life. When I read this, it seemed theoretically reasonable, but did not ring true in my experience. I have always been, I told myself, 100 percent heterosexual! The group process of analyzing my own autobiographical stories challenged the concept I had developed of myself, and also shed light on the way in which the institutional context of sport provided a context for the development of my definition of myself as "100 percent straight." Here is one of the stories.

When I was in the ninth grade I played on a "D" basketball team, set up especially for the smallest of high school boys. Indeed, though I was pudgy with baby fat, I was a short 5'2", still prepubescent with no facial hair and a high voice that I artificially tried to lower. The first day of practice I was immediately attracted to a boy I'll call Timmy, because he looked like the boy who played in the *Lassie* TV show. Timmy was short, with a high voice, like me. And like me, he had no facial hair yet.

Unlike me, he was very skinny. I liked Timmy right away, and soon we were together a lot. I noticed things about him that I didn't notice about other boys: he said some words a certain way, and it gave me pleasure to try to talk like him. I remember liking the way the light hit his boyish, nearly hairless body. I thought about him when we weren't together. He was in the school band, and at the football games I'd squint to see where he was in the mass of uniforms. In short, though I wasn't conscious of it at the time, I was infatuated with Timmy—I had a crush on him. Later that basketball season, I decided—for no reason that I could really articulate then—that I hated Timmy. I aggressively rejected him, began to make fun of him around other boys. He was, we all agreed, a geek. He was a faggot.

Three years later Timmy and I were both on the varsity basketball team, but had hardly spoken a word to each other since we were freshmen. Both of us now had lower voices, had grown to around 6 feet tall, and we both shaved, at least a bit. But Timmy was a skinny, somewhat stigmatized reserve on the team, while I was the team captain and starting point guard. But I wasn't so happy or secure about this. I'd always dreamed of dominating games, of being the hero. Halfway through my senior season, however, it became clear that I was not a star, and I figured I knew why. I was not aggressive enough.

I had always liked the beauty of the fast break, the perfectly executed pick and roll play between two players, and especially the long 20-foot shot that touched nothing but the bottom of the net. But I hated and feared the sometimes brutal contact under the basket. In fact, I stayed away from the rough fights for rebounds and was mostly a perimeter player, relying on my long shots or my passes to more aggressive teammates under the basket. But now it became apparent to me that time was running out in my quest for greatness: I needed to change my game, and fast. I decided one day before practice that I was gonna get aggressive. While practicing one of our standard plays, I passed the ball to a teammate, and then ran to the spot at which I was to set a pick on a defender. I knew that one could sometimes get away with setting a face-up screen on a player, and then as he makes contact with you, roll your back to him and plant your elbow hard in his stomach. The beauty of this move is that your own body "roll" makes the elbow look like an accident. So I decided to try this move. I approached the defensive player, Timmy, rolled, and planted my elbow deeply into his solar plexus. Air exploded audibly from Timmy's mouth, and he crumbled to the floor momentarily.

Play went on as though nothing had happened, but I felt bad about it. Rather than making me feel better, it made me feel guilty and weak. I had to admit to myself why I'd chosen Timmy as the target against whom to test out my new aggression. He was the skinniest and weakest player on the team.

At the time, I hardly thought about these incidents, other than to try to brush them off as incidents that made me feel extremely uncomfortable. Years later I can now interrogate this as a sexual story, and as a gender story unfolding within the context of the heterosexualized and masculinized institution of sport. Examining my story in light of research conducted by Alfred Kinsey a half century ago, I can recognize in myself what Kinsey saw as a very common fluidity and changeability of sexual desire over the life-course. Put simply, Kinsey found that large numbers of adult "heterosexual" men had previously, as adolescents and young adults, experienced sexual desire for males. A surprisingly large number of these men had experienced sexual contact to the point of orgasm with other males during adolescence or early adulthood. Similarly, my story invited me to consider what is commonly called the "Freudian theory of bisexuality." Sigmund Freud shocked the post-Victorian world by suggesting that all people go through a stage, early in life, when they are attracted to people of the same sex.[1] Adult experiences, Freud argued, eventually led most people to shift their sexual desire to what he called an appropriate "love object"—a person of the opposite sex. I also considered my experience in light of what lesbian feminist author Adrienne Rich called the institution of compulsory heterosexuality. Perhaps the extremely high levels of homophobia that are often endemic in boys' and men's organized sports led me to deny and repress my own homoerotic desire through a direct and overt rejection of Timmy, through homophobic banter with male peers, and the resultant stigmatization of the feminized Timmy. Eventually I considered my experience in the light of what radical theorist Herbert Marcuse called the sublimation of homoerotic desire into an aggressive, violent act as serving to construct a clear line of demarcation between self and other. Sublimation, according to Marcuse, involves the driving underground, into the unconscious, of sexual desires that might appear dangerous due to their socially stigmatized status. But sublimation involves more than simple repression into the unconscious. It involves a transformation of sexual desire into something else—often into aggressive and violent acting out toward others. These acts clarify the boundaries between oneself and others and therefore lessen any anxieties that might be attached to the repressed homoerotic desire.

Importantly, in our analysis of my story, the memory group went beyond simply discussing the events in psychological terms. The story did perhaps suggest some deep psychological processes at work, but it also revealed the importance of social context—in this case, the context of the athletic team. In short, my rejection of Timmy and the joining with teammates to stigmatize him in ninth grade stands as an example of what sociologist R. W. Connell calls a moment of engagement with hegemonic masculinity, where I actively took up the male group's task of constructing heterosexual/masculine identities in the context of sport. The elbow in Timmy's gut three years later can be seen as a punctuation mark that occurred precisely because of my fears that I might be failing in this goal.

It is helpful, I think, to compare my story with gay and lesbian "coming out" stories in sport. Though we have a few lesbian and bisexual coming out stories among women athletes, there are very few from gay males. Tom Waddell, who as a closeted gay man finished sixth in the decathlon in the 1968 Olympics, later came out and started the Gay Games, an athletic and cultural festival that draws tens of thousands of people every four years. When I interviewed Tom Waddell over a decade ago about his sexual identity and athletic career, he made it quite clear that for many years sports was his closet:

> When I was a kid, I was tall for my age, and was very thin and very strong. And I was usually faster than most other people. But I discovered rather early that I liked gymnastics and I liked dance. I was very interested in being a ballet dancer . . . [but] something became obvious to me right away—that male ballet dancers were effeminate, that they were what most people would call faggots. And I thought I just couldn't handle that. . . . I was totally closeted and very concerned about being male. This was the fifties, a terrible time to live, and everything was stacked against me. Anyway, I realized that I had to do something to protect my image of myself as a male—because at that time homosexuals were thought of primarily as men who wanted to

be women. And so I threw myself into athletics—I played football, gymnastics, track and field . . . I was a jock—that's how I was viewed, and I was comfortable with that.

Tom Waddell was fully conscious of entering sports and constructing a masculine/heterosexual athletic identity precisely because he feared being revealed as gay. It was clear to him, in the context of the 1950s, that being known as gay would undercut his claims to the status of manhood. Thus, though he described the athletic closet as "hot and stifling," he remained there until several years after his athletic retirement. He even knowingly played along with locker room discussions about sex and women as part of his "cover."

> I wanted to be viewed as male, otherwise I would be a dancer today. I
> wanted the male, macho image of an athlete. So I was protected by a
> very hard shell. I was clearly aware of what I was doing. . . . I often felt
> compelled to go along with a lot of locker room garbage because I
> wanted that image—and I know a lot of others who did too.

Like my story, Waddell's points to the importance of the athletic institution as a context in which peers mutually construct and reconstruct narrow definitions of masculinity. Heterosexuality is considered to be a rock-solid foundation of this concept of masculinity. But unlike my story, Waddell's may invoke a dramaturgical analysis.[2] He seemed to be consciously "acting" to control and regulate others' perceptions of him by constructing a public "front stage" persona that differed radically from what he believed to be his "true" inner self. My story, in contrast, suggests a deeper, less consciously strategic repression of my homoerotic attraction. Most likely, I was aware on some level of the dangers of such feelings, and was escaping the risks, disgrace, and rejection that would likely result from being different. For Waddell, the decision to construct his identity largely within sport was to step into a fiercely heterosexual/masculine closet that would hide what he saw as his "true" identity. In contrast, I was not so much stepping into a "closet" that would hide my identity; rather, I was stepping out into an entire world of heterosexual privilege. My story also suggests how a threat to the promised privileges of hegemonic masculinity—my failure as an athlete—might trigger a momentary sexual panic that can lay bare the constructedness, indeed, the instability of the heterosexual/masculine identity.

In either case, Waddell's or mine, we can see how, as young male athletes, heterosexuality and masculinity was not something we "were," but something we were doing. It is significant, I think, that although each of us was "doing heterosexuality," neither of us was actually "having sex" with women (though one of us desperately wanted to). This underscores a point made by some recent theorists that heterosexuality should not be thought of simply as sexual acts between women and men. Rather, heterosexuality is a constructed identity, a performance, and an institution that is not necessarily linked to sexual acts. Though for one of us it was more conscious than for the other, we were both "doing heterosexuality" as an ongoing practice through which we sought to do two things:

- avoid stigma, embarrassment, ostracism, or perhaps worse if we were even suspected of being gay;
- link ourselves into systems of power, status, and privilege that appear to be the birthright of "real men" (i.e., males who are able to compete successfully with other males in sport, work, and sexual relations with women).

In other words, each of us actively scripted our own sexual and gender performances, but these scripts were constructed within the constraints of a socially organized (institutionalized) system of power and pleasure.

Questions for Future Research

As I prepared to tell this sexual story publicly to my colleagues at the sport studies conference, I felt extremely nervous. Part of the nervousness was due to the fact that I knew some of them would object to my claim that telling personal stories can be a source of sociological insights. But a larger part of the reason for my nervousness was due to the fact that I was revealing something very personal about my sexuality in such a public way. Most of us are not accustomed to doing this, especially in the context of a professional conference. But I had learned long ago, especially from feminist women scholars, and from gay and lesbian scholars, that biography is linked to history. Part of "normal" academic discourse has been to hide "the personal" (including the fact that the researchers are themselves people with values, feelings, and, yes, biases) behind a carefully constructed facade of "objectivity." Rather than trying to hide or be ashamed of one's subjective experience of the world, I was challenging myself to draw on my experience of the world as a resource. Not that I should trust my experience as the final word on "reality." White, heterosexual males like me have made the mistake for centuries of calling their own experience "objectivity," and then punishing anyone who does not share their worldview by casting them as "deviant." Instead, I hope to use my experience as an example of how those of us who are in dominant sexual/racial/gender/class categories can get a new perspective on the "constructedness" of our identities by juxtaposing our subjective experiences against the recently emerging worldviews of gay men and lesbians, women, and people of color.

Finally, I want to stress that in juxtaposition neither my own nor Tom Waddell's story sheds much light on the question of why some individuals "become gay" while others "become" heterosexual or bisexual. Instead, I should like to suggest that this is a dead-end question, and that there are far more important and interesting questions to be asked:

- How has heterosexuality, as an institution and as an enforced group practice, constrained and limited all of us— gay, straight, and bi?
- How has the institution of sport been an especially salient institution for the social construction of heterosexual masculinity?
- Why is it that when men play sports they are almost always automatically granted masculine status, and thus assumed to be heterosexual, while when women play sports, questions are raised about their "femininity" and sexual orientation?

These kinds of questions aim us toward an analysis of the workings of power within institutions—including the ways that these workings of power shape and constrain our identities and relationships—and point us toward imagining alternative social arrangements that are less constraining for everyone.

Notes

1. The fluidity and changeability of sexual desire over the life-course is now more obvious in evidence from prison and military populations and single-sex boarding schools. The theory of bisexuality is evident, for example, in childhood crushes on same-sex primary schoolteachers.

2. Dramaturgical analysis, associated with Erving Goffman, uses the theater and performance to develop an analogy with everyday life.

References

Haug, Frigga. 1987. *Female Sexualization: A Collective Work of Memory.* London: Verso.

Lenskyj, Helen. 1986. *Out of Bounds: Women, Sport and Sexuality.* Toronto: Women's Press.

———. 1997. "No Fear? Lesbians in Sport and Physical Education," *Women in Sport and Physical Activity Journal 6* (2): 7–22.

Messner, Michael A. 1992. *Power at Play: Sports and the Problem of Masculinity.* Boston: Beacon Press.

———. 1994. "Gay Athletes and the Gay Games: An Interview with Tom Waddell," in M. A. Messner and D. F. Sabo (eds.), *Sex, Violence and Power in Sports: Rethinking Masculinity.* Freedom, CA: The Crossing Press, pp. 113–19.

Pronger, Brian. 1990. *The Arena of Masculinity: Sports, Homosexuality, and the Meaning of Sex.* New York: St. Martin's Press.

6

The Heterosexual Questionnaire

M. Rochlin

Purpose: The purpose of this exercise is to examine the manner in which the use of heterosexual norms may bias the study of gay men's and lesbians' lives.

Instructions: Heterosexism is a form of bias in which heterosexual norms are used in studies of homosexual relationships. Gay men and lesbians are seen as deviating from a heterosexual norm, and this often leads to marginalization and pathologizing of their behavior.

Read the questionnaire below with this definition in mind. Then respond to the questions that follow.

1. What do you think caused your heterosexuality?
2. When and how did you first decide you were a heterosexual?
3. Is it possible that your heterosexuality is just a phase you may grow out of?
4. Is it possible that your heterosexuality stems from a neurotic fear of others of the same sex?

5. If you have never slept with a person of the same sex, is it possible that all you need is a good gay lover?

6. Do your parents know that you are straight? Do your friends and/or roommate(s) know? How did they react?

7. Why do you insist on flaunting your heterosexuality? Can't you just be who you are and keep it quiet?

8. Why do heterosexuals place so much emphasis on sex?

9. Why do heterosexuals feel compelled to seduce others into their lifestyle?

10. A disproportionate majority of child molesters are heterosexual. Do you consider it safe to expose children to heterosexual teachers?

11. Just what do men and women *do* in bed together? How can they truly know how to please each other, being so anatomically different?

12. With all the societal support marriage receives, the divorce rate is spiraling. Why are there so few stable relationships among heterosexuals?

13. Statistics show that lesbians have the lowest incidence of sexually transmitted diseases. Is it really safe for a woman to maintain a heterosexual lifestyle and run the risk of disease and pregnancy?

14. How can you become a whole person if you limit yourself to compulsive, exclusive heterosexuality?

15. Considering the menace of overpopulation, how could the human race survive if everyone were heterosexual?

16. Could you trust a heterosexual therapist to be objective? Don't you feel s/he might be inclined to influence you in the direction of her/his own leanings?

17. There seem to be very few happy heterosexuals. Techniques have been developed that might enable you to change if you really want to. Have you considered trying aversion therapy?

18. Would you want your child to be heterosexual, knowing the problems that s/he would face?

19. What were your first reactions upon reading this questionnaire?

PART TWO

Understanding Privilege

7

Privilege, Power, Difference, and Us

Allan Johnson

To do something about the trouble around difference, we have to talk about it, but most of the time we don't, because it feels too risky. This is true for just about everyone, but especially for members of privileged categories, for whites, for men, and for heterosexuals. As Paul Kivel writes, for example, "Rarely do we whites sit back and listen to people of color without interrupting, without being defensive, without trying to regain attention to ourselves, without criticizing or judging."

The discomfort, defensiveness, and fear come in part from not knowing how to talk about privilege without feeling vulnerable to anger and blame. They will continue until we find a way to reduce the risk of talking about privilege. The key to reducing the risk is to understand what makes talking about privilege *seem* risky. I don't mean that risk is an illusion. There is no way to do this work without the possibility that people will feel uncomfortable or frightened or threatened. But the risk isn't nearly as big as it seems, for like the proverbial (and mythical) human fear of the strange and unfamiliar, the problem begins with how people *think* about things and who they are in relation to them.

Individualism, or the Myth That Everything Is Somebody's Fault

We live in a society that encourages us to think that the social world begins and ends with individuals. It's as if an organization or a society is just a collection of people, and everything that happens in it begins with what each one thinks, feels, and intends. If you understand people, the reasoning goes, then you also understand social life. It's an appealing way to think because it's grounded in our experience as individuals, which is what we know best. But it's also misleading, because it boxes us into a narrow and distorted view of reality. In other words, it isn't true.

If we use individualism to explain sexism, for example, it's hard to avoid the idea that sexism exists simply because men *are* sexist—men have sexist feelings, beliefs, needs, and motivations that lead them to behave in sexist ways. If sexism produces evil consequences, it's because men *are* evil, hostile, and malevolent toward women. In short, everything bad in the world is seen as somebody's fault, which is why talk about privilege so often turns into a game of hot potato.

Individualistic thinking keeps us stuck in the trouble by making it almost impossible to talk seriously about it. It encourages women, for example, to blame and distrust men. It sets men up to feel personally attacked if anyone mentions gender issues, and to define those issues as a "women's problem." It also encourages men who don't think or behave in overtly sexist ways—the ones most likely to become part of the solution—to conclude that sexism has nothing to do with them, that it's just a problem for "bad" men. The result is a kind of paralysis: people either talk about sexism in the most superficial, unthreatening, trivializing, and even stupid way ("The Battle of the Sexes," *Men Are from Mars, Women Are from Venus*) or they don't talk about it at all.

Breaking the paralysis begins with realizing that the social world consists of a lot more than individuals. We are always participating in something larger than ourselves—what sociologists call social systems—and systems are more than collections of people. A university, for example, is a social system, and people participate in it. But the people aren't the university and the university isn't the people. This means that to understand what happens in it, we have to look at both the university and how individual people participate in it. If patterns of racism exist in a society, for example, the reason is never just a matter of white people's personalities, feelings, or intentions. We also have to understand how they participate in particular kinds of behavior, and what consequences it produces.

Individuals, Systems, and Paths of Least Resistance

To see the difference between a system and the people who participate in it, consider a game like *Monopoly.* I used to play *Monopoly,* but I don't anymore because I don't like the way I behave when I do. Like everyone else, as a *Monopoly* player I try to take everything from the other players—all their money, all their property—which then forces them out of the game. The point of the game is to ruin everyone else and be the only one left in the end. When you win, you feel good, because you're *supposed* to feel good. Except that one day I realized that I felt good about winning—about taking everything from everyone else—even when I played with my children, who were pretty young at the time. But there didn't seem to be much point to playing without trying to win, because winning is what the game is *about.* Why land on a property and not buy it, or own a property and not improve it, or have other players land on your property and not collect the rent? So I stopped playing.

And it worked, because the fact is that I don't behave in such greedy ways when I'm not playing *Monopoly,* even though it's still me, Allan, in either case. So what's all this greedy behavior about? Do we behave in greedy ways simply because we *are* greedy? In a sense, the answer is yes, in that greed is part of the human repertoire of possible motivations, just like compassion, altruism, or fear. But how, then, do I explain the absence of such behavior when I'm not playing *Monopoly?* Clearly, the answer has to include both me as an individual human being who's capable of making all kinds of choices *and* something about the social situation in which I make those choices. It's not one or the other; it's both in relation to each other.

If we think of *Monopoly* as a social system—as "something larger than ourselves that we participate in"—then we can see how people and systems come together in a dynamic relationship that produces the patterns of social life, including problems around difference and privilege. People are indisputably the ones who make social systems happen. If no one plays *Monopoly,* it's just a box full of stuff with writing inside the cover. When people open it up and identify themselves as players, however, *Monopoly* starts to *happen.* This makes people very important, but we shouldn't confuse that with *Monopoly* itself. We aren't *Monopoly* and *Monopoly* isn't us. I can describe the game and how it works without saying anything about the personal characteristics of all the people who play it or might play it.

People make *Monopoly* happen, but *how?* How do we know what to do? How do we choose from the millions of things that, as human beings, we *could* do at any given moment? The answer is the other half of the dynamic relation between individuals and systems. As we sit around the table, we make *Monopoly* happen from one minute to the next. But our participation in the game also shapes how *we* happen as people—what we think and feel and do. This doesn't mean that systems control us in a rigid and predictable way. Instead, systems load the odds in certain directions by offering what I call "paths of least resistance" for us to follow.

In every social situation, we have an almost limitless number of choices we might make. Sitting in a movie theater, for example, we could go to sleep, sing, eat dinner, undress, dance, take out a flashlight and read the newspaper, carry on loud conversations, dribble a basketball up and down the aisles—these are just a handful of the millions of behaviors people are capable of. All of these possible paths vary in how much resistance we run into if we try to follow them. We discover this as soon as we choose paths we're not supposed to. Jump up and start singing, for example, and you'll quickly feel how much resistance the management and the rest of the audience offer up to discourage you from going any further. By comparison, the path of least resistance is far more appealing, which is why it's the one we're most likely to choose.

The odds are loaded toward a path of least resistance in several ways. We often choose a path because it's the only one we see. When I get on an elevator, for example, I turn and face front along with everyone else. It rarely occurs to me to do it another way, such as facing the rear. If I did, I'd soon feel how some paths have more resistance than others.

I once tested this idea by walking to the rear of an elevator and standing with my back toward the door. As the seconds ticked by, I could feel people looking at me, wondering what I was up to, and actually wanting me to turn around. I wasn't saying anything or doing anything to anyone. I was only standing there minding my own business. But that wasn't all that I was doing, for I was also violating a social norm that makes facing the door a path of least resistance. The path is there all the time—it's built in to riding the elevator as a social situation—but the path wasn't clear until I stepped onto a different one and felt the greater resistance rise up around it.

Similar dynamics operate around issues of difference and privilege. In many corporations, for example, the only way to get promoted is to have a mentor or sponsor pick you out as a promising person and bring you along by teaching you what you need to know and acting as an advocate who opens doors and creates opportunities. In a society that separates and privileges people by gender and race, there aren't many opportunities to get comfortable with people across difference. This means that senior managers will feel drawn to employees who resemble them, which usually means those who are white, straight, and male.

Managers who are white and/or male probably won't realize they're following a path of least resistance that shapes their choice until they're asked to mentor an African American woman or someone else they don't resemble. The greater resistance toward the path of mentoring across difference may result from something as subtle as feeling "uncomfortable" in the other person's presence. But that's all it takes to make the relationship ineffective or to ensure that it never happens in the first place. And as each manager follows the system's path to mentor and support those who most resemble them, the patterns of white dominance and male dominance in the system as a whole are perpetuated, regardless of what people consciously feel or intend.

In other cases, people know alternative paths exist but they stick to the path of least resistance anyway, because they're afraid of what will happen if they don't. Resistance can take many forms, ranging from mild disapproval to being fired from a job, beaten up, run out of town, imprisoned, tortured, or killed. When managers are told to lay off large numbers of workers, for example, they may hate the assignment and feel a huge amount of distress. But the path of *least* resistance is to do what they're told, because the alternative may be for them to lose their own jobs. To make it less unpleasant, they may use euphemisms like "downsizing" and "outplacement" to soften the painful reality of people losing their jobs. (Note in this example how the path of least resistance isn't necessarily an easy path to follow.)

In similar ways, a man may feel uncomfortable when he hears a friend tell a sexist joke, and feel compelled to object in some way. But the path of least resistance in that situation is to go along and avoid the risk of being ostracized or ridiculed for challenging his friend and making *him* feel uncomfortable. The path of least resistance is to smile or laugh or just remain silent.

What we experience as social life happens through a complex dynamic between all kinds of systems—families, schools, workplaces, communities, entire societies—and the choices people make as they participate in them and help make them happen. How we experience the world and ourselves, our sense of other people, and the ongoing reality of the systems themselves all arise, take shape, and happen through this dynamic. In this way, social life produces a variety of consequences, including privilege and oppression. To understand that and what we can do to change it, we have to see how systems are organized in ways that encourage people to follow paths of least resistance. The existence of those paths and the choice we make to follow them are keys to what creates and perpetuates all the forms that privilege and oppression can take in people's lives.

What It Means to Be Involved in Privilege and Oppression

Individuals and systems are connected to each other through a dynamic relationship. If we use this relationship as a model for thinking about the world and ourselves, it's easier to bring problems like racism, sexism, and heterosexism out into the open and talk about them. In particular, it's easier to see the problems in relation to us, and to see ourselves in relation to them.

If we think the world is just made up of individuals, then a white woman who's told she's "involved" in racism is going to think you're telling her she's a racist person who harbors ill will toward people of color. She's using an individualistic model of the world that limits her to interpreting words like *racist* as personal characteristics, personality flaws. Individualism divides the world up into different kinds of people—good people and bad, racists and nonracists, "good guys" and sexist pigs. It encourages us to think of racism, sexism, and heterosexism as diseases that infect people and make them sick. And so we look for a "cure" that will turn diseased, flawed individuals into healthy, "good" ones, or at least isolate them so that they can't infect others. And if we can't cure them, then we can at least try to control their behavior.

But what about everyone else? How do we see *them* in relation to the trouble around difference? What about the vast majority of whites, for example, who tell survey interviewers that they aren't racist and don't hate or even dislike people of color? Or what about the majority of men who say they favor an Equal Rights Amendment to the U.S. Constitution? From an individualistic perspective, if you aren't consciously or openly prejudiced or hurtful, then you aren't part of the problem. You might show disapproval of "bad" people and even try to help out the people who are hurt by them. Beyond that, however, the trouble doesn't have anything to do with you so far as you can see. If your feelings and thoughts and outward behavior are good, then *you* are good, and that's all that matters.

Unfortunately, that isn't all that matters. There's more, because patterns of oppression and privilege are rooted in systems that we all participate in and make happen. Those patterns are built into paths of least resistance that people feel drawn to follow every day, regardless of whether they think about where they lead or the consequences they produce. When male professors take more seriously students who look like themselves, for example, they don't have to be self-consciously sexist in order to help perpetuate patterns of gender privilege. They don't have to be bad people in order to play a "game" that produces oppressive consequences. It's the same as when people play *Monopoly*—it always ends with someone winning and everyone else losing, *because that's how the game is set up to work as a system.* The only way to change the outcome is to change how we see and play the game and, eventually, the *system itself* and its paths of least resistance. If we have a vision of what we want social life to look like, we have to create paths that lead in that direction.

Of course there are people in the world who have hatred in their hearts—such as neo-Nazi skinheads who make a sport of harassing and killing blacks or homosexuals—and it's important not to minimize the damage they do. Paradoxically, however, even though they cause a lot of trouble, they aren't the key to understanding privilege or to doing something about it. They are participating in something larger than themselves that, among other things, steers them toward certain targets for their rage. It's no accident that their hatred is rarely directed at privileged groups, but instead those who are culturally devalued and excluded. Hate-crime perpetrators may have personality disorders that bend them toward victimizing *someone*, but their choice of whom to victimize isn't part of a mental illness. That's something they have to learn, and culture is everyone's most powerful teacher. In choosing their targets, they follow paths of least resistance built into a society that everyone participates in, that everyone makes happen, regardless of how they feel or what they intend.

So if I notice that someone plays *Monopoly* in a ruthless way, it's a mistake to explain that simply in terms of their personality. I also have to ask how a system like *Monopoly* rewards ruthless behavior more than other games we might play. I have to ask how it creates conditions that make such behavior appear to be the path of least resistance, normal and unremarkable. And since I'm playing the game, too, I'm one of the people who make it happen as a system, and its paths must affect me, too.

My first reaction might be to deny that I follow that path. I'm not a ruthless person or anything close to it. But this misses the key difference between systems and the people who participate in them: We don't have to be ruthless *people* in order to support or follow paths of least resistance that lead to behavior with ruthless *consequences*. After all, we're all trying to win, because that's the point of the game. However gentle and kind I am as I take your money when you land on my Boardwalk with its four houses, take it I will, and gladly, too. "Thank you," I say in my most sincerely unruthless tone, or even "Sorry," as I drive you out of the game by taking your last dollar and your mortgaged properties. Me, ruthless? Not at all. I'm just playing the game the way it's supposed to be played. And even if I don't try hard to win, the mere fact that I play the game supports its existence and makes it possible, especially if I remain silent about the consequences it produces. Just my going along makes the game appear normal and acceptable, which reinforces the paths of least resistance for everyone else.

This is how most systems work and how most people participate in them. It's also how systems of privilege work. Good people with good intentions make systems happen that produce all kinds of injustice and suffering for people in culturally devalued and excluded groups. Most of the time, people don't even know the paths are there in the first place, and this is why it's important to raise awareness that everyone is always following them in one way or another. If you weren't following a path of least resistance, you'd certainly know it, because you'd be on an alternative path with greater resistance that would make itself felt. In other words, if you're not going along with the system, it won't be long before people notice and let you know it. All you have to do is show up for work wearing "inappropriate" clothes to see how quickly resistance can form around alternative paths.

The trouble around difference is so pervasive, so long-standing, so huge in its consequences for so many millions of people that it can't be written off as the misguided doings of a small minority of people with personality problems. The people who get labeled as bigots, misogynists, or homophobes are all following racist, sexist, heterosexist paths of least resistance that are built into the entire society.

In a way, "bad people" are like ruthless *Monopoly* players who are doing just what the game calls for even if their "style" is a bit extreme. Such extremists may be the ones who grab the headlines, but they don't have enough power to create and sustain trouble of this magnitude. The trouble appears in the daily workings of every workplace, every school and university, every government agency, every community. It involves every major kind of social system, and since systems don't exist without the involvement of people, there's no way to escape being involved in the trouble that comes out of them. If we participate in systems the trouble comes out of, and if those systems exist only through our participation, then this is enough to involve us in the trouble itself.

Reminders of this reality are everywhere. I see it, for example, every time I look at the label in a piece of clothing. I just went upstairs to my closet and noted where each of my shirts was made. Although each carries a U.S. brand name, only three were made here; the rest were made in the Philippines, Thailand, Mexico, Taiwan, Macao, Singapore, or Hong Kong. And although each cost me twenty to forty dollars, it's a good bet that the people who actually made them—primarily women—were paid pennies for their labor performed under terrible conditions that can sometimes be so extreme as to resemble slavery.

The only reason people exploit workers in such horrible ways is to make money in a capitalist system. To judge from the contents of my closet, that clearly includes *my* money. By itself, that fact doesn't make me a bad person, because I certainly don't intend that people suffer for the sake of my wardrobe. But it does mean that I'm involved in their suffering because I participate in a system that produces that suffering. As someone who helps make the system happen, however, I can also be a part of the solution.

But isn't the difference I could make a tiny one? The question makes me think of the devastating floods of 1993 along the Mississippi and Missouri rivers. The news was full of powerful images of people from all walks of life working feverishly side by side to build dikes to hold back the raging waters that threatened their communities. Together, they filled and placed thousands of sandbags. When the waters receded, much had been lost, but a great deal had been saved as well. I wonder how it felt to be one of those people. I imagine they were proud of their effort and experienced a satisfying sense of solidarity with the people they'd worked with. The sandbags each individual personally contributed were the tiniest fraction of the total, but each felt part of the group effort and was proud to identify with the consequences it produced. They didn't have to make a big or even measurable difference to feel involved.

It works that way with the good things that come out of people pulling together in all the systems that make up social life. It also works that way with the bad things, with each sandbag adding to the problem instead of the solution. To perpetuate privilege and oppression, we don't even have to do anything consciously to support it. Just our silence is crucial for ensuring its future, for the simple fact is that no system of social oppression can continue to exist without most people choosing to remain silent about it. If most whites spoke out about racism; if most men talked about sexism; if most heterosexuals came out of their closet of silence and stood openly against heterosexism, it would be a critical first step toward revolutionary change. But the vast majority of "good" people are silent on these issues, and it's easy for others to read their silence as support.

As long as we participate in social systems, we don't get to choose whether to be involved in the consequences they produce. We're involved simply through the fact that we're here. As such, we can only choose *how* to be involved, whether to be just part of the problem or also to be part of the solution. That's where our power lies, and also our responsibility.

8

How Jews
Became White

Karen Brodkin Sacks

*The American nation was founded and developed by the Nordic race,
but if a few more million members of the Alpine, Mediterranean and
Semitic races are poured among us, the result must inevitably be a hy-
brid race of people as worthless and futile as the good-for-nothing mon-
grels of Central America and Southeastern Europe.*
      —Kenneth Roberts, quoted in *Carlson and Colburn* 1972:312

It is clear that Kenneth Roberts did not think of my ancestors as white
like him. The late nineteenth and early decades of the twentieth centuries saw a steady stream of warnings by scientists, policymakers, and the
popular press that "mongrelization" of the Nordic or Anglo-Saxon race—
the real Americans—by inferior European races (as well as inferior non-
European ones) was destroying the fabric of the nation. I continue to be
surprised to read that America did not always regard its immigrant European workers as white, that they thought people from different nations
were biologically different. My parents, who are first-generation U.S.-born

Eastern European Jews, are not surprised. They expect anti-Semitism to be a part of the fabric of daily life, much as I expect racism to be part of it. They came of age in a Jewish world in the 1920s and 1930s at the peak of anti-Semitism in the United States. They are proud of their upward mobility and think of themselves as pulling themselves up by their own bootstraps. I grew up during the 1950s in the Euroethnic New York suburb of Valley Stream, where Jews were simply one kind of white folks and where ethnicity meant little more to my generation than food and family heritage. Part of my familized ethnic heritage was the belief that Jews were smart and that our success was the result of our own efforts and abilities, reinforced by a culture that valued sticking together, hard work, education, and deferred gratification. Today, this belief in a Jewish version of Horatio Alger has become an entry point for racism by some mainstream Jewish organizations against African Americans especially, and for their opposition to affirmative action for people of color (Gordon 1964; Sowell 1981; Steinberg 1989: chap. 3).

It is certainly true that the United States has a history of anti-Semitism and of beliefs that Jews were members of an inferior race. But Jews were hardly alone. American anti-Semitism was part of a broader pattern of late-nineteenth-century racism against all southern and eastern European immigrants, as well as against Asian immigrants. These views justified all sorts of discriminatory treatment, including closing the doors to immigration from Europe and Asia in the 1920s.[1] This picture changed radically after World War II. Suddenly the same folks who promoted nativism and xenophobia were eager to believe that the Euro-origin people whom they had deported, reviled as members of inferior races, and prevented from immigrating only a few years earlier were now model middle-class white suburban citizens.

It was not an educational epiphany that made those in power change their hearts, their minds, and our race. Instead, it was the biggest and best affirmative action program in the history of our nation, and it was for Euromales. There are similarities and differences in the ways each of the European immigrant groups became "whitened." I want to tell the story in a way that links anti-Semitism to other varieties of anti-European racism, because this foregrounds what Jews shared with other Euroimmigrants and shows changing notions of whiteness to be part of America's larger system of institutional racism.

Euroraces

The U.S. "discovery" that Europe had inferior and superior races came in response to the great waves of immigration from southern and eastern Europe in the late nineteenth century. Before that time, European immigrants—including Jews—had been largely assimilated into the white population. The twenty-three million European immigrants who came to work in U.S. cities after 1880 were too many and too concentrated to disperse and blend. Instead, they piled up in the country's most dilapidated urban areas, where they built new kinds of working-class ethnic communities. Since immigrants and their children made up more than 70 percent of the population of most of the country's largest cities, urban America came to take on a distinctly immigrant flavor. The golden age of industrialization in the United States was also the golden age of class struggle between the captains of the new industrial empires and the masses of manual workers whose labor made them rich. As the majority of mining and manufacturing workers, immigrants were visibly major players in these struggles (Higham 1955:226; Steinberg 1989:36).[2]

The Red Scare of 1919 clearly linked anti-immigrant to anti-working-class sentiment—to the extent that the Seattle general strike of native-born workers was blamed on foreign agitators. The Red Scare was fueled by economic depression, a massive postwar strike wave, the Russian revolution, and a new wave of postwar immigration. [. . .]

Not surprisingly, the belief in European races took root most deeply among the wealthy U.S.-born Protestant elite, who feared a hostile and seemingly unassimilable working class. By the end of the nineteenth century, Senator Henry Cabot Lodge pressed Congress to cut off immigration to the United States; Teddy Roosevelt raised the alarm of "race suicide" and took Anglo-Saxon women to task for allowing "native" stock to be outbred by inferior immigrants. In the twentieth century, these fears gained a great deal of social legitimacy thanks to the efforts of an influential network of aristocrats and scientists who developed theories of eugenics—breeding for a "better" humanity—and scientific racism. Key to these efforts was Madison Grant's influential *Passing of the Great Race,* in which he shared his discovery that there were three or four major European races ranging from the superior Nordics of northwestern Europe to the inferior southern and eastern races of Alpines, Mediterraneans, and, worst of all, Jews, who seemed to be everywhere in his native New York City. Grant's nightmare was race mixing among Europeans. For him, "the cross between any of the three European races and a Jew is a Jew" (quoted in Higham 1955:156). He didn't have good things to say about Alpine or Mediterranean "races" either. For Grant, race and class were interwoven: the upper class was racially pure Nordic, and the lower classes came from the lower races.

Far from being on the fringe, Grant's views resonated with those of the nonimmigrant middle class. A *New York Times* reporter wrote of his visit to the Lower East Side:

> This neighborhood, peopled almost entirely by the people who claim to have been driven from Poland and Russia, is the eyesore of New York and perhaps the filthiest place on the Western continent. It is impossible for a Christian to live there because he will be driven out, either by blows or the dirt and stench. Cleanliness is an unknown quantity to these people. They cannot be lifted up to a higher plane because they do not want to be. If the cholera should ever get among these people, they would scatter its germs as a sower does grain. (quoted in Schoener 1967:58)[3]

Such views were well within the mainstream of the early-twentieth-century scientific community. Grant and eugenicist Charles B. Davenport organized the Galton Society in 1918 in order to foster research and to otherwise promote eugenics and immigration restriction.[4] [. . .]

By the 1920s, scientific racism sanctified the notion that real Americans were white and real whites came from northwest Europe. Racism animated laws excluding and expelling Chinese in 1882, and then closing the door to immigration by virtually all Asians and most Europeans in 1924 (Saxton 1971, 1990). Northwestern European ancestry as a requisite for whiteness was set in legal concrete when the Supreme Court denied Bhagat Singh Thind the right to become a naturalized citizen under a 1790 federal law that allowed whites the right to become naturalized citizens. Thind argued that East Indians were the real Aryans and Caucasians, and therefore white. The Court countered that the United States only wanted blond Aryans and Caucasians, "that the blond Scandinavian and the brown Hindu have a common ancestor in the dim reaches of antiquity, but the average man knows perfectly well that there are unmistakable and profound differences between them today" (Takaki 1989:298–299). A narrowly defined white, Christian race was also built into the 1705 Virginia "Act concerning servants and slaves." This statute stated "that no negroes, mulattos and Indians or other infidels or jews, Moors, Mahometans or other infidels shall, at any time, purchase any christian servant, nor any other except of their own complexion" (Martyn 1979:111).[5]

The 1930 census added its voice, distinguishing not only immigrant from "native" whites, but also native whites of native white parentage, and native whites of immigrant (or mixed) parentage. In distinguishing immigrant (southern and eastern Europeans) from "native" (northwestern Europeans), the census reflected the racial distinctions of the eugenicist-inspired intelligence tests.[6]

Racism and anti-immigrant sentiment in general and anti-Semitism in particular flourished in higher education. Jews were the first of the Euroimmigrant groups to enter colleges in significant numbers, so it wasn't surprising that they faced the brunt of discrimination there.[7] The Protestant elite complained that Jews were unwashed, uncouth, unrefined, loud, and pushy. Harvard University President A. Lawrence Lowell, who was also a vice president of the Immigration Restriction League, was openly opposed to Jews at Harvard. The Seven Sisters schools had a reputation for "flagrant discrimination." [. . .]

Anti-Semitic patterns set by these elite schools influenced standards of other schools, made anti-Semitism acceptable, and "made the aura of exclusivity a desirable commodity for the college-seeking clientele" (Synott 1986:250; and see Karabel 1984; Silberman 1985; Steinberg 1989: chaps. 5, 9). Fears that colleges "might soon be overrun by Jews" were publicly expressed at a 1918 meeting of the Association of New England Deans. In 1919 Columbia University took steps to decrease the number of entering Jews by a set of practices that soon came to be widely adopted. [. . .]

Columbia's quota against Jews was well known in my parents' community. My father is very proud of having beaten it and of being admitted to Columbia Dental School on the basis of his sculpting skill. In addition to demonstrating academic qualifications, he was asked to carve a soap ball, which he did so well and fast that his Protestant interviewer was willing to accept him. Although he became a teacher instead because the dental school tuition was too high, he took me to the dentist every week of my childhood and prolonged the agony by discussing the finer points of tooth filling and dental care. My father also almost failed the speech test required for his teaching license because he didn't speak "standard"—that is, non-immigrant, nonaccented—English. For my parents and most of their friends, English was a second language learned when they went to school, since their home language was Yiddish. They saw the speech test as designed to keep all ethnics, not just Jews, out of teaching. [. . .]

My parents' conclusion is that Jewish success, like their own, was the result of hard work and of placing a high value on education. They went to Brooklyn College during the Depression. My mother worked days and started school at night, and my father went during the day. Both their families encouraged them. More accurately, their families expected this effort from them. Everyone they knew was in the same boat, and their world was made up of Jews who advanced as they did. The picture of New York—where most Jews lived—seems to back them up. In 1920, Jews made up 80 percent of the students at New York's City College, 90 percent of Hunter College, and before World War I, 40 percent of private Columbia University. By 1934, Jews made up almost 24 percent of all law students nationally, and 56 percent of those in New York City. Still, more Jews became public school teachers, like my parents and their friends, than doctors or lawyers (Steinberg 1989:137, 227). Steinberg has debunked the myth that Jews advanced because of the cultural value placed on education. This is not to say that Jews did not advance. They did. "Jewish success in America was a matter of historical timing. . . . [T]here was a fortuitous match between the experience and skills of Jewish immigrants, on the one hand, and the manpower needs and opportunity structures, on the other" (1989:103). Jews were the only ones among the southern and eastern European immigrants who came from urban, commercial, craft, and manufacturing backgrounds, not least of which was garment manufacturing. They entered the United States in New York, center of the nation's booming garment industry, soon came to dominate its skilled (male) and "unskilled" (female) jobs, and found it an industry amenable to low-capital entrepreneurship. As a result, Jews were the first of the new European immigrants to create a middle class of small businesspersons early in the twentieth century. Jewish educational advances followed this business success and depended upon it, rather than creating it (see also Bodnar 1985 for a similar argument about mobility).

In the early twentieth century, Jewish college students entered a contested terrain in which the elite social mission was under challenge by a newer professional training mission. Pressure for change had begun to transform the curriculum and reorient college from a gentleman's bastion to a training ground for the middle-class professionals needed by an industrial economy. "The curriculum was overhauled to prepare students for careers in business, engineering, scientific farming, and the arts, and a variety of new professions such as accounting and pharmacy that were making their appearance in American colleges for the first time" (Steinberg 1989:229). Occupational training was precisely what drew Jews to college. In a setting where disparagement of intellectual pursuits and the gentleman's C were badges of distinction, it was not hard for Jews to excel.

How we interpret Jewish social mobility in this milieu depends on whom we compare Jews to. Compared with other immigrants, Jews were upwardly mobile. But compared with that of nonimmigrant whites, their mobility was very limited and circumscribed. Anti-immigrant racist and anti-Semitic barriers kept the Jewish middle class confined to a small number of occupations. Jews were excluded from mainstream corporate management and corporately employed professions, except in the garment and movie industries, which they built. Jews were almost totally excluded from university faculties (and the few that made it had powerful patrons). Jews were concentrated in small businesses, and in professions where they served a largely Jewish clientele (Davis 1990:146 n. 25; Silberman 1985:88–117; Sklare 1971:63–67). [. . .]

My parents' generation believed that Jews overcame anti-Semitic barriers because Jews are special. My belief is that the Jews who were upwardly mobile were special among Jews (and were also well placed to write the story). My generation might well counter our parents' story of pulling themselves up by their own bootstraps with, "But think what you might have been without the racism and with some affirmative action!" And that is precisely what the postwar boom, the decline of systematic, public anti-immigrant racism and anti-Semitism, and governmental affirmative action extended to white males.

Euroethnics into Whites

By the time I was an adolescent, Jews were just as white as the next white person. Until I was eight, I was a Jew in a world of Jews. Everyone on Avenue Z in Sheepshead Bay was Jewish. I spent my days playing and going to school on three blocks of Avenue Z, and visiting my grandparents in the nearby Jewish neighborhoods of Brighton Beach and Coney Island. There were plenty of Italians in my neighborhood, but they lived around the corner. They were a kind of Jew, but on the margins of my social horizons. Portuguese were even more distant, at the end of the bus ride, at Sheepshead Bay. [. . .] We left that world in 1949 when we moved to Valley Stream, Long Island, which was Protestant, Republican, and even had farms until Irish, Italian, and Jewish exurbanites like us gave it a more suburban and Democratic flavor. Neither religion nor ethnicity separated us at school or in the neighborhood. Except temporarily. In elementary school years, I remember a fair number of dirt-bomb (a good suburban weapon) wars on the block. Periodically one of the Catholic boys would accuse me or my brother of killing his God, to which we would reply, "Did not" and start lobbing dirt-bombs. Sometimes he would get his friends from Catholic school, and I would get mine from public school kids on the block, some of whom were Catholic. Hostilities lasted no more than a couple of hours and punctuated an otherwise friendly relationship. They ended by junior high years, when other things became more important. Jews, Catholics, and Protestants, Italians, Irish, Poles, and "English" (I don't remember hearing WASP as a kid) were mixed up on the block and in school. We thought of ourselves as middle class and very enlightened because our ethnic backgrounds seemed so irrelevant to high school culture. We didn't see race (we thought), and racism was not part of our peer consciousness, nor were the immigrant or working-class histories of our families.

Like most chicken and egg problems, it's hard to know which came first. Did Jews and other Euroethnics become white because they became middle class? That is, did money whiten? Or did being incorporated in an expanded version of whiteness open up the economic doors to a middle-class status? Clearly, both tendencies were at work. Some of the changes set in motion during the war against fascism led to a more inclusive version of whiteness. Anti-Semitism and anti-European racism lost respectability. The 1940 census no longer distinguished native whites of native parentage from those, like my parents, of immigrant parentage, so that Euroimmigrants and their children were more securely white by submersion in an expanded notion of whiteness. (This census also changed the race of Mexicans to white [U.S. Bureau of the Census, 1940:4].) Theories of nurture and culture replaced theories of nature and biology. Instead of dirty and dangerous races who would destroy U.S. democracy, immigrants became ethnic groups whose children had successfully assimilated into the mainstream and risen to the middle class. In this new myth, Euroethnic suburbs like mine became the measure of U.S. democracy's victory over racism. Jewish mobility became a new Horatio Alger story. In time and with hard work, every ethnic group would get a piece of the pie, and the United States would be a nation with equal opportunity for all its people to become part of a prosperous middle-class majority. And it seemed that Euroethnic immigrants and their children were delighted to join middle America.[8]

This is not to say that anti-Semitism disappeared after World War II, only that it fell from fashion and was driven underground. [. . .]

Although changing views on who was white made it easier for Euroethnics to become middle class, it was also the case that economic prosperity played a very powerful role in the whitening process. Economic mobility of Jews and other Euroethnics rested ultimately on U.S. postwar economic prosperity with its enormously expanded need for professional, technical, and managerial labor, and on government assistance in providing it. The United States emerged from the war with the strongest economy in the world. [. . .] The postwar period was a historic moment for real class mobility and for the affluence we have erroneously come to believe was the U.S. norm. It was a time when the old white and the newly white masses became middle class.

The GI Bill of Rights, as the 1944 Serviceman's Readjustment Act was known, was arguably the most massive affirmative action program in U.S. history. It was created to develop needed labor-force skills, and to provide those who had them with a lifestyle that reflected their value to the economy. The GI benefits ultimately extended to sixteen million GIs (veterans of the Korean War as well) included priority in jobs—that is, preferential hiring, but no one objected to it then; financial support during the job search; small loans for starting up businesses; and, most important, low-interest home loans and educational benefits, which included tuition and living expenses (Brown 1946; Hurd 1946; Mosch 1975; *Postwar Jobs for Veterans* 1945; Willenz 1983). This legislation was rightly regarded as one of the most revolutionary postwar programs. I call it affirmative action because it was aimed at and disproportionately helped male, Euro-origin GIs. [. . .]

Education and Occupation

It is important to remember that prior to the war, a college degree was still very much a "mark of the upper class" (Willenz 1983:165). Colleges were largely finishing schools for Protestant elites. Before the postwar boom, schools could not begin to accommodate the American masses. Even in New York City before the 1930s, neither the public schools nor City College had room for more than a tiny fraction of potential immigrant students.

Not so after the war. The almost eight million GIs who took advantage of their educational benefits under the GI bill caused "the greatest wave of college building in American history" (Nash et al. 1986:885). White male GIs were able to take advantage of their educational benefits for college and technical training, so they were particularly well positioned to seize the opportunities provided by the new demands for professional, managerial, and technical labor. "It has been well documented that the GI educational benefits transformed American higher education and raised the educational level of that generation and generations to come. With many provisions for assistance in upgrading their educational attainments veterans pulled ahead of nonveterans in earning capacity. In the long run it was the nonveterans who had fewer opportunities" (Willenz 1983:165).[9] [. . .]

Even more significantly, the postwar boom transformed the U.S. class structure—or at least its status structure—so that the middle class expanded to encompass most of the population. Before the war, most Jews, like most other Americans, were working class. Already upwardly mobile before the war relative to other immigrants, Jews floated high on this rising economic tide, and most of them entered the middle class. Still, even the high tide missed some Jews. As late as 1973, some 15 percent of New York's Jews were poor or near-poor, and in the 1960s, almost 25 percent of employed Jewish men remained manual workers (Steinberg 1989:89–90).

Educational and occupational GI benefits really constituted affirmative action programs for white males because they were decidedly not extended to African Americans or to women of any race. White male privilege was shaped against the backdrop of wartime racism and postwar sexism. During and after the war, there was an upsurge in white racist violence against black servicemen in public schools, and in the KKK, which spread to California and New York (Dalfiume 1969:133–134). The number of lynchings rose during the war, and in 1943 there were antiblack race riots in several large northern cities. Although there was a wartime labor shortage, black people were discriminated against in access to well-paid defense industry jobs and in housing. In 1946 there were white riots against African Americans across the South, and in Chicago and Philadelphia as well. Gains made as a result of the wartime Civil Rights movement, especially employment in defense-related industries, were lost with peace-time conversion as black workers were the first fired, often in violation of seniority (Wynn 1976:114, 116). White women were also laid off, ostensibly to make jobs for demobilized servicemen, and in the long run women lost most of the gains they had made in wartime (Kessler-Harris 1982). We now know that women did not leave the labor force in any significant numbers but instead were forced to find inferior jobs, largely nonunion, part-time, and clerical.

Theoretically available to all veterans, in practice women and black veterans did not get anywhere near their share of GI benefits. Because women's units were not treated as part of the military, women in them were not considered veterans and were ineligible for Veterans' Administration (VA) benefits (Willenz 1983:168). The barriers that almost completely shut African-American GIs out of their benefits were more complex. In Wynn's portrait (1976:115), black GIs anticipated starting new lives, just like their white counterparts. Over 43 percent hoped to return to school and most expected to relocate, to find better jobs in new lines of work. The exodus from the South toward the North and far West was particularly large. So it wasn't a question of any lack of ambition on the part of African-American GIs.

Rather, the military, the Veterans' Administration, the U.S. Employment Service, and the Federal Housing Administration (FHA) effectively denied African-American GIs access to their benefits and to the new educational, occupational, and residential opportunities. Black GIs who served in the thoroughly segregated armed forces during World War II served under white officers, usually southerners (Binkin and Eitelberg 1982: Dalfiume 1969; Foner 1974; Johnson 1967; Nalty and MacGregor 1981). African-American soldiers were disproportionately given dishonorable discharges, which denied them veterans' rights under the GI Bill. Thus between August and November 1946, 21 percent of white soldiers and 39 percent of black soldiers were dishonorably discharged. Those who did get an honorable discharge then faced the Veterans' Administration and the U.S. Employment Service. The latter, which was responsible for job placements, employed very few African Americans, especially in the South. This meant that black veterans did not receive much employment information, and that the offers they did receive were for low-paid and menial jobs. "In one survey of 50 cities, the movement of blacks into peacetime employment was found to be lagging far behind that of white veterans: in Arkansas 95 percent of the placements made by the USES for Afro-Americans were in service or unskilled jobs" (Nalty and MacGregor 1981:218, and see 60–61). African Americans were also less likely than whites, regardless of GI status, to gain new jobs commensurate with their wartime jobs, and they suffered more heavily. For example, in San Francisco by 1948, Black Americans "had dropped back halfway to their prewar employment status" (Wynn 1976:114, 116).[10]

Black GIs faced discrimination in the educational system as well. Despite the end of restrictions on Jews and other Euroethnics, African Americans were not welcome in white colleges. Black colleges were overcrowded, and the combination of segregation and prejudice made for few alternatives. About twenty thousand black veterans attended college by 1947, most in black colleges, but almost as many, fifteen thousand, could not gain entry. Predictably, the disproportionately few African Americans who did gain access to their educational benefits were able, like their white counterparts, to become doctors and engineers, and to enter the black middle class (Walker 1970).

Suburbanization

In 1949, ensconced at Valley Stream, I watched potato farms turn into Levittown and into Idlewild (later Kennedy) Airport. This was a major spectator sport in our first years on suburban Long Island. A typical weekend would bring various aunts, uncles, and cousins out from the city. After a huge meal we would pile in the car—itself a novelty—to look at the bulldozed acres and comment on the match-box construction. During the week, my mother and I would look at the houses going up within walking distance.

Bill Levitt built a basic 900–1,000-square-foot, somewhat expandable house for a lower-middle-class and working-class market on Long Island, and later in Pennsylvania and New Jersey (Gans 1967). Levittown started out as two thousand units of rental housing at sixty dollars a month, designed to meet the low-income housing needs of returning war vets, many of whom, like my Aunt Evie and Uncle Julie, were living in Quonset huts. By May 1947, Levitt and Sons had acquired enough land in Hempstead

Township on Long Island to build four thousand houses, and by the next February, he'd built six thousand units and named the development after himself. After 1948, federal financing for the construction of rental housing tightened, and Levitt switched to building houses for sale. By 1951 Levittown was a development of some fifteen thousand families. [. . .]

At the beginning of World War II, about 33 percent of all U.S. families owned their houses. That percentage doubled in twenty years. Most Levittowners looked just like my family. They came from New York City or Long Island; about 17 percent were military, from nearby Mitchell Field; Levittown was their first house; and almost everyone was married. The 1947 inhabitants were over 75 percent white collar, but by 1950 more blue-collar families moved in, so that by 1951, "barely half" of the new residents were white collar, and by 1960 their occupational profile was somewhat more working class than for Nassau County as a whole. By this time too, almost one-third of Levittown's people were either foreign-born or, like my parents, first-generation U.S. born (Dobriner 1963:91, 100).

The FHA was key to buyers and builders alike. Thanks to it, suburbia was open to more than GIs. People like us would never have been in the market for houses without FHA and VA low-down-payment, low-interest, long-term loans to young buyers.[11] [. . .]

The FHA believed in racial segregation. Throughout its history, it publicly and actively promoted restrictive covenants. Before the war, these forbade sale to Jews and Catholics as well as to African Americans. The deed to my house in Detroit had such a covenant, which theoretically prevented it from being sold to Jews or African Americans. Even after the Supreme Court ended legal enforcement of restrictive covenants in 1948, the FHA continued to encourage builders to write them against African Americans. FHA underwriting manuals openly insisted on racially homogeneous neighborhoods, and their loans were made only in white neighborhoods. I bought my Detroit house in 1972 from Jews who were leaving a largely African-American neighborhood. By that time, after the 1968 Fair Housing Act, restrictive covenants were a dead letter (although blockbusting by realtors was rapidly replacing it).

With the federal government behind them, virtually all developers refused to sell to African Americans. Palo Alto and Levittown, like most suburbs as late as 1960, were virtually all white. Out of 15,741 houses and

65,276 people, averaging 4.2 people per house, only 220 Levittowners, or 52 households, were "nonwhite." In 1958 Levitt announced publicly at a press conference to open his New Jersey development that he would not sell to black buyers. This caused a furor, since the state of New Jersey (but not the U.S. government) prohibited discrimination in federally subsidized housing. Levitt was sued and fought it, although he was ultimately persuaded by township ministers to integrate. [. . .]

The result of these policies was that African Americans were totally shut out of the suburban boom. An article in *Harper's* described the housing available to black GIs. "On his way to the base each morning, Sergeant Smith passes an attractive air-conditioned, FHA-financed housing project. It was built for service families. Its rents are little more than the Smiths pay for their shack. And there are half-a-dozen vacancies, but none for Negroes" (quoted in Foner 1974:195).

Where my family felt the seductive pull of suburbia, Marshall Berman's experienced the brutal push of urban renewal. In the Bronx in the 1950s, Robert Moses's Cross-Bronx Expressway erased "a dozen solid, settled, densely populated neighborhoods like our own; . . . something like 60,000 working- and lower-middle-class people, mostly Jews, but with many Italians, Irish and Blacks thrown in, would be thrown out of their homes. . . . For ten years, through the late 1950s and early 1960s, the center of the Bronx was pounded and blasted and smashed."

Urban renewal made postwar cities into bad places to live. At a physical level, urban renewal reshaped them, and federal programs brought private developers and public officials together to create downtown central business districts where there had formerly been a mix of manufacturing, commerce, and working-class neighborhoods. Manufacturing was scattered to the peripheries of the city, which were ringed and bisected by a national system of highways. Some working-class neighborhoods were bulldozed, but others remained (Hartman 1975). In Los Angeles, as in New York's Bronx, the postwar period saw massive freeway construction right through the heart of old working-class neighborhoods. In East Los Angeles and Santa Monica, Chicano and African-American communities were divided in half or blasted to smithereens by the highways bringing Angelenos to the new white suburbs, or to make way for civic monuments like Dodger Stadium (Pardo 1990).

Urban renewal was the other side of the process by which Jewish and other working-class Euroimmigrants became middle class. It was the push to suburbia's seductive pull. The fortunate white survivors of urban renewal headed disproportionately for suburbia, where they could partake of prosperity and the good life. [. . .]

If the federal stick of urban renewal joined the FHA carrot of cheap mortgages to send masses of Euros to the suburbs, the FHA had a different kind of one-two punch for African Americans. Segregation kept them out of the suburbs, and redlining made sure they could not buy or repair their homes in the neighborhoods where they were allowed to live. The FHA practiced systematic redlining. This was a system developed by its predecessor, the Home Owners Loan Corporation (HOLC), which in the 1930s developed an elaborate neighborhood rating system that placed the highest (green) value on all-white, middle-class neighborhoods, and the lowest (red) on racially nonwhite or mixed and working-class neighborhoods. High ratings meant high property values. The idea was that low property values in redlined neighborhoods made them bad investments. The FHA was, after all, created by and for banks and the housing industry. Redlining warned banks not to lend there, and the FHA would not insure mortgages in such neighborhoods. Redlining created a self-fulfilling prophecy. "With the assistance of local realtors and banks, it assigned one of the four ratings to every block in every city. The resulting information was then translated into the appropriate color [green, blue, yellow, and red] and duly recorded on secret 'Residential Security Maps' in local HOLC offices. The maps themselves were placed in elaborate 'City Survey Files,' which consisted of reports, questionnaires, and workpapers relating to current and future values of real estate" (Jackson 1985:197).[12]

FHA's and VA's refusal to guarantee loans in redlined neighborhoods made it virtually impossible for African Americans to borrow money for home improvement or purchase. Because these maps and surveys were quite secret, it took the 1960s Civil Rights movement to make these practices and their devastating consequences public. As a result, those who fought urban renewal or who sought to make a home in the urban ruins found themselves locked out of the middle class. They also faced an ideological assault that labeled their neighborhoods slums and called those who lived in them slum dwellers (Gans 1962).

The record is very clear that instead of seizing the opportunity to end institutionalized racism, the federal government did its best to shut and double seal the postwar window of opportunity in African Americans' faces. It consistently refused to combat segregation in the social institutions that were key for upward mobility: education, housing, and employment. Moreover, federal programs that were themselves designed to assist demobilized GIs and young families systematically discriminated against African Americans. Such programs reinforced white/nonwhite racial distinctions even as intrawhite racialization was falling out of fashion. This other side of the coin, that white men of northwestern or southeastern European ancestry were treated equally in theory and in practice with regard to the benefits they received, was part of the larger postwar whitening of Jews and other eastern and southern Europeans.

The myth that Jews pulled themselves up by their own bootstraps ignores the fact that it took federal programs to create the conditions whereby the abilities of Jews and other European immigrants could be recognized and rewarded rather than denigrated and denied. The GI Bill and FHA and VA mortgages were forms of affirmative action that allowed male Jews and other Euro-American men to become suburban homeowners and to get the training that allowed them—but not women vets or war workers—to become professionals, technicians, salesmen, and managers in a growing economy. Jews' and other white ethnics' upward mobility was the result of programs that allowed us to float on a rising economic tide. To African Americans, the government offered the cement boots of segregation, redlining, urban renewal, and discrimination.

Those racially skewed gains have been passed across the generations, so that racial inequality seems to maintain itself "naturally," even after legal segregation ended. Today, in a shrinking economy where downward mobility is the norm, the children and grandchildren of the postwar beneficiaries of the economic boom have some precious advantages. For example, having parents who own their own homes or who have decent retirement benefits can make a real difference in young people's ability to take on huge college loans or to come up with a down payment for a house. Even this simple inheritance helps perpetuate the gap between whites and nonwhites. Sure Jews needed ability, but ability was not enough to make it. The same applies even more in today's long recession.

Notes

This is a revised and expanded version of a paper published in *Jewish Currents* in June 1992 and delivered at the 1992 meetings of the American Anthropological Association in the session *Blacks and Jews, 1992: Reaching across the Cultural Boundaries* organized by Angela Gilliam. I would like to thank Emily Abel, Katya Gibel Azoulay, Edna Bonacich, Angela Gilliam, Isabelle Gunning, Valerie Matsumoto, Regina Morantz-Sanchez, Roger Sanjek, Rabbi Chaim Seidler-Feller, Janet Silverstein, and Eloise Klein Healy's writing group for uncovering wonderful sources and for critical readings along the way.

1. Indeed, Boasian and Du Boisian anthropology developed in active political opposition to this nativism.

2. On immigrants as part of the industrial work force, see Steinberg 1989:36.

3. I thank Roger Sanjek for providing me with this source.

4. It was intended, as Davenport wrote to the president of the American Museum of Natural History, Henry Fairfield Osborne, as "an anthropological society . . . with a central governing body, self-elected and self-perpetuating, and very limited in members, and also confined to native Americans who are anthropologically, socially and politically sound, no Bolsheviki need apply."

5. I thank Valerie Matsumoto for telling me about the Thind case and Katya Gibel Azoulay for providing this information to me on the Virginia statute.

6. "The distinction between white and colored" has been "the only racial classification which has been carried through all the 15 censuses." "Colored" consisted of "Negroes" and "other races": Mexican, Indian, Chinese, Japanese, Filipino, Hindu, Korean, Hawaiian, Malay, Siamese, and Samoan. (U.S. Bureau of the Census, 1930:25, 26).

7. For why Jews entered colleges earlier than other immigrants, and for a challenge to views that attribute it to Jewish culture, see Steinberg 1989.

8. Indeed, Jewish social scientists were prominent in creating this ideology of the United States as a meritocracy. Most prominent of course was Nathan Glazer, but among them also were Charles Silberman and Marshall Sklare.

9. The belief was widespread that "the GI Bill . . . helped millions of families move into the middle class" (Nash et al. 1986:885). A study that compares mobility among veterans and nonveterans provides a kind of confirmation. In an unnamed small city in Illinois, Havighurst and his colleagues (1951) found no significant

difference between veterans and nonveterans, but this was because apparently very few veterans used any of their GI benefits.

10. African Americans and Japanese Americans were the main target of wartime racism. By contrast, there were virtually no anti-German American or anti-Italian American policies in World War II (see Takaki 1989:357–406).

11. See Eichler 1982:5 for homeowning percentages; Jackson (1985:205) found an increase in families living in owner-occupied buildings, rising from 44 percent in 1934 to 63 percent in 1972.

12. These ideas from the real estate industry were "codified and legitimated in 1930s work by University of Chicago sociologist Robert Park and real estate professor Homer Hoyt" (Jackson 1985:198–199).

References

Binkin, Martin, and Mark J. Eitelberg. 1982. *Blacks and the Military.* Washington, D.C.: Brookings.

Bodnar, John. 1985. *The Transplanted: A History of Immigrants in Urban America.* Bloomington: Indiana University Press.

Brody, David. 1980. *Workers in Industrial America: Essays of the Twentieth Century Struggle.* New York: Oxford University Press.

Brown, Francis J. 1946. *Educational Opportunities for Veterans.* Washington, D.C.: Public Affairs Press, American Council on Public Affairs.

Carlson, Lewis H., and George A. Colburn. 1972. *In Their Place: White America Defines Her Minorities, 1850–1950.* New York: Wiley.

Dalfiume, Richard M. 1969. *Desegregation of the U.S. Armed Forces: Fighting on Two Fronts, 1939–1953.* Columbia: University of Missouri Press.

Davis, Mike. 1990. *City of Quartz.* London: Verso.

Dobriner, William M. 1963. *Class in Suburbia.* Englewood Cliffs, N.J.: Prentice-Hall.

Eichler, Ned. 1982. *The Merchant Builders.* Cambridge, Mass.: MIT Press.

Fields, Barbara Jeanne. 1990. Slavery, Race, and Ideology in the United States of America. *New Left Review* 181:95–118.

Foner, Jack. 1974. *Blacks and the Military in American History: A New Perspective.* New York: Praeger.

Gans, Herbert. 1962. *The Urban Villagers.* New York: Free Press.

———. 1967. *The Levittowners.* New York: Pantheon.

Gordon, Milton. 1964. *Assimilation in American Life.* New York: Oxford University Press.

Hartman, Chester. 1975. *Housing and Social Policy.* Englewood Cliffs, N.J.: Prentice-Hall.

Higham, John. 1955. *Strangers in the Land.* New Brunswick, N.J.: Rutgers University Press.

Hurd, Charles. 1946. *The Veterans' Program: A Complete Guide to Its Benefits, Rights, and Options.* New York: McGraw-Hill.

Jackson, Kenneth T. 1985. *Crabgrass Frontier: The Suburbanization of the United States.* New York: Oxford University Press.

Johnson, Jesse J. 1967. *Ebony Brass: An Autobiography of Negro Frustration amid Aspiration.* New York: Frederick.

Karabel, Jerome. 1984. Status-Group Struggle, Organizational Interests, and the Limits of Institutional Autonomy. *Theory and Society* 13:1–40.

Kessler-Harris, Alice. 1982. *Out to Work: A History of Wage-Earning Women in the United States.* New York: Oxford University Press.

Martyn, Byron Curti. 1979. Racism in the U.S.: A History of Anti-Miscegenation Legislation and Litigation. Ph.D. diss., University of Southern California.

Mosch, Theodore R. 1975. *The GI Bill: A Breakthrough in Educational and Social Policy in the United States.* Hicksville, N.Y.: Exposition.

Nalty, Bernard C., and Morris J. MacGregor, eds. 1981. *Blacks in the Military: Essential Documents.* Wilmington, Del.: Scholarly Resources.

Nash, Gary B., Julie Roy Jeffrey, John R. Howe, Allen F. Davis, Peter J. Frederick, and Allen M. Winkler. 1986. *The American People: Creating a Nation and a Society.* New York: Harper and Row.

Pardo, Mary. 1990. Mexican-American Women Grassroots Community Activists: "Mothers of East Los Angeles." *Frontiers* 11:1–7.

Postwar Jobs for Veterans. 1945. *Annals of the American Academy of Political and Social Science* 238 (March).

Saxton, Alexander. 1971. *The Indispensable Enemy.* Berkeley and Los Angeles: University of California Press.

———. 1990. *The Rise and Fall of the White Republic.* London: Verso.

Silberman, Charles. 1985. *A Certain People: American Jews and Their Lives Today.* New York: Summit.

Sklare, Marshall. 1971. *America's Jews.* New York: Random House.

Sowell, Thomas. 1981. *Ethnic America: A History.* New York: Basic.

Steinberg, Stephen. 1989. *The Ethnic Myth: Race, Ethnicity, and Class in America.* 2d ed. Boston: Beacon.

Synott, Marcia Graham. 1986. Anti-Semitism and American Universities: Did Quotas Follow the Jews? In *Anti-Semitism in American History,* ed. David A. Gerber. Urbana: University of Illinois Press, 233–274.

Takaki, Ronald. 1989. *Strangers from a Different Shore.* Boston: Little, Brown.

Tobin, Gary A., ed. 1987. *Divided Neighborhoods: Changing Patterns of Racial Segregation.* Beverly Hills: Sage.

U.S. Bureau of the Census. 1930. *Fifteenth Census of the United States.* Vol. 2. Washington, D.C.: U.S. Government Printing Office.

_____. 1940. *Sixteenth Census of the United States.* Vol. 2. Washington, D.C.: U.S. Government Printing Office.

Walker, Olive. 1970. The Windsor Hills School Story. *Integrated Education: Race and Schools* 8(3):4–9.

Willenz, June A. 1983. *Women Veterans: America's Forgotten Heroines.* New York: Continuum.

Wynn, Neil A. 1976. *The Afro-American and the Second World War.* London: Elek.

9

Masculinity as Homophobia

Fear, Shame, and Silence in the Construction of Gender Identity

Michael S. Kimmel

"Funny thing," [Curley's wife] said. "If I catch any one man, and he's alone, I get along fine with him. But just let two of the guys get together an' you won't talk. Jus' nothin' but mad." She dropped her fingers and put her hands on her hips. "You're all scared of each other, that's what. Ever'one of you's scared the rest is goin' to get something on you."
—John Steinbeck, *Of Mice and Men* (1937)

We think of manhood as eternal, a timeless essence that resides deep in the heart of every man. We think of manhood as a thing, a quality that one either has or doesn't have. We think of manhood as innate, residing in the particular biological composition of the human male, the result of androgens or the possession of a penis. We think of manhood as a transcendent tangible property that each man must manifest in the world, the reward presented with great ceremony to a young novice by his elders for having successfully completed an arduous initiation ritual. In the words of poet Robert Bly (1990), "the structure at the bottom of the male psyche is still as firm as it was twenty thousand years ago" (p. 230).

In this chapter, I view masculinity as a constantly changing collection of meanings that we construct through our relationships with ourselves, with each other, and with our world. Manhood is neither static nor timeless; it is historical. Manhood is not the manifestation of an inner essence; it is socially constructed. Manhood does not bubble up to consciousness from our biological makeup; it is created in culture. Manhood means different things at different times to different people. We come to know what it means to be a man in our culture by setting our definitions in opposition to a set of "others"—racial minorities, sexual minorities, and, above all, women.

Our definitions of manhood are constantly changing, being played out on the political and social terrain on which the relationships between women and men are played out. In fact, the search for a transcendent, timeless definition of manhood is itself a sociological phenomenon—we tend to search for the timeless and eternal during moments of crisis, those points of transition when old definitions no longer work and new definitions are yet to be firmly established.

This idea that manhood is socially constructed and historically shifting should not be understood as a loss, that something is being taken away from men. In fact, it gives us something extraordinarily valuable—agency, the capacity to act. It gives us a sense of historical possibilities to replace the despondent resignation that invariably attends timeless, ahistorical essentialisms. Our behaviors are not simply "just human nature," because "boys will be boys." From the materials we find around us in our culture—other people, ideas, objects—we actively create our worlds, our identities. Men, both individually and collectively, can change.

In this chapter, I explore this social and historical construction of both hegemonic masculinity and alternate masculinities, with an eye toward offering a new theoretical model of American manhood.[1] To accomplish this I first uncover some of the hidden gender meanings in classical statements of social and political philosophy, so that I can anchor the emergence of contemporary manhood in specific historical and social contexts. I then spell out the ways in which this version of masculinity emerged in the United States, by tracing both psychoanalytic developmental sequences and a historical trajectory in the development of marketplace relationships.

Classical Social Theory as a Hidden Meditation of Manhood
Begin this inquiry by looking at four passages from that set of texts commonly called classical social and political theory. You will, no doubt, recognize them, but I invite you to recall the way they were discussed in your undergraduate or graduate courses in theory:

> The bourgeoisie cannot exist without constantly revolutionizing the instruments of production, and thereby the relations of production, and with them the whole relations of society. Conservation of the old modes of production in unaltered form, was, on the contrary, the first condition of existence for all earlier industrial classes. Constant revolutionizing of production, uninterrupted disturbance of all social conditions, everlasting uncertainty and agitation distinguish the bourgeois epoch from all earlier ones. All fixed, fast-frozen relations, with their train of ancient and venerable prejudices and opinions are swept away, all new-formed ones become antiquated before they can ossify. All that is solid melts into air, all that is holy is profaned, and man is at last compelled to face with sober senses, his real conditions of life, and his relation with his kind. (Marx and Engels, 1848/1964)

> An American will build a house in which to pass his old age and sell it before the roof is on; he will plant a garden and rent it just as the trees are coming into bearing; he will clear a field and leave others to reap the harvest; he will take up a profession and leave it, settle in one place and soon go off elsewhere with his changing desires. . . . At first sight there is something astonishing in this spectacle of so many lucky men restless in the midst of abundance. But it is a spectacle as old as the world; all that is new is to see a whole people performing in it. (Tocqueville, 1835/1967)

> Where the fulfillment of the calling cannot directly be related to the highest spiritual and cultural values, or when, on the other hand, it

need not be felt simply as economic compulsion, the individual generally abandons the attempt to justify it at all. In the field of its highest
development, in the United States, the pursuit of wealth, stripped of
its religious and ethical meaning, tends to become associated with
purely mundane passions, which often actually give it the character of
sport. (Weber, 1905/1966)

■   ■   ■

We are warned by a proverb against serving two masters at the same
time. The poor ego has things even worse: it serves three severe masters and does what it can to bring their claims and demands into harmony with one another. These claims are always divergent and often
seem incompatible. No wonder that the ego so often fails in its task.
Its three tyrannical masters are the external world, the super ego and
the id. . . . It feels hemmed in on three sides, threatened by three kinds
of danger, to which, if it is hard pressed, it reacts by generating anxiety. . . . Thus the ego, driven by the id, confined by the super ego, re-
pulsed by reality, struggles to master its economic task of bringing
about harmony among the forces and influences working in and
upon it; and we can understand how it is that so often we cannot suppress a cry: "Life is not easy!" (Freud, "The Dissection of the Psychical
Personality," 1933/1966)

If your social science training was anything like mine, these were offered as descriptions of the bourgeoisie under capitalism, of individuals in
democratic societies, of the fate of the Protestant work ethic under the
ever rationalizing spirit of capitalism, or of the arduous task of the autonomous ego in psychological development. Did anyone ever mention
that in all four cases the theorists were describing men? Not just "man" as
in generic mankind, but a particular type of masculinity, a definition of
manhood that derives its identity from participation in the marketplace,
from interaction with other men in that marketplace—in short, a model
of masculinity for whom identity is based on homosocial competition?
Three years before Tocqueville found Americans "restless in the midst of
abundance," Senator Henry Clay had called the United States "a nation of
self-made men."

What does it mean to be "self-made"? What are the consequences of self-making for the individual man, for other men, for women? It is this notion of manhood—rooted in the sphere of production, the public arena, a masculinity grounded not in landownership or in artisanal republican virtue but in successful participation in marketplace competition—this has been the defining notion of American manhood. Masculinity must be proved, and no sooner is it proved that it is again questioned and must be proved again—constant, relentless, unachievable, and ultimately the quest for proof becomes so meaningless that it takes on the characteristics, as Weber said, of a sport. He who has the most toys when he dies wins.

Where does this version of masculinity come from? How does it work? What are the consequences of this version of masculinity for women, for other men, and for individual men themselves? These are the questions I address in this chapter.

Masculinity as History and the History of Masculinity

The idea of masculinity expressed in the previous extracts is the product of historical shifts in the grounds on which men rooted their sense of themselves as men. To argue that cultural definitions of gender identity are historically specific goes only so far; we have to specify exactly what those models were. In my historical inquiry into the development of these models of manhood[2] I chart the fate of two models for manhood at the turn of the 19th century and the emergence of a third in the first few decades of that century.

In the late 18th and early 19th centuries, two models of manhood prevailed. The *Genteel Patriarch* derived his identity from landownership. Supervising his estate, he was refined, elegant, and given to casual sensuousness. He was a doting and devoted father, who spent much of his time supervising the estate and with his family. Think of George Washington or Thomas Jefferson as examples. By contrast, the *Heroic Artisan* embodied the physical strength and republican virtue that Jefferson observed in the yeoman farmer, independent urban craftsman, or shopkeeper. Also a devoted father, the Heroic Artisan taught his son his craft, bringing him through ritual apprenticeship to status as master craftsman. Economically autonomous, the Heroic Artisan also cherished his democratic community, delighting in the participatory democracy of the town meeting.

Think of Paul Revere at his pewter shop, shirtsleeves rolled up, a leather apron—a man who took pride in his work.

Heroic Artisans and Genteel Patriarchs lived in casual accord, in part because their gender ideals were complementary (both supported participatory democracy and individual autonomy, although patriarchs tended to support more powerful state machineries and also supported slavery) and because they rarely saw one another: Artisans were decidedly urban and the Genteel Patriarchs ruled their rural estates. By the 1830s, though, this casual symbiosis was shattered by the emergence of a new vision of masculinity, *Marketplace Manhood.*

Marketplace Man derived his identity entirely from his success in the capitalist marketplace, as he accumulated wealth, power, status. He was the urban entrepreneur, the businessman. Restless, agitated, and anxious, Marketplace Man was an absentee landlord at home and an absent father with his children, devoting himself to his work in an increasingly homosocial environment—a male-only world in which he pits himself against other men. His efforts at self-making transform the political and economic spheres, casting aside the Genteel Patriarch as an anachronistic feminized dandy—sweet, but ineffective and outmoded, and transforming the Heroic Artisan into a dispossessed proletarian, a wage slave.

As Tocqueville would have seen it, the coexistence of the Genteel Patriarch and the Heroic Artisan embodied the fusion of liberty and equality. Genteel Patriarchy was the manhood of the traditional aristocracy, the class that embodied the virtue of liberty. The Heroic Artisan embodied democratic community, the solidarity of the urban shopkeeper or craftsman. Liberty and democracy, the patriarch and the artisan, could, and did, coexist. But Marketplace Man is capitalist man, and he makes both freedom and equality problematic, eliminating the freedom of the aristocracy and proletarianizing the equality of the artisan. In one sense, American history has been an effort to restore, retrieve, or reconstitute the virtues of Genteel Patriarchy and Heroic Artisanate as they were being transformed in the capitalist marketplace.

Marketplace Manhood was a manhood that required proof, and that required the acquisition of tangible goods as evidence of success. It reconstituted itself by the exclusion of "others"—women, nonwhite men, nonnative-born men, homosexual men—and by terrified flight into a pristine mythic homosocial Eden where men could, at last, be real men among other men. The story of the ways in which Marketplace Man becomes American Everyman is a tragic tale, a tale of striving to live up to impossible ideals of success leading to chronic terrors of emasculation, emotional emptiness, and a gendered rage that leave a wide swath of destruction in their wake.

Masculinities as Power Relations

Marketplace Masculinity describes the normative definition of American masculinity. It describes his characteristics—aggression, competition, anxiety—and the arena in which those characteristics are deployed—the public sphere, the marketplace. If the marketplace is the arena in which manhood is tested and proved, it is a gendered arena, in which tensions between women and men and tensions among different groups of men are weighted with meaning. These tensions suggest that cultural definitions of gender are played out in a contested terrain and are themselves power relations.

All masculinities are not created equal; or rather, we are all *created* equal, but any hypothetical equality evaporates quickly because our definitions of masculinity are not equally valued in our society. One definition of manhood continues to remain the standard against which other forms of manhood are measured and evaluated. Within the dominant culture, the masculinity that defines white, middle class, early middle-aged, heterosexual men is the masculinity that sets the standards for other men, against which other men are measured and, more often than not, found wanting. Sociologist Erving Goffman (1963) wrote that in America, there is only "one complete, unblushing male":

> a young, married, white, urban, northern heterosexual, Protestant father of college education, fully employed, of good complexion, weight and height, and a recent record in sports. Every American male tends to look out upon the world from this perspective. . . . Any male who fails to qualify in any one of these ways is likely to view himself . . . as unworthy, incomplete, and inferior. (p. 128)

This is the definition that we will call "hegemonic" masculinity, the image of masculinity of those men who hold power, which has become the standard in psychological evaluations, sociological research, and self-help and advice literature for teaching young men to become "real men" (Connell, 1987). The hegemonic definition of manhood is a man *in* power, a man *with* power, and a man *of* power. We equate manhood with being strong, successful, capable, reliable, in control. The very definitions of manhood we have developed in our culture maintain the power that some men have over other men and that men have over women.

Our culture's definition of masculinity is thus several stories at once. It is about the individual man's quest to accumulate those cultural symbols that denote manhood, signs that he has in fact achieved it. It is about those standards being used against women to prevent their inclusion in public life and their consignment to a devalued private sphere. It is about the differential access that different types of men have to those cultural resources that confer manhood and about how each of these groups then develop their own modifications to preserve and claim their manhood. It is about the power of these definitions themselves to serve to maintain the real-life power that men have over women and that some men have over other men.

This definition of manhood has been summarized cleverly by psychologist Robert Brannon (1976) into four succinct phrases:

1. "No Sissy Stuff!" One may never do anything that even remotely suggests femininity. Masculinity is the relentless repudiation of the feminine.
2. "Be a Big Wheel." Masculinity is measured by power, success, wealth, and status. As the current saying goes, "He who has the most toys when he dies wins."
3. "Be a Sturdy Oak." Masculinity depends on remaining calm and reliable in a crisis, holding emotions in check. In fact, proving you're a man depends on never showing your emotions at all. Boys don't cry.
4. "Give 'em Hell." Exude an aura of manly daring and aggression. Go for it. Take risks.

These rules contain the elements of the definition against which virtually all American men are measured. Failure to embody these rules, to affirm the power of the rules and one's achievement of them is a source of men's confusion and pain. Such a model is, of course, unrealizable for any man. But we keep trying, valiantly and vainly, to measure up. American masculinity is a relentless test.[3] The chief test is contained in the first rule.

Whatever the variations by race, class, age, ethnicity, or sexual orientation, being a man means "not being like women." This notion of anti-femininity lies at the heart of contemporary and historical conceptions of manhood, so that masculinity is defined more by what one is not rather than who one is.

Masculinity as the Flight From the Feminine

Historically and developmentally, masculinity has been defined as the flight from women, the repudiation of femininity. Since Freud, we have come to understand that developmentally the central task that every little boy must confront is to develop a secure identity for himself as a man. As Freud had it, the oedipal project is a process of the boy's renouncing his identification with and deep emotional attachment to his mother and then replacing her with the father as the object of identification. Notice that he reidentifies but never reattaches. This entire process, Freud argued, is set in motion by the boy's sexual desire for his mother. But the father stands in the son's path and will not yield his sexual property to his puny son. The boy's first emotional experience, then, the one that inevitably follows his experience of desire, is fear—fear of the bigger, stronger, more sexually powerful father. It is this fear, experienced symbolically as the fear of castration, Freud argues, that forces the young boy to renounce his identification with mother and seek to identify with the being who is the actual source of his fear, his father. In so doing, the boy is now symbolically capable of sexual union with a motherlike substitute, that is, a woman. The boy becomes gendered (masculine) and heterosexual at the same time.

Masculinity, in this model, is irrevocably tied to sexuality. The boy's sexuality will now come to resemble the sexuality of his father (or at least the way he imagines his father)—menacing, predatory, possessive, and possibly punitive. The boy has come to identify with his oppressor; now he can become the oppressor himself. But a terror remains, the terror that the young man will be unmasked as a fraud, as a man who has not completely and irrevocably separated from mother. It will be other men who will do the unmasking. Failure will de-sex the man, make him appear as not fully a man. He will be seen as a wimp, a Mama's boy, a sissy.

After pulling away from his mother, the boy comes to see her not as a source of nurturance and love, but as an insatiably infantilizing creature, capable of humiliating him in front of his peers. She makes him dress up in uncomfortable and itchy clothing, her kisses smear his cheeks with lipstick, staining his boyish innocence with the mark of feminine dependency. No wonder so many boys cringe from their mothers' embraces with groans of "Aw, Mom! Quit it!" Mothers represent the humiliation of infancy, help-lessness, dependency. "Men act as though they were being guided by (or re-belling against) rules and prohibitions enunciated by a moral mother," writes psychohistorian Geoffrey Gorer (1964). As a result, "all the niceties of masculine behavior—modesty, politeness, neatness, cleanliness—come to be regarded as concessions to feminine demands, and not good in them-selves as part of the behavior of a proper man" (pp. 56, 57).

The flight from femininity is angry and frightened, because the mother can so easily emasculate the young boy by her power to render him depen-dent or at least remind him of dependency. It is relentless; manhood be-comes a lifelong quest to demonstrate its achievement, as if to prove the unprovable to others, because we feel so unsure of it ourselves. Women don't often feel compelled to "prove their womanhood"—the phrase itself sounds ridiculous. Women have different kinds of gender identity crises; their anger and frustration, and their own symptoms of depression, come more from being excluded than from questioning whether they are femi-nine enough.[4]

The drive to repudiate the mother as the indication of the acquisi-tion of masculine gender identity has three consequences for the young boy. First, he pushes away his real mother, and with her the traits of nurturance, compassion, and tenderness she may have embodied. Sec-ond, he suppresses those traits in himself, because they will reveal his incomplete separation from mother. His life becomes a lifelong project to demonstrate that he possesses none of his mother's traits. Masculine identity is born in the renunciation of the feminine, not in the direct affirmation of the masculine, which leaves masculine gender identity tenuous and fragile.

Third, as if to demonstrate the accomplishment of these first two tasks, the boy also learns to devalue all women in his society, as the living em-bodiments of those traits in himself he has learned to despise. Whether or not he was aware of it, Freud also described the origins of sexism—the sys-tematic devaluation of women—in the desperate efforts of the boy to sep-arate from mother. We may *want* "a girl just like the girl that married dear old Dad," as the popular song had it, but we certainly don't want to *be like* her.

This chronic uncertainty about gender identity helps us understand several obsessive behaviors. Take, for example, the continuing problem of the school-yard bully. Parents remind us that the bully is the *least* secure about his manhood, and so he is constantly trying to prove it. But he "proves" it by choosing opponents he is absolutely certain he can defeat; thus the standard taunt to a bully is to "pick on someone your own size." He can't, though, and after defeating a smaller and weaker opponent, which he was sure would prove his manhood, he is left with the empty gnawing feeling that he has not proved it after all, and he must find another opponent, again one smaller and weaker, that he can again defeat to prove it to himself.[5]

One of the more graphic illustrations of this lifelong quest to prove one's manhood occurred at the Academy Awards presentation in 1992. As aging, tough guy actor Jack Palance accepted the award for Best Supporting Actor for his role in the cowboy comedy *City Slickers,* he commented that people, especially film producers, think that because he is 71 years old, he's all washed up, that he's no longer competent. "Can we take a risk on this guy?" he quoted them as saying, before he dropped to the floor to do a set of one-armed push-ups. It was pathetic to see such an accomplished actor still having to prove that he is virile enough to work and, as he also commented at the podium, to have sex.

When does it end? Never. To admit weakness, to admit frailty or fragility, is to be seen as a wimp, a sissy, not a real man. But seen by whom?

Masculinity as a Homosocial Enactment

Other men: We are under the constant careful scrutiny of other men. Other men watch us, rank us, grant our acceptance into the realm of manhood. Manhood is demonstrated for other men's approval. It is other men who evaluate the performance. Literary critic David Leverenz (1991) argues that "ideologies of manhood have functioned primarily in relation to the gaze of male peers and male authority" (p. 769). Think of how men boast to one another of their accomplishments—from their latest sexual conquest to the size of the fish they caught—and how we constantly parade the markers of manhood—wealth, power, status, sexy women—in front of other men, desperate for their approval.

That men prove their manhood in the eyes of other men is both a consequence of sexism and one of its chief props. "Women have, in men's minds, such a low place on the social ladder of this country that it's useless to define yourself in terms of a woman," noted playwright David Mamet. "What men need is men's approval." Women become a kind of currency that men use to improve their ranking on the masculine social scale. (Even those moments of heroic conquest of women carry, I believe, a current of homosocial evaluation.) Masculinity is a *homosocial* enactment. We test ourselves, perform heroic feats, take enormous risks, all because we want other men to grant us our manhood.

Masculinity as a homosocial enactment is fraught with danger, with the risk of failure, and with intense relentless competition. "Every man you meet has a rating or an estimate of himself which he never loses or forgets," wrote Kenneth Wayne (1912) in his popular turn-of-the-century advice book. "A man has his own rating, and instantly he lays it alongside of the other man" (p. 18). Almost a century later, another man remarked to psychologist Sam Osherson (1992) that "[b]y the time you're an adult, it's easy to think you're always in competition with men, for the attention of women, in sports, at work" (p. 291).

Masculinity as Homophobia

If masculinity is a homosocial enactment, its overriding emotion is fear. In the Freudian model, the fear of the father's power terrifies the young boy to renounce his desire for his mother and identify with his father. This model links gender identity with sexual orientation: The little boy's identification with father (becoming masculine) allows him to now engage in sexual relations with women (he becomes heterosexual). This is the origin of how we can "read" one's sexual orientation through the successful performance of gender identity. Second, the fear that the little boy feels does not send him scurrying into the arms of his mother to protect him from his father. Rather, he believes he will overcome his fear by identifying with its source. We become masculine by identifying with our oppressor.

But there is a piece of the puzzle missing, a piece that Freud, himself, implied but did not follow up.[6] If the pre-oedipal boy identifies with mother, he *sees the world through mother's eyes.* Thus, when he confronts father during his great oedipal crisis, he experiences a split vision: He sees his father as his mother sees his father, with a combination of awe, wonder, terror, *and desire.* He simultaneously sees the father as he, the boy, would like to see him—as the object not of desire but of emulation. Repudiating mother and identifying with father only partially answers his dilemma. What is he to do with that homoerotic desire, the desire he felt because he saw father the way that his mother saw father?

He must suppress it. Homoerotic desire is cast as feminine desire, desire for other men. Homophobia is the effort to suppress that desire, to purify all relationships with other men, with women, with children of its taint, and to ensure that no one could possibly ever mistake one for a homosexual. Homophobic flight from intimacy with other men is the repudiation of the homosexual within—never completely successful and hence constantly reenacted in every homosocial relationship. "The lives of most American men are bounded, and their interests daily curtailed by the constant necessity to prove to their fellows, and to themselves, that they are not sissies, not homosexuals," writes psychoanalytic historian Geoffrey Gorer (1964). "Any interest or pursuit which is identified as a feminine interest or pursuit becomes deeply suspect for men" (p. 129).

Even if we do not subscribe to Freudian psychoanalytic ideas, we can still observe how, in less sexualized terms, the father is the first man who evaluates the boy's masculine performance, the first pair of male eyes before whom he tries to prove himself. Those eyes will follow him for the rest of his life. Other men's eyes will join them—the eyes of role models such as teachers, coaches, bosses, or media heroes; the eyes of his peers, his friends, his workmates; and the eyes of millions of other men, living and dead, from whose constant scrutiny of his performance he will never be free. "The tradition of all the dead generations weighs like a nightmare on the brain of the living," was how Karl Marx put it over a century ago (1848/1964, p. 11). "The birthright of every American male is a chronic sense of personal inadequacy" is how two psychologists describe it today (Woolfolk & Richardson, 1978, p. 57).

That nightmare from which we never seem to awaken is that those other men will see that sense of inadequacy, they will see that in our own eyes we are not who we are pretending to be. What we call masculinity is often a hedge against being revealed as a fraud, an exaggerated set of activities that keep others from seeing through us, and a frenzied effort to keep at bay those fears within ourselves. Our real fear "is not fear of women but of being ashamed or humiliated in front of other men, or being dominated by stronger men" (Leverenz, 1986, p. 451).

This, then, is the great secret of American manhood: *We are afraid of other men.* Homophobia is a central organizing principle of our cultural definition of manhood. Homophobia is more than the irrational fear of gay men, more than the fear that we might be perceived as gay. "The word 'faggot' has nothing to do with homosexual experience or even with fears of homosexuals," writes David Leverenz (1986). "It comes out of the depths of manhood: a label of ultimate contempt for anyone who seems sissy, untough, uncool" (p. 455). Homophobia is the fear that other men will unmask us, emasculate us, reveal to us and the world that we do not measure up, that we are not real men. We are afraid to let other men see that fear. Fear makes us ashamed, because the recognition of fear in ourselves is proof to ourselves that we are not as manly as we pretend, that we are, like the young man in a poem by Yeats, "one that ruffles in a manly pose for all his timid heart." Our fear is the fear of humiliation. We are ashamed to be afraid.

Shame leads to silence—the silences that keep other people believing that we actually approve of the things that are done to women, to minorities, to gays and lesbians in our culture. The frightened silence as we scurry past a woman being hassled by men on the street. That furtive silence when men make sexist or racist jokes in a bar. That clammy-handed silence when guys in the office make gay-bashing jokes. Our fears are the sources of our silences, and men's silence is what keeps the system running. This might help to explain why women often complain that their male friends or partners are often so understanding when they are alone and yet laugh at sexist jokes or even make those jokes themselves when they are out with a group.

The fear of being seen as a sissy dominates the cultural definitions of manhood. It starts so early. "Boys among boys are ashamed to be unmanly," wrote one educator in 1871 (cited in Rotundo, 1993, p. 264). I have a standing bet with a friend that I can walk onto any playground in America where 6-year-old boys are happily playing and by asking one question, I can provoke a fight. That question is simple: "Who's a sissy around here?" Once posed, the challenge is made. One of two things is likely to happen. One boy will accuse another of being a sissy, to which that boy will respond that he is not a sissy, that the first boy is. They may have to fight it out to see who's lying. Or a whole group of boys will surround one boy and all shout "He is! He is!" That boy will either burst into tears and run home crying, disgraced, or he will have to take on several boys at once, to prove that he's not a sissy. (And what will his father or older brothers tell him if he chooses to run home crying?) It will be some time before he regains any sense of self-respect.

Violence is often the single most evident marker of manhood. Rather it is the willingness to fight, the desire to fight. The origin of our expression that one has a chip on one's shoulder lies in the practice of an adolescent boy in the country or small town at the turn of the century, who would literally walk around with a chip of wood balanced on his shoulder—a signal of his readiness to fight with anyone who would take the initiative of knocking the chip off (see Gorer, 1964, p. 38; Mead, 1965).

As adolescents, we learn that our peers are a kind of gender police, constantly threatening to unmask us as feminine, as sissies. One of the favorite tricks when I was an adolescent was to ask a boy to look at his fingernails. If he held his palm toward his face and curled his fingers back to see them, he passed the test. He'd looked at his nails "like a man." But if he held the back of his hand away from his face, and looked at his fingernails with arm outstretched, he was immediately ridiculed as a sissy.

As young men we are constantly riding those gender boundaries, checking the fences we have constructed on the perimeter, making sure that nothing even remotely feminine might show through. The possibilities of being unmasked are everywhere. Even the most seemingly insignificant thing can pose a threat or activate that haunting terror. On the day the students in my course "Sociology of Men and Masculinities" were scheduled to discuss homophobia and male-male friendships, one student provided a touching illustration. Noting that it was a beautiful day, the first day of spring after a brutal northeast winter, he decided to wear shorts to class. "I had this really nice pair of new Madras shorts," he commented. "But then I thought to myself, these shorts have lavender and pink in them. Today's class topic is homophobia. Maybe today is not the best day to wear these shorts."

Our efforts to maintain a manly front cover everything we do. What we wear. How we talk. How we walk. What we eat. Every mannerism, every movement contains a coded gender language. Think, for example, of how you would answer the question: How do you "know" if a man is homosexual? When I ask this question in classes or workshops, respondents invariably provide a pretty standard list of stereotypically effeminate behaviors. He walks a certain way, talks a certain way, acts a certain way. He's very emotional; he shows his feelings. One woman commented that she "knows" a man is gay if he really cares about her; another said she knows he's gay if he shows no interest in her, if he leaves her alone.

Now alter the question and imagine what heterosexual men do to make sure no one could possibly get the "wrong idea" about them. Responses typically refer to the original stereotypes, this time as a set of negative rules about behavior. Never dress that way. Never talk or walk that way. Never show your feelings or get emotional. Always be prepared to demonstrate sexual interest in women that you meet, so it is impossible for any woman to get the wrong idea about you. In this sense, homophobia, the fear of being perceived as gay, as not a real man, keeps men exaggerating all the traditional rules of masculinity, including sexual predation with women. Homophobia and sexism go hand in hand.

The stakes of perceived sissydom are enormous—sometimes matters of life and death. We take enormous risks to prove our manhood, exposing ourselves disproportionately to health risks, workplace hazards, and stress-related illnesses. Men commit suicide three times as often as women. Psychiatrist Willard Gaylin (1992) explains that it is "invariably because of perceived social humiliation," most often tied to failure in business:

> Men become depressed because of loss of status and power in the world of men. It is not the loss of money, or the material advantages that money could buy, which produces the despair that leads to self-destruction. It is the "shame," the "humiliation," the sense of personal "failure." . . . A man despairs when he has ceased being a man among men. (p. 32)

In one survey, women and men were asked what they were most afraid of. Women responded that they were most afraid of being raped and murdered. Men responded that they were most afraid of being laughed at (Noble, 1992, pp. 105–106).

Homophobia as a Cause of Sexism, Heterosexism, and Racism

Homophobia is intimately interwoven with both sexism and racism. The fear—sometimes conscious, sometimes not—that others might perceive us as homosexual propels men to enact all manner of exaggerated masculine behaviors and attitudes to make sure that no one could possibly get the wrong idea about us. One of the centerpieces of that exaggerated masculinity is putting women down, both by excluding them from the public sphere and by the quotidian put-downs in speech and behaviors that organize the daily life of the American man. Women and gay men become the "other" against which heterosexual men project their identities, against whom they stack the decks so as to compete in a situation in which they will always win, so that by suppressing them, men can stake a claim for their own manhood. Women threaten emasculation by representing the home, workplace, and familial responsibility, the negation of fun. Gay men have historically played the role of the consummate sissy in the American popular mind because homosexuality is seen as an inversion of normal gender development. There have been other "others." Through American history, various groups have represented the sissy, the non-men against whom American men played out their definitions of manhood, often with vicious results. In fact, these changing groups provide an interesting lesson in American historical development.

At the turn of the 19th century, it was Europeans and children who provided the contrast for American men. The "true American was vigorous, manly, and direct, not effete and corrupt like the supposed Europeans," writes Rupert Wilkinson (1986). "He was plain rather than ornamented, rugged rather than luxury seeking, a liberty loving common man or natural gentleman rather than an aristocratic oppressor or servile minion" (p. 96). The "real man" of the early 19th century was neither noble nor serf. By the middle of the century, black slaves had replaced the effete nobleman. Slaves were seen as dependent, helpless men, incapable of defending their women and children, and therefore less than manly. Native Americans were cast as foolish and naive children, so they could be infantilized as the "Red Children of the Great White Father" and therefore excluded from full manhood.

By the end of the century, new European immigrants were also added to the list of the unreal men, especially the Irish and Italians, who were seen as too passionate and emotionally volatile to remain controlled sturdy oaks, and Jews, who were seen as too bookishly effete and too physically puny to truly measure up. In the mid-20th century, it was also Asians—first the Japanese during the Second World War, and more recently, the Vietnamese during the Vietnam War—who have served as unmanly templates against which American men have hurled their gendered rage. Asian men were seen as small, soft, and effeminate—hardly men at all.

Such a list of "hyphenated" Americans—Italian-, Jewish-, Irish-, African-, Native-, Asian-, gay—composes the majority of American men. So man-hood is only possible for a distinct minority, and the definition has been constructed to prevent the others from achieving it. Interestingly, this emasculation of one's enemies has a flip side—and one that is equally gendered. These very groups that have historically been cast as less than manly were also, often simultaneously, cast as hypermasculine, as sexually aggressive, violent rapacious beasts, against whom "civilized" men must take a decisive stand and thereby rescue civilization. Thus black men were depicted as rampaging sexual beasts, women as carnivorously carnal, gay men as sexually insatiable, southern European men as sexually predatory and voracious, and Asian men as vicious and cruel torturers who were immorally disinterested in life itself, willing to sacrifice their entire people for their whims. But whether one saw these groups as effeminate sissies or as brutal uncivilized savages, the terms with which they were perceived were gendered. These groups become the "others," the screens against which traditional conceptions of manhood were developed.

Being seen as unmanly is a fear that propels American men to deny manhood to others, as a way of proving the unprovable—that one is fully manly. Masculinity becomes a defense against the perceived threat of humiliation in the eyes of other men, enacted through a "sequence of postures"—things we might say, or do, or even think, that, if we thought carefully about them, would make us ashamed of ourselves (Savran, 1992, p. 16). After all, how many of us have made homophobic or sexist remarks, or told racist jokes, or made lewd comments to women on the street? How many of us have translated those ideas and those words into actions, by physically attacking gay men, or forcing or cajoling a woman to have sex even though she didn't really want to because it was important to score?

Power and Powerlessness in the Lives of Men

I have argued that homophobia, men's fear of other men, is the animating condition of the dominant definition of masculinity in America, that the reigning definition of masculinity is a defensive effort to prevent being emasculated. In our efforts to suppress or overcome those fears, the dominant culture exacts a tremendous price from those deemed less than fully manly: women, gay men, nonnative-born men, men of color. This perspective may help clarify a paradox in men's lives, a paradox in which men have virtually all the power and yet do not feel powerful (see Kaufman, 1993).

Manhood is equated with power—over women, over other men. Everywhere we look, we see the institutional expression of that power—in state and national legislatures, on the boards of directors of every major U.S. corporation or law firm, and in every school and hospital administration. Women have long understood this, and feminist women have spent the past three decades challenging both the public and the private expressions of men's power and acknowledging their fear of men. Feminism as a set of theories both explains women's fear of men and empowers women to confront it both publicly and privately. Feminist women have theorized that masculinity is about the drive for domination, the drive for power, for conquest.

This feminist definition of masculinity as the drive for power is theorized from women's point of view. It is how women experience masculinity. But it assumes a symmetry between the public and the private that does not conform to men's experiences. Feminists observe that women, as a group, do not hold power in our society. They also observe that individually, they, as women, do not feel powerful. They feel afraid, vulnerable. Their observation of the social reality and their individual experiences are therefore symmetrical. Feminism also observes that men, as a group, *are* in power. Thus, with the same symmetry, feminism has tended to assume that individually men must feel powerful.

This is why the feminist critique of masculinity often falls on deaf ears with men. When confronted with the analysis that men have all the power, many men react incredulously. "What do you mean, men have all the power?" they ask, "What are you talking about? My wife bosses me around. My kids boss me around. My boss bosses me around. I have no power at all! I'm completely powerless!"

Men's feelings are not the feelings of the powerful, but of those who see themselves as powerless. These are the feelings that come inevitably from the discontinuity between the social and the psychological, between the aggregate analysis that reveals how men are in power as a group and the psychological fact that they do not feel powerful as individuals. They are the feelings of men who were raised to believe themselves entitled to feel that power, but do not feel it. No wonder many men are frustrated and angry.

This may explain the recent popularity of those workshops and retreats designed to help men to claim their "inner" power, their "deep manhood," or their "warrior within." Authors such as Bly (1990), Moore and Gillette (1991, 1992, 1993a, 1993b), Farrell (1986, 1993), and Keen (1991) honor and respect men's feelings of powerlessness and acknowledge those feelings to be both true and real. "They gave white men the semblance of power," notes John Lee, one of the leaders of these retreats (quoted in *Newsweek*, p. 41). "We'll let you run the country, but in the meantime, stop feeling, stop talking, and continue swallowing your pain and your hurt." (We are not told who "they" are.)

Often the purveyors of the mythopoetic men's movement, that broad umbrella that encompasses all the groups helping men to retrieve this mythic deep manhood, use the image of the chauffeur to describe modern man's position. The chauffeur appears to have the power—he's wearing the uniform, he's in the driver's seat, and he knows where he's going. So, to the observer, the chauffeur looks as though he is in command. But to the chauffeur himself, they note, he is merely taking orders. He is not at all in charge.[7]

Despite the reality that everyone knows chauffeurs do not have the power, this image remains appealing to the men who hear it at these weekend workshops. But there is a missing piece to the image, a piece concealed by the framing of the image in terms of the individual man's experience. That missing piece is that the person who is giving the orders is also a man. Now we have a relationship *between* men—between men giving orders and other men taking those orders. The man who identifies with the chauffeur is entitled to be the man giving the orders, but he is not. ("They," it turns out, are other men.)

The dimension of power is now reinserted into men's experience not only as the product of individual experience but also as the product of relations with other men. In this sense, men's experience of powerlessness is *real*—the men actually feel it and certainly act on it—but it is not *true*, that is, it does not accurately describe their condition. In contrast to women's lives, men's lives are structured around relationships of power and men's differential access to power, as well as the differential access to that power of men as a group. Our imperfect analysis of our own situation leads us to believe that we men need *more* power, rather than leading us to support feminists' efforts to rearrange power relationships along more equitable lines.

Philosopher Hannah Arendt (1970) fully understood this contradictory experience of social and individual power:

> Power corresponds to the human ability not just to act but to act in concert. Power is never the property of an individual; it belongs to a group and remains in existence only so long as the group keeps together. When we say of somebody that he is "in power" we actually refer to his being empowered by a certain number of people to act in their name. The moment the group, from which the power originated to begin with . . . disappears, "his power" also vanishes. (p. 44)

Why, then, do American men feel so powerless? Part of the answer is because we've constructed the rules of manhood so that only the tiniest fraction of men come to believe that they are the biggest of wheels, the sturdiest of oaks, the most virulent repudiators of femininity, the most daring and aggressive. We've managed to disempower the overwhelming majority of American men by other means—such as discriminating on the basis of race, class, ethnicity, age, or sexual preference.

Masculinist retreats to retrieve deep, wounded, masculinity are but one of the ways in which American men currently struggle with their fears and their shame. Unfortunately, at the very moment that they work to break down the isolation that governs men's lives, as they enable men to express those fears and that shame, they ignore the social power that men continue to exert over women and the privileges from which they (as the middle-aged, middle-class white men who largely make up these retreats) continue to benefit—regardless of their experiences as wounded victims of oppressive male socialization.[8]

Others still rehearse the politics of exclusion, as if by clearing away the playing field of secure gender identity of any that we deem less than manly—women, gay men, nonnative-born men, men of color—middle-class, straight, white men can reground their sense of themselves without those haunting fears and that deep shame that they are unmanly and will be exposed by other men. This is the manhood of racism, of sexism, of homophobia. It is the manhood that is so chronically insecure that it trembles at the idea of lifting the ban on gays in the military, that is so threatened by women in the workplace that women become the targets of sexual harassment, that is so deeply frightened of equality that it must ensure that the playing field of male competition remains stacked against all newcomers to the game.

Exclusion and escape have been the dominant methods American men have used to keep their fears of humiliation at bay. The fear of emasculation by other men, of being humiliated, of being seen as a sissy, is the leitmotif in my reading of the history of American manhood. Masculinity has become a relentless test by which we prove to other men, to women, and ultimately to ourselves, that we have successfully mastered the part. The restlessness that men feel today is nothing new in American history; we have been anxious and restless for almost two centuries. Neither exclusion nor escape has ever brought us the relief we've sought, and there is no reason to think that either will solve our problems now. Peace of mind, relief from gender struggle, will come only from a politics of inclusion, not exclusion, from standing up for equality and justice, and not by running away.

Notes

1. Of course, the phrase "American manhood" contains several simultaneous fictions. There is no single manhood that defines all American men; "America" is meant to refer to the United States proper, and there are significant ways in which this "American manhood" is the outcome of forces that transcend both gender and nation, that is, the global economic development of industrial capitalism. I use it, therefore, to describe the specific hegemonic version of masculinity in the United States, that normative constellation of attitudes, traits, and behaviors that became the standard against which all other masculinities are measured and against which individual men measure the success of their gender accomplishments.

2. Much of this work is elaborated in Kimmel, 1996.

3. Although I am here discussing only American masculinity, I am aware that others have located this chronic instability and efforts to prove manhood in the particular cultural and economic arrangements of Western society. Calvin, after all, inveighed against the disgrace "for men to become effeminate," and countless other theorists have described the mechanics of manly proof. (See, for example, Seidler, 1994.)

4. I do not mean to argue that women do not have anxieties about whether they are feminine enough. Ask any woman how she feels about being called aggressive; it sends a chill into her heart because her femininity is suspect. (I believe that the reason for the enormous recent popularity of sexy lingerie among women is that it enables women to remember they are still feminine underneath their corporate business suit—a suit that apes masculine styles.) But I think the stakes are not as great for women and that women have greater latitude in defining their identities around these questions than men do. Such are the ironies of sexism: The powerful have a narrower range of options than the powerless, because the powerless can *also* imitate the powerful and get away with it. It may even enhance status, if done with charm and grace—that is, is not threatening. For the powerful, any hint of behaving like the powerless is a fall from grace.

5. Such observations also led journalist Heywood Broun to argue that most of the attacks against feminism came from men who were shorter than 5 ft. 7 in. "The man who, whatever his physical size, feels secure in his own masculinity and in his own re-lation to life is rarely resentful of the opposite sex" (cited in Symes, 1930, p. 139).

6. Some of Freud's followers, such as Anna Freud and Alfred Adler, did follow up on these suggestions. (See especially, Adler, 1980.) I am grateful to Terry Ku-pers for his help in thinking through Adler's ideas.

7. The image is from Warren Farrell, who spoke at a workshop I attended at the First International Men's Conference, Austin, Texas, October 1991.

8. For a critique of these mythopoetic retreats, see Kimmel and Kaufman, 1995.

References

Adler, A. (1980). *Cooperation between the sexes: Writings on women, love and mar-riage, sexuality and its disorders* (H. Ansbacher and R. Ansbacher, Eds. and Trans.). New York: Jason Aronson.

Arendt, H. (1970). *On revolution.* New York: Viking.

Bly, R. (1990). *Iron John: A book about men.* Reading, MA: Addison-Wesley.

Brannon, R. (1976). The male sex role—and what it's done for us lately. In R. Brannon & D. David (Eds.), *The forty-nine percent majority* (pp. 1–40). Read-ing, MA: Addison-Wesley.

Connell, R. W. (1987). *Gender and power.* Stanford, CA: Stanford University Press.

Farrell, W. (1986). *Why men are the way they are.* New York: McGraw-Hill.

Farrell, W. (1993). *The myth of male power: Why men are the disposable sex.* New York: Simon & Schuster.

Freud, S. (1933/1966). *New introductory lectures on psychoanalysis* (L. Strachey, Ed.). New York: Norton.

Gaylin, W. (1992). *The male ego.* New York: Viking.

Goffman, E. (1963). *Stigma.* Englewood Cliffs, NJ: Prentice Hall.

Gorer, G. (1964). *The American people: A study in national character.* New York: Norton.

Kaufman, M. (1993). *Cracking the armour: Power and pain in the lives of men.* Toronto: Viking Canada.

Keen, S. (1991). *Fire in the belly.* New York: Bantam.

Kimmel, M. S. (1996). *Manhood in America: A cultural history.* New York: Free Press.

Kimmel, M., and M. Kaufman (1995). Weekend warriors: The new men's movement. In H. Brod and M. Kaufman (Eds.), *Theorizing masculinities.* Thousand Oaks, CA: Sage Publications.

Leverenz, D. (1986). Manhood, humiliation and public life: Some stories. *Southwest Review, 71,* Fall.

Leverenz, D. (1991). The last real man in America: From Natty Bumppo to Batman. *American Literary Review, 3.*

Marx, K., & F. Engels. (1848/1964). The communist manifesto. In R. Tucker (Ed.), *The Marx-Engels reader.* New York: Norton.

Mead, M. (1965). *And keep your powder dry.* New York: William Morrow.

Moore, R., & D. Gillette. (1991). *King, warrior, magician, lover.* New York: HarperCollins.

Moore, R., & D. Gillette. (1992). *The king within: Accessing the king in the male psyche.* New York: William Morrow.

Moore, R., & D. Gillette. (1993a). *The warrior within: Accessing the warrior in the male psyche.* New York: William Morrow.

Moore, R., & D. Gillette. (1993b). *The magician within: Accessing the magician in the male psyche.* New York: William Morrow.

Noble, V. (1992). A helping hand from the guys. In K. L. Hagan (Ed.), *Women respond to the men's movement.* San Francisco: HarperCollins.

Osherson, S. (1992). *Wrestling with love: How men struggle with intimacy, with women, children, parents, and each other.* New York: Fawcett.

Rotundo, E. A. (1993). *American manhood: Transformations in masculinity from the revolution to the modern era.* New York: Basic Books.

Savran, D. (1992). *Communists, cowboys and queers: The politics of masculinity in the work of Arthur Miller and Tennessee Williams.* Minneapolis: University of Minnesota Press.

Seidler, V. J. (1994). *Unreasonable men: Masculinity and social theory.* New York: Routledge.

Symes, L. (1930). The new masculinism. *Harper's Monthly, 161,* January.

Tocqueville, A. de. (1835/1967). *Democracy in America.* New York: Anchor.

Wayne, K. (1912). *Building the young man.* Chicago: A. C. McClurg.

Weber, M. (1905/1966). *The Protestant ethic and the spirit of capitalism.* New York: Charles Scribner's.

What men need is men's approval. (1993, January 3). *The New York Times,* p. C-11.

Wilkinson, R. (1986). *American tough: The tough-guy tradition and American character.* New York: Harper & Row.

Woolfolk, R. L., & F. Richardson. (1978). *Sanity, stress and survival.* New York: Signet.

10

On White Pride, Reverse Racism, and Other Delusions

Tim Wise

It seems like every week I get an e-mail from someone demanding to know why there's no White History Month or White Entertainment Television or why whites aren't allowed to have organizations to defend "our" interests, the way people of color are, without being thought of as racists.

That so many people find this kind of argumentation persuasive would be humorous were it not so dangerous and so indicative of the way in which our nation has yet to come to grips with its racist history. Had we honestly confronted racism as an issue, past and present, it is unlikely that such positions would make sense to anyone. After all, *every month* has been white history month, even if it wasn't called that. White history has been made the normative history, the default position, and when your narrative is taken as the norm—indeed, when it gets to be viewed as synonymous with *American* history—the need to racially designate its origins is obviously a less pressing concern. White folks' contributions have never been ignored, diminished, or overlooked. To now demand special time to teach about the people we've already learned about from the start seems a bit preposterous.

On a similar note, to think that whites working for white empowerment or "white rights" is no different than people of color working for the empowerment of *their* group (through such mechanisms as the NAACP or the Congressional Black Caucus, for instance), can only make sense if one takes a fundamentally dishonest glimpse at the nation's past.

After all, groups representing persons of color were created to address the unique *disempowerment* experienced by those groups' members. Blacks, Latinos/Latinas, Asians, and Native Americans have been systematically denied opportunities in the United States *solely* because of their group membership. Their "race" was the basis for housing discrimination, restrictions on educational opportunities, exclusion from jobs, and other forms of mistreatment. Whites have never been the targets of institutional oppression in the United States *as whites* such that organizing *as whites* would have made sense. Sure, whites have been marginalized on the basis of ethnicity—the Irish, for example, or Italians, or Jews—and have long organized around ethnicity as a support system for job networking, educational benefits, or other purposes. But as whites, persons of European descent have been the dominant group. So to organize on that basis would be to come together for the purpose of providing collective support for their existing domination and hegemony. It would be redundant in the extreme.

And contrary to popular belief, affirmative action programs haven't altered the fundamental truth that whites continue to dominate in every arena of American life. So, for instance, whites hold more than 90 percent of all the management level jobs in this country,[1] receive about 94 percent of government contract dollars,[2] and hold 90 percent of tenured faculty positions on college campuses.[3] Contrary to popular belief, and in spite of affirmative action programs, whites are more likely than members of any other racial group to be admitted to their college of first choice.[4] Furthermore, white men with only a high school diploma are more likely to have a job than black and Latino men with college degrees,[5] and even when they have a criminal record, white men are more likely than black men without one to receive a call back for a job interview, even when all their credentials are the same.[6] Despite comparable rates of school rule infractions, white students are only half to one-third as likely as blacks and Latino youth to be suspended or expelled;[7] and despite *higher* rates of drug use, white youth are far less likely to be arrested, prosecuted, or incarcerated for a drug offense than are youth of color.[8]

So when it comes to jobs, education, housing, contracting, or anything else, people of color are the ones facing discrimination and restricted opportunities, and whites remain on top, making the idea of organizing for our collective interests little more than piling dominance on top of dominance. Not to ensure a place at the table, so to speak, but to secure the table itself and to control who gets to be seated around it for now and always.

It is for this reason that white pride is more objectionable than "black pride" or "Latino pride." In the case of the latter two, those exhibiting pride are not doing so as a celebration of their presumed superiority or dominance over others. If anything, they are celebrating the perseverance of their people against great obstacles, such as those placed in their way by discrimination, conquest, and enslavement. In the case of white pride, whites *as whites* have not overcome obstacles in the same fashion, because we have always been the dominant group. Although Irish pride or Italian pride makes sense given the way in which persons of those ethnicities have faced real oppression in the past (and even today, in the case of Italians, who sometimes face negative stereotypes), white pride, given the historic meaning of whiteness, can mean little *but* pride in presumed superiority.

Minority Scholarships and the Myth of White Disadvantage

Nowhere is the myth of white disadvantage—and thus, the need for some collective response by the white community—more prevalent than on college campuses, regarding the issue of so-called minority scholarships. Enraged by what they see as unfair preferences and the sacrifice of pure merit on the altar of political correctness, whites at some colleges have even sought to create "whites-only" scholarships, less as legitimate awards than as a way to highlight the "injustice" of financial assistance efforts targeted to students of color.

To hear many such students tell it, persons of color are taking up all the financial aid money and receiving unfair preferences based solely on the color of their skin. But in truth, less than 4 percent of scholarship money in the United States is represented by awards that consider race as a factor at all, while only *0.25 percent* of all undergrad scholarship dollars come from awards that are restricted to persons of color alone.[9] What's more, only 3.5 percent of college students of color receive any scholarship even *partially* based on race, suggesting that such programs remain a pathetically small piece of the financial aid picture in this country.[10]

Additionally, to suggest that race-based scholarships are a unique and illegitimate break with an otherwise meritocratic system is preposterous. The fact is, there are plenty of scholarships that have nothing to do with merit per se, but about which the critics of "minority" scholarships say nothing: scholarships for people who are left-handed, or kids whose parents sell Tupperware, or the children of horse-breeders, or descendants of the signers of the Declaration of Independence, among many thousands of such awards.[11] Apparently, it's okay to ensure opportunity for members of these groups despite the fact that none of them have faced systemic oppression before, but it's the height of immorality to do the same for students of color, who have indeed faced explicitly racial obstacles in their lives.

Of course, on an even more basic level, to complain about so-called unfair preferences for students of color, be it in terms of scholarships or affirmative action policies in admissions, is to ignore the many ways in which the nation's educational system provides unfair advantages to whites from beginning to end.

It ignores the fact that the average white student in the United States attends school with half as many poor kids as the average black or Latino/a student, which in turn has a direct effect on performance, because attending a low-poverty school generally means having more resources available for direct instruction.[12] Indeed, schools with high concentrations of students of color are eleven to fifteen times more likely than mostly white schools to have high concentrations of student poverty.[13] It ignores the fact that white students are twice as likely as their African American or Latino/Latina counterparts to be taught by the most highly qualified teachers, and half as likely to have the least qualified instructors in class.[14] This too directly benefits whites, as research suggests being taught by highly qualified teachers is one of the most important factors in school achievement.[15] It ignores the fact that whites are twice as likely, relative to black students, to be placed in honors or advanced placement (AP) classes, and that even when academic performance would justify lower placement for whites and higher placement for blacks, it is the African American students who are disproportionately tracked low and whites who are tracked higher.[16] Indeed, schools serving mostly white students have three times as many honors or AP classes offered per capita as those serving mostly students of color.[17]

To ignore this background context and to award scholarships based solely on so-called merit is to miss the ways in which the academic success and accomplishments of white students have been structured by unequal and preferential opportunity and the ways in which students of color have been systematically denied the same opportunity to achieve. It is to compound the original injury and to extend white privilege at the point of admissions or financial aid awards beyond the level to which it has already been operating in the lives of white students. In other words, to award scholarships on the basis of so-called merit, when merit itself has been accumulated due to an unfair head start, is to perpetuate a profound injustice. However, to offer scholarship monies to capable and high-achieving students of color who through no fault of their own have been restricted in their ability to accumulate "merit" to the same degree is to ensure as equitable and fair a competition as possible and to do justice in an otherwise unjust system.

In effect, these are not scholarships based on race but rather scholarships based on recognition of *racism* and how it has shaped the opportunity structure in the United States. Because race has been the basis for oppression, and continues to play such a large role in one's life chances, it is perfectly legitimate to then offer scholarships on the basis of the category that has triggered the oppression. If people of color have been denied opportunity because of their race, then why is it so hard to understand the validity of remedying that denial and its modern-day effects by also taking into account their race? After all, *that* was the source of the injury, so why shouldn't it also be the source of the solution?

White Bonding as a Dangerous Distraction

But beyond the facts of white advantage and ongoing disadvantage for people of color, there is another deeply disturbing aspect of modern white backlash, and the attempt by some whites to bond around presumed white victim status. Namely, that by seeking to bond on the basis of whiteness, those pushing the concept end up ignoring the way in which white identity has actually *harmed* persons of European descent, by causing most of us to ignore our real interests, all for the sake of phony racial bonding. To understand why this is so, it might help to have some historical perspective on how the notion of whiteness came into being in the first place and for what purpose.

Contrary to popular belief, the white race is a quite modern creation that only emerged as a term and concept to describe Europeans in the late 1600s and after, specifically in the colonies of what would become the United States. Prior to that time, "whites" had been a collection of Europeans with little in common, and often long histories of conflict, bloodshed, and conquest of one another's lands and peoples. The English, for example, did not consider themselves to be of the same group as the Irish, Germans, Italians, or French. The notion of the white race found traction in the North American colonies not because it described a clear scientific concept, or some true historical bond between persons of European descent but rather because the elites of the colonies (who were small in number but controlled the largest part of colonial wealth) needed a way to secure their power. At the time, the wealthy landowners feared rebellions in which poor European peasants might join with African slaves to overthrow aristocratic governance; after all, these poor Europeans were barely above the level of slaves themselves, especially if they worked as indentured servants.[18]

In 1676, for example, Bacon's Rebellion prompted a new round of colonial laws to extend rights and privileges to despised poor Europeans so as to divide them from those slaves with whom they had much in common, economically speaking. By allowing the lowest of Europeans to be placed legally above all Africans, and by encouraging (or even requiring) them to serve on slave patrols, the elite gave poor "whites" a stake in the system that had harmed them. Giving poor Europeans the right to own land, ending indentured servitude in the early 1700s, and in some cases allowing them to vote, were all measures implemented so as to convince lower-caste Europeans that their interests were closer to those of the rich than to those of blacks. It was within this context that the term "white" to describe Europeans en masse was born as an umbrella term to capture the new pan-Euro unity needed to defend the system of African slavery and Indian genocide going on in the Americas.[19] And the trick worked marvelously, dampening down the push for rebellion by poor whites on the basis of class interest and encouraging them to cast their lot with the elite, if only in aspirational terms.

This divide-and-conquer tactic would be extended and refined in future generations as well. Indeed, the very first law passed by the newly established Congress of the United States was the Naturalization Act of

1790, which extended citizenship to all "free white persons" and *only* free white persons, including newly arrived immigrants, as long as the latter would make their homes in the United States for a year. Despite long-standing animosities between persons of European descent, all blood feuds were put aside for the purpose of extending pan-Euro or white hegemony over the United States.[20]

During the Civil War, the process of using "whiteness" to further divide working people from one another continued. So, for example, southern elites made it quite clear that their reason for secession from the Union was the desire to maintain and extend the institution of slavery and white supremacy, institutions they felt were threatened by the rise of Lincoln and the Republican Party. One might think that seceding and going to war to defend slavery would hardly meet with the approval of poor white folks, who didn't own slaves. After all, if slaves can be made to work for free, any working-class white person who must charge for his or her labor will be undercut by slave labor and find it harder to make ends meet. Yet by convincing poor whites that their interests were racial rather than economic, and that whites in the South had to band together to defend "their way of life," the elites in the South conned these same lower-caste Europeans into joining a destructive war effort that cost hundreds of thousands of lives—*their* lives, in fact.[21]

Then, during the growth of the labor union movement, white union workers barred blacks from apprenticeship programs and unions because of racism, encouraged in this by owners and bosses who would use workers of color to break white labor strikes for better wages and working conditions. By bringing in blacks and others of color to break strikes, bosses counted on white workers turning on those replacing them rather than turning on the bosses themselves. And indeed, this is what happened time and again, further elevating whiteness above class interest in the minds of European Americans.[22]

Today, whiteness continues to serve as a distraction to working-class persons of European descent. So in the debate over immigration, it is often claimed that immigrants of color are driving down the wages of white workers and that sealing the border is necessary to secure jobs and decent incomes for the working class. But such an argument presumes that the only thing keeping employers from giving white workers a raise (or black workers for that matter) is the presence of easily exploited foreign labor, as if closing the border would suddenly convince them to open up their wallets and give working people a better deal. In truth, however, were companies unable to exploit immigrant labor, they would simply move their entire operations to Mexico or elsewhere to take advantage of low-wage labor or nonexistent regulations on their activities. And if they were the kind of companies that couldn't move their operations abroad (such as construction firms, for example), they would likely shift to more contingent, part-time and temp labor, which would mean that whoever ended up with those jobs would still have little or no benefits and insecure wages. This is hardly the recipe for real improvement in the conditions of working people.

White workers would be far better off joining up with workers of color, including the undocumented, to push for higher wages and better working conditions; and they would surely be better off if those coming from Mexico were made legal and organized into unions. But thinking as whites has made this kind of cross-racial solidarity virtually unthinkable. Instead of focusing on the trade agreements that allow companies to move wherever they can get the best return on investment—agreements that have even by the government's admission resulted in the loss of hundreds of thousands of well-paying jobs—white workers are encouraged by racism and white bonding to focus their ire on the workers themselves. After all, the workers are brown, and the owners are almost all white, which is to say that the latter are the ones with whom the white working class has been convinced to identify.

Conclusion: White Solidarity Illogical and Hurtful for All

It is perhaps understandable that young whites uninformed about the history of racism in America might fall prey to the lure of "white rights" thinking. After all, without a full understanding of the way in which whites have been elevated above people of color and continue to be favored in employment, housing, criminal justice, and education, it would make sense for whites to wonder why things like affirmative action or Black History Month were necessary or why groups that advocate for the interests of persons of color were still needed. If you start from the assumption that the United States is a level playing field, then these kinds of things might seem odd, even racially preferential. But given the historical context, not to mention the vital information regarding ongoing discrimination in the present, the importance and legitimacy of these initiatives and organizations becomes evident to all but the most unreasonable.

What is most important for white folks to understand is that our interests do not lie with the white intraracial bonding we are being asked to embrace. Indeed, the very concept of the white race was invented by the wealthy so as to trick poor and working-class European Americans into accepting an economic system that exploited them even as it elevated them in relative terms over persons of color. For whites to organize on the basis of whiteness is to codify as legitimate a category the meaning of which was always and forever about domination and privilege relative to those who couldn't qualify for membership in the club.

Finally, to organize as whites in a white-dominated society where whites have eleven times the average net worth of blacks and eight times the average net worth of Latinos/Latinas,[23] where they have unemployment rates half that of blacks and poverty rates one-third as high as that for blacks and Latinos/Latinas,[24] and where they run virtually every major institution in the nation is by definition to organize for the continuation of that domination and supremacy. It is to seek to enshrine their head start; to seek the perpetuation of hegemony established in a system of formal apartheid, as if to say that that system was perfectly legitimate and worthy of survival. It is fundamentally different than for a minority group to organize collectively so as to secure its interests, because minority interests and opportunities cannot be assumed or taken for granted as a function of their lesser power, whereas those of the majority typically can.

And to organize on the basis of whiteness is to cast one's lot with the elite who desperately wish for working-class people to believe their enemies are each other rather than the bosses who cut their wages, raid their pension funds, and limit their health care coverage. The more white working people fight working people who are black and brown, the less they'll be likely to take aim at those who pick their pockets every day they show up for work—paying them only a fraction of the value of the products and services they provide, all in the name of profits they have no intention of truly sharing with their employees. Whiteness is a trick, but sadly one that has worked for nearly three-and-a-half centuries. Only when white folks wise up and realize that whiteness itself is our problem will we ever stand a chance of true liberation. Until then, our whiteness will provide us privileges and advantages but only in relation to those at the bottom of the racial caste structure. It will provide a psychological wage, as W. E. B. Du Bois put it, as an alternative to real wages. Not a bad deal, until you're struggling to feed your family and keep a roof over your heads. For in times like that, real currency works a bit better.

Notes

1. U.S. Federal Glass Ceiling Commission, *Good for Business: Making Full Use of the Nation's Human Capital* (Washington, DC: Bureau of National Affairs, March 1995).

2. Fred L. Pincus, *Reverse Discrimination: Dismantling the Myth* (Boulder, CO: Lynne Rienner, 2003), 18.

3. Roberta J. Hill, "Far More Than Frybread," in *Race in the College Classroom: Pedagogy and Politics*, ed. Bonnie TuSmith and Maureen T. Reddy (New Brunswick, NJ: Rutgers University Press, 2002), 169.

4. Sylvia Hurtado and Christine Navia, "Reconciling College Access and the Affirmative Action Debate," in *Affirmative Action's Testament of Hope*, ed. Mildred Garcia (Albany: State University of New York Press, 1997), 115.

5. *The State of Black America 2007: Portrait of the Black Male* (New York: National Urban League, 2007).

6. Devah Pager, "The Mark of a Criminal Record," *American Journal of Sociology* 108, no. 5 (March 2003): 937–975.

7. Russell J. Skiba, Robert S. Michael, Abra Carroll Nardo, and Reece Peterson, *The Color of Discipline: Sources of Racial and Gender Disproportionality in School Punishment,* Policy Research Report SRS1 (Bloomington, IN: Education Policy Center, June 2000), 4.

8. "Young White Offenders Get Lighter Treatment," *Tennessean*, April 26, 2000, 8A; Substance Abuse and Mental Health Services Administration (SAMHSA), *Results from the 2003 National Survey on Drug Use and Health* (Rockville, MD: Office of Applied Studies, Department of Health and Human Services, 2004); see also the same report for 2003, 2002, 2001, 2000, 1999; Federal Bureau of Investigation, *Crime in the United States, 2001* (Washington, DC: U.S. Department of Justice, 2002); Coramae Richey Mann, *Unequal Justice: A Question of Color* (Indianapolis: Indiana University Press, 1993), 224; Jim Sidanius, Shana Levin, and Felicia Pratto, "Hierarchical Group Relations, Institutional Terror, and the Dynamics of the Criminal Justice System," in *Confronting Racism: The Problem and the Response,*

ed. Jennifer Eberhardt and Susan T. Fiske (London: Sage, 1998), 142; SAMHSA, *Summary of Findings from the National Household Survey on Drug Abuse* (Rockville, MD: Office of Applied Studies, Department of Health and Human Services, 2003), Table H.1, and calculations by the author. According to the SAMHSA report, as of 2003, there were 19.5 million current users of illegal narcotics. According to the data in the report, there were 165.4 million whites age twelve and over in the United States that year, and 8.5 percent of these were current users, which translates to 14 million white users. Fourteen million as a share of 19.5 million is 72 percent. According to the same report, there were 26.8 million blacks twelve and over in the United States, of whom 9.7 percent were current drug users. This translates into 2.6 million current black drug users, which, as a share of 19.5 million is 13 percent. According to the report, there were 29 million Hispanics, of whom 7.2 percent, or 2 million, were current drug users. Two million as a share of 19.5 million is 10 percent. Combined then, the black and Latino users come to 23 percent of all drug users. See also Human Rights Watch, *Punishment and Prejudice: Racial Disparities in the War on Drugs* 12, n. 2 (May 2000); Michael K. Brown, Martin Carnoy, Elliott Currie, Troy Duster, David B. Oppenheimer, Marjorie M. Shultz, and David Wellman, *Whitewashing Race: The Myth of a Color-Blind Society* (Berkeley: University of California Press, 2003), 144.

9. U.S. General Accounting Office, *Information on Minority Targeted Scholarships*, B251634 (Washington, DC: U.S. Government Printing Office, January 1994).

10. Stephen L. Carter, "Color-Blind and Color-Active," *Recorder*, January 3, 1992.

11. National Scholarship Research Service, *The Scholarship Book* (Upper Saddle River, NJ: Prentice-Hall, 2002).

12. Judith Blau, *Race in the Schools: Perpetuating White Dominance?* (Boulder, CO: Lynne Rienner, 2004), 204.

13. Gary Orfield, Mark Bachmeier, David R. James, and Tamela Eitle, "Deepening Segregation in American Public Schools: A Special Report from the Harvard Project on School Desegregation," *Equity and Excellence in Education* 30 (1997): 5–24; Valerie Martinez-Ebers, "Latino Interests in Education, Health, and Criminal Justice Policy," *Political Science and Politics* (September 2000).

14. Linda Darling-Hammond, "Unequal Opportunity: Race and Education," *Brookings Review* (Spring 1998): 31.

15. Michael K. Brown et al. *Whitewashing Race: The Myth of a Color-Blind Society* (Berkeley: University of California Press, 2003), 111; Jawanza Kunjufu, *Black Students, Middle-Class Teachers* (Chicago: African American Images, 2002), 57–58.

16. Rebecca Gordon, *Education and Race* (Oakland: Applied Research Center, 1998), 48–49; Claude S. Fischer, Michael Hout, Martin Sanchez Jankowski, Samuel R. Lucas, Ann Swidler, and Kim Voss, *Inequality by Design: Cracking the Bell Curve Myth* (Princeton, NJ: Princeton University Press, 1996), 164–165; Leonard Steinhorn and Barbara Diggs-Brown, *By the Color of Our Skin: The Illusion of Integration and the Reality of Race* (New York: Dutton, 1999), 47.

17. Gary Orfield and Susan Eaton, *Dismantling Desegregation* (New York: New Press, 1996), 68.

18. Paul Rubio, *A History of Affirmative Action, 1619–2000* (Jackson: University Press of Mississippi, 2000); James Loewen, *Lies My Teacher Told Me* (New York: New Press, 1995); Herbert Gutman and the American Social History Project, *Who Built America? Working People and the Nation's Economy, Politics, Culture, and Society.* Two vol. (New York: Pantheon, 1989); Theodore Allen, *The Invention of the White Race,* vol. 1: *Racial Oppression and Social Control* (New York: Verso, 1994); Allen, *The Invention of the White Race,* vol. 2: *The Origin of Racial Oppression in Anglo-America* (New York: Verso, 1997).

19. Rubio, *A History of Affirmative Action;* Thandeka, *Learning to Be White: Money, Race, and God in America* (New York: Continuum, 2000).

20. Rubio, *A History of Affirmative Action;* Noel Ignatiev, *How the Irish Became White* (New York: Routledge, 1994); Jennifer Guglielmo, ed., *Are Italians White? How Race Is Made in America* (New York: Routledge, 2003).

21. Chandra Manning, *What This Cruel War Was Over: Soldiers, Slavery, and the Civil War* (New York: Knopf, 2007).

22. Loewen, *Lies My Teacher Told Me;* Gutman, and the American Social History Project, *Who Built America? Working People and the Nation's Economy, Politics, Culture, and Society.*

23. Shawna Orzechowski and Peter Sepielli, *Net Worth and Asset Ownership of Households: 1998 and 2000,* Current Population Reports, P70–88 (Washington, DC: U.S. Bureau of the Census, May 2003), 2.

24. *The State of Black America 2007: Portrait of the Black Male* (New York: National Urban League, 2007).

11

Class: Still Alive and Reproducing in the United States

Diana Kendall

The report of my death was an exaggeration.

—Mark Twain, May 1897

Like Mark Twain's famous statement that rumors of his death had been greatly exaggerated, are those social scientists and media analysts who argue that social class in the United States is dead overstating their case?

Is class still relevant in contemporary sociological analysis? Does class shape the material interests and lived experiences of people in the twenty-first century? I argue that class is not only relevant, remaining alive and well but also that it is constantly being socially reproduced, particularly by elites who desire to maintain their privilege and pass it on to their children and grandchildren. If it can be shown, for example, that an upper class exists not only economically but also socially and in terms of identity and class consciousness, it is reasonable to assume that other classes still exist and have meaning in daily life. My study of the upper-class members documents how this top class possesses a distinct demographic identity and routinely engages in boundary maintenance activities, two attributes of class that "death of class" advocates believe to be in serious decline in the United States.

The core argument to the effect that we are moving toward a classless society or that class has "dissolved" as a salient category in sociological analysis is not a new one; however, it has been revitalized in recent decades by analysts such as Jan Pakulski and Malcolm Waters (1996a, 1996b) and Paul W. Kingston (2000). Among other things, death-of-class proponents assert that, although economic inequality is still present—and may be increasing—in the United States, cohesive social classes no longer exist.

I address some, but not all, of the death-of-class issues. My study of social reproduction shows that many people in local and regional upper classes do form stable identities in class terms and that these identities remain features of contemporary life. I agree with Vanneman and Cannon (1987), Erik O. Wright (1996), and other scholars that it is premature to dismiss class as a useful concept in analyzing inequality. According to studies of high-income regions, class is alive and class divisions have intensified, rather than diminished, through the process of globalization. Although some individuals may rise "from rags to riches," that does not mean that the playing field is equal or that those with great wealth do not protect it (i.e., protect class interests). The rising standard of living in the West over the past fifty years basically has concealed increasing inequality, and even poor people are less inclined to notice the fact that the well-off have become richer (Seabrook 2002). Nonetheless, class is still there.

Class exists as a salient factor when people think in terms of "us" and "them" based at least in part upon wealth. The us-versus-them mentality of class-based relations in the local community has been a topic of sociological interest for many years. In the 1950s, scholars showed how members of the upper class created a set of exclusive clubs, luxury residential enclaves, and private social occasions unique to the upper class to ensure that many elites had a protective inner social circle that provided them with proximity to each other and a shield against having to deal with those who were "not our kind of people." There was also elaboration on how the upper-class debutante presentation served as a mechanism by which elites not only introduced their daughters to eligible bachelors but also introduced the young women to high society. This "coming out" ritual indicated that the daughters of privileged families were now full-fledged members of a restricted and exclusive group for which they and their families had fulfilled certain class-based prerequisites. This is an example of stratification by status based on a positive or negative social estimation of honor that is associated with a particular lifestyle expected of people in a specific social circle (Gerth and Mills 1958). Implicit in these early studies of the upper class was the idea that elites were in the "inner circle," whereas people in other classes were outsiders, not only socially but also in the opportunity structure of the community and perhaps the larger society. In addition to these earlier studies of the upper class, a number of well-known community-based studies have addressed the issue of how class is reproduced not only biologically, but socially.

My research took place over a ten-year period in which I interviewed and observed privileged women in Texas (see Kendall 2002). The participants generally are from wealthy, old-guard families who share not only an interest in the arts but also an interest—whether or not openly acknowledged—in the social reproduction of the upper class. Almost all of the women in the groups I studied are members of households with an annual income that would place them in the top 1–5 percent of households in this nation. I found that social elites across cities typically engage in similar behavior and have somewhat similar outlooks.

Maintenance and Social Reproduction of the Upper Class

Long-established elite families are in a unique economic and social position to perpetuate the advantages they hold because they have possessed wealth and privilege for several generations. They are not newcomers to privilege and exclusivity, and, for many of them, their primary goal is to maintain the boundaries that protect their elite position and that make it possible for them to pass their advantages on to their children.

My study focused on privileged women because, throughout the history of elite social reproduction, women have played a significant role in maintaining class-based boundaries and fostering cohesion among members of the upper class (Daniels 1988; Domhoff 1970, 1998; Odendahl 1990; Ostrander 1984; Ostrower 1995, 2002). Boundary maintenance involves both geographic and social dimensions. In Texas, there is a distinct social geography of the upper class that is reflected in residential housing patterns, exclusive private schools many privileged children attend, by-invitation-only clubs and organizations, and seemingly archaic rituals such as debutante presentations that bring members of the upper class (and some who aspire to the inner circles of the upper class) together as a class-conscious, socially cohesive group.

The Upper-Class Residence, Children's Peer Groups, and "The Bubble"

One of the most significant ways that social class boundary maintenance occurs is through the selection of the family residence, an activity in which privileged women play a major role. The establishment of an upper-class home within a proper upper-class neighborhood is one key way in which both visible and invisible barriers can be created to keep others out and to provide the right social environment for the socialization of the next generation. Another mechanism of boundary maintenance is the highly selective nature of children's peer groups, which I also examine.

Whether stay-at-home moms, full-time community volunteers, or professional women, the women in my study typically indicated that they had been actively involved in the choice of residential location and style for their families. Based on location, type, and quality, an elite family's residence may be both a showplace of conspicuous consumption and a part of the social "bubble": a safe haven that provides the family with comfort, safety, and isolation from those of other social classes. Geographic isolation and exclusivity may be seen by elite parents as related to safety issues and often are described to the children as such. A number of women in my study recalled being repeatedly told during their childhood not to stray outside their own residential area without the protection and supervision of their own or a friend's parents or household employees. Furthermore, elite residences tend to be in exclusive urban enclaves, affluent suburbs, and multi-million-dollar gated communities where housing costs prohibit all but the wealthiest families from acquiring a home. As a result, no middle- or lower-income families and few families of color will be the neighbors of elite white families.

Although anyone with sufficient financial resources can acquire a residence in one of the affluent neighborhoods, the goal of elites—particularly those with children—is sufficient social distance and geographical isolation to separate themselves from people of other classes, races, or ethnic groupings and to be in the proximity of others from their own social group. This separation becomes part of the social reproduction of the upper class; whether parents explicitly use such terms or not, elite children quickly learn that some people are "our kind of people" and all others are not. Members of the upper class and the more affluent members of the upper middle class seek, perhaps above all else, to purchase a home in a prestigious urban neighborhood or a wealthy suburban enclave. Social science literature affirms that residential choice patterns of elites and others are not strictly individual choices: other practices are also at work at the macro, social structural level of society that keep people in divergent class groupings segregated.

Residential boundary maintenance is a powerful force in perpetuating class distinctions because upper-class children are taught to have pride in their neighborhoods, and they do not realize that these neighborhoods are not representative of the larger social world. For the most part, elite children are surrounded by others (except for household help) who are similar to themselves. As one respondent stated, "When I was a kid, I thought everybody lived like we did." Preserving the social bubble for children in settings such as these is especially important to elite women because it provides a safe and protective environment from which the children only emerge in supervised and special circumstances.

To further insulate and isolate children in the "bubble," privileged women are careful about their children's play groups. Building social networks and controlling outsiders' access to these networks begins in early childhood for the typical upper-class child, and one early manifestation of such networks is the play group. Although play groups and play dates are popular ideas among middle- and upper-middle-class parents, elite mothers appear to be uniquely fond of this approach for building their children's social networks. For most of these women, the intended function of the play group has nothing to do with excluding outsiders but rather is based on the belief that children should interact with "others like us who share our family values and act like we want our kids to behave." However, the result of parental play-group management is largely one of promoting upper-class segregation.

Taking control of play groups is also a mechanism used by upper-class parents to ensure that their children will receive the appropriate socialization for an upper-class lifestyle and will not come to question their family's wealth or social position. For upper-class parents, careful selection of members of their child's play group is the key to building social networks for the child, but also has the effect of instilling notions of entitlement in the children. When upper-class children interact only with other privileged children, they compare themselves to others on a within-economic-class basis rather than looking across class lines where invidious distinctions in wealth and opportunity are highly visible. For example, children come to assume that the ownership of multiple luxury vehicles or possession of extravagant amenities in their homes is not unusual.

Prep Schools, Universities, and Upper-Class Reproduction

Children of the upper classes typically attend either private preparatory schools or even highly regarded public schools located within wealthy residential enclaves. Upper-class beliefs and values initially taught at home are strengthened in elite private schools and public schools primarily populated by elites, where students are encouraged to develop a sense of collective identity that involves school, peers, and one's place within the larger society. As privileged young people create a web of affiliations in dormitories, sporting events, classrooms, and other settings within their schools, they establish ties that, because they are interwoven in such a way as to become indistinguishable from the students' individual identity, will grow and become even more important after graduation. Consequently, to develop solidarity with one's classmates is to develop a form of class solidarity because of the commonalities in beliefs and lived experiences shared over a period of time, frequently without the students being exposed to countervailing belief systems or social networks. Over time, identity with others in the same class is a stronger link than merely some vague perception that they share similar values. Additionally, and most importantly, elite schools convey to students the idea that their privilege is justified (Cookson and Persell 1985); this attitude is essential for maintaining an upper-class outlook.

Do Upper-Class Mechanisms of Social Reproduction Work?

Because of the need to socially (as well as biologically) reproduce the upper class in each new generation, elite women use the mechanisms set forth in this article to maintain class-based boundaries and to convey to their children social and cultural capital not as easily available to those in other classes. Do the class reproduction strategies described in this article actually work? I believe the answer is "yes." The social reproduction processes engaged in by privileged women do, in fact, help elite young people become class actors who support upper-class ideologies, and those same processes deny many other children the opportunities that might be available for them in a true democracy.

Do the advantages of the upper class disadvantage other people? Any form of exclusionary practice based on class (or race/ethnicity and gender), even in voluntary organizations and charitable activities, reproduces inequality in the United States. Exclusionary practices provide an unfair advantage to those elites who assume that it is their *right* to possess the most wealth in society, to hold the top positions, and to create a world of advantage for their children. They show little concern for those in the bottom tiers of society whose labor often helps privileged elites to maintain their dominant position in a capitalist economy, where they enjoy a consumer-oriented, leisure-class lifestyle.

References

Cookson, Peter W., Jr., and Caroline Hodges Persell. 1985. *Preparing for Power: America's Elite Boarding Schools.* New York: Basic Books.

Daniels, Arlene Kaplan. 1988. *Invisible Careers.* Chicago: University of Chicago Press.

Domhoff, G. William. 1970. *The Higher Circles.* New York: Random House.

———. 1998. *Who Rules America? Power and Politics in the Year 2000.* Mountain View, CA: Mayfield.

Gerth, H. H., and C. Wright Mills. 1958. *From Max Weber: Essays in Sociology.* New York: Oxford University Press.

Kendall, Diana. 2002. *The Power of Good Deeds: Privileged Women and the Social Reproduction of the Upper Class.* Lanham, MD: Rowman & Littlefield.

Kingston, Paul W. 2000. *The Classless Society.* Stanford, CA: Stanford University Press.

Odendahl, Teresa. 1990. *Charity Begins at Home: Generosity and Self-Interest among the Philanthropic Elite.* New York: Basic Books.

Ostrander, Susan. 1984. *Women of the Upper Class.* Philadelphia, PA: Temple University Press.

Ostrower, Francie. 1995. *Why the Wealthy Give: The Culture of Elite Philanthropy.* Princeton, NJ: Princeton University Press.

———. 2002. *Trustees of Culture: Power, Wealth, and Status on Elite Arts Boards.* Chicago: University of Chicago Press.

Pakulski, Jan, and Malcolm Waters. 1996a. *The Death of Class.* Thousand Oaks, CA: Sage Publications.

———. 1996b. "The Reshaping and Dissolution of Social Class in Advanced Society." *Theory and Society* 25: 667–691.

Seabrook, Jeremy. 2002. *The No-Nonsense Guide to Class, Caste, and Hierarchies.* London: Verso.

Vanneman, Reeve, and Lynn Weber Cannon. 1987. *The American Perception of Class.* Philadelphia, PA: Temple University Press.

Wright, Erik O. 1996. "The Continuing Significance of Class Analysis—Comments." *Theory and Society* 25: 693–716.

PART THREE

Examining Intersections

12

Invisibility/Hypervisibility: The Paradox of Normative Whiteness

Maureen T. Redding

The current national political climate is powerfully influenced by a fantasy—a very public fantasy—of white loss of privilege, especially in employment and education. We could probably come up with several dozen plausible explanations for this fantasy's imperviousness to hard facts, but I think a central factor in its persistence is the invisibility of whiteness as whiteness. That social and political context—that fantasy of privilege lost—is the broader context for my remarks here. Just as racism is sexualized, sexism and heterosexism are racialized. Over a decade ago, Angela Davis pointed out the tight link established between white supremacy and male supremacy by the turn of this century, and the economic motives for that linkage. Other writers on race and sex have examined the ways that systems of oppression, such as racism, sexism, and heterosexism, reinforce each other. I want to shift the angle a bit, to look at some ways that systems of privilege—particularly normative whiteness and normative heterosexuality—are mutually reinforcing.

Let me take a moment to explain what I mean by "invisibility/hypervisibility" in my title. Whiteness and heterosexuality seem invisible, transparent, to those who are white and/or heterosexual; they are simply norms. In contrast, whiteness makes itself hypervisible to those who are not white, much as heterosexuality forces itself upon the consciousnesses of gays and lesbians. And one way that these constructs reinforce their invisibility to those who benefit from them is precisely through this hypervisibility to those who do not. I want to tell you a few stories from my life as a mother and a teacher that I think can be used to probe constructions of whiteness and heterosexuality:

The first story: Out in public without my family, I am often the dismayed recipient of other white people's confidences about race. For instance, several months ago, I was waiting on a very long, slow-moving line at the bank. The woman ahead of me—also white—was reading the local paper, which evidently had a story about Providence public schools. She frowned and said to me, "The schools are really in a mess." Thinking she meant some recently announced budget cuts, I said, "Yes, they are." Misinterpreting my agreement, the woman continued, "I'm thinking of moving my son to a private school. His school has just about been taken over by colored kids. And they fight!" Staying as calm as possible, I asked, "What do you mean by 'colored kids'?" Still no clue. "You know, blacks," she answered. "Let me understand this," I said. "Are the white kids attacking the Black kids? Who is fighting?" Beginning to realize she had chosen her audience badly, the woman mumbled some inadequate answer and looked back at her paper.

The second story: Some years ago, toward the end of an introductory literature course, my students and I were all discussing Barbara Smith's essay "Toward a Black Feminist Criticism," in which she reads Toni Morrison's *Sula* as a lesbian novel. An older student, a woman whom I respected and who had made intelligent, sensitive comments on other texts—and who, coincidentally, had been my son's second-grade French teacher—began attacking Smith's argument, seeming terribly offended by it. I asked Helene why she was so agitated. She answered, "Morrison wrote a beautiful novel about women's friendship, perfectly innocent friendship, and this critic is trying to ruin the book by talking about all this lesbian stuff that just isn't there." Taken aback, I said, "Ruin the book? Why would that reading 'ruin' the book?" "Oh, come on," Helene said. "You're a mother. Wouldn't the worst thing that could happen to you be your child telling you he's a homosexual? Wouldn't that wreck your life?" As you can imagine, we ended up very far from *Sula;* I'm fairly sure Helene never believed my assertion that my son's telling me he is gay would not even make my top 1,000 list of "bad" things that could happen, never mind be "the worst" thing.

The third story: I was shopping at the local market with my daughter, who was then two. As we stood on line, another customer—whom I had never seen before—said of my daughter, "She's a real beauty. You're going to have to watch out, 'cause the boys will be chasing her. She's going to break some hearts." The woman was obviously trying to be complimentary, but I was stunned at her casting a two-year-old's appearance in sexual terms AND by her assumption that my daughter would be heterosexual. Who can know about a two-year-old? Why assume? Within a few months of this incident, I heard numerous similar remarks, including comments that began "when she gets married" and even coy remarks from a child care provider about my daughter's "boyfriend." My many objections usually met with puzzled looks.

The last story: For three years now, since he was eleven, my son has been conscious of the homophobia and heterosexism of many of his peers, and has often spoken up in situations where this homophobia gets expressed. He attended a very progressive middle school that emphasizes community and that acts swiftly whenever that community might be undermined. During an eighth-grade class meeting last year, Brendan raised as a topic for discussion homophobic name-calling, and was deeply disappointed when his teacher did not take the lead in the discussion and also when other kids in the class, whom he knew shared his views, failed to speak out. He came home disgusted, and said he felt like giving up; he was especially angry with one boy whom Brendan had counted on but who remained silent during the discussion. Now, what I knew—but Brendan did not—is that this boy had told several trusted adults that he thought he might be gay. My husband and I tried, without outing his friend, to suggest reasons that kids might be frightened into silence and encouraged Brendan to continue speaking up. Brendan had a hard time making the connection between his own willingness to speak up and the fact that he was not a target of the anti-gay slurs; that is, his own heterosexual privilege was invisible to him at the very same time he was strenuously objecting to that privilege.

If gender, race, and sexuality are not biological givens but social con-structs—as of course they are—then they are learned and performed. Coming of age with the second wave of feminism, I was always conscious of gender and of the ways in which I could deliberately dissent from tradi-tional gender roles by "performing" gender differently. To a lesser extent, again thanks to feminism, I was also at least somewhat aware of sexuality and of the ways that I could dissent from restrictive constructs of sexuality by "performing" sexuality differently. Like most white people, however, I was far less conscious of race as a social construct that affected me; that is, I never really thought about whiteness itself or its implications for my life until I married a Black man and—far more consciousness-changing—had a Black child. However, I surely was "performing whiteness and heterosex-uality"—more accurately, performing white heterosexuality—quite un-consciously, in many areas of my life.

Talking about whiteness is difficult. Being white—unless you are an out-and-out racist or a highly aware antiracist—generally does not in-clude much consciousness of whiteness as a social signifier, as a state or condition of being freighted with meaning. Because white heterosexuality is treated as the norm, identical to humanity, whiteness and heterosexual-ity do not get marked as categories in most white, heterosexual people's lives. We do not think of "white writers" or "heterosexual writers" for in-stance as subsets of the general category of "writers," although we do mark writers of color and gay or lesbian writers this way: writer = white and heterosexual unless otherwise noted. This widely shared sense of whiteness and heterosexuality as norms, as going without saying, is not easily disrupted. To say someone's cultural background is white, or to say that he or she is heterosexual, is to say nothing at all. Richard Dyer, in his brilliant essay on representations of whiteness in film, "White," notes that this (false) sense of whiteness as a natural norm is an important compo-nent of white power, which "secures its dominance by seeming not to be anything in particular," by pretending to be invisible (44). I would argue that the same is true of heterosexuality. Few people ask how one "be-comes" heterosexual or what "causes" heterosexuality, for instance. Mak-ing whiteness and heterosexuality visible, becoming aware of whiteness and heterosexuality as social constructs, is the first step in shifting loca-tion, in expanding one's subjectivity, and in beginning to alter those con-structs.

In trying to talk about whiteness clearly in an essay called "White Woman Feminist," Marilyn Frye makes a move that I find very helpful, first separating the physical traits that evidently cause one to be assigned by others to the category "white." She dubs these traits whiteness. But being white, she points out, "is not a biological condition. It is being a member of a certain social/political category, a category that is persistently maintained by those people who are, in their own and each other's perception, unquestionably in it" (115). Assenting to this category, which "defines itself as the paradigm of humanity," both requires and demonstrates what Frye calls "whiteliness." Whiteliness is a way of being in the world, with a relation to whiteness analogous to the relation between masculinity and maleness; it is performing whiteness as presently constructed. Although I do not consistently use Frye's terminology, I think her distinction is useful, and it is "whiteliness" that I am really trying to get at. "Whiteliness" is open not only to those already in the category "white." Learning "whiteliness" is how various immigrant groups, initially defined as "other" by the white majority in the U.S., become white. Whiteliness is learned and therefore can be unlearned; it can be engaged in by people who are not white, and rejected by those who are. Not all white people are whitely; not all whitely people are white.

I want to make a parallel distinction between heterosexuality and "straightliness." I have no idea whether sexual orientation is genetically or environmentally determined. Furthermore, I don't see that origins make a material difference. Wherever it begins, the particular forms that sexuality takes are socially constructed; that is, desire is mediated. Sexuality is not just one's experience of one's own body, in relation to others or not; it is also a public choice that affects every aspect of one's life. Being heterosexual, then, is not a biological condition but it is "being a member of a social/political category, a category that is persistently maintained"—policed—"by those people who are, in their own and each other's perception, unquestionably in it." Assenting to this category, which also "defines itself as the paradigm of humanity," both requires and demonstrates what I call "straightliness." Straightliness is a way of being in the world, with a relation to heterosexuality analogous to the relation between whiteliness and whiteness; it is performing heterosexuality as presently constructed. "Straightliness" is open not only to those already in the category "heterosexual." Learning "straightliness" is one way that children and young adults establish a seemingly secure place in their social worlds. Straightliness is learned and therefore can be unlearned; it can be engaged in by people who are not heterosexual and rejected by those who are. Not all heterosexual people are "straightly"; not all straightly people are heterosexual.

Lack of consciousness about whiteness is a central component of performing whiteness, and of whiteliness. I think that people raised in countries other than the U.S. have a different relationship to race than do those raised here, and so want to clarify that I am speaking now of those of us socialized in the U.S. For us, race is always in play, so to speak, whether we recognize that or not. We live in a racialized and racist society in which race is a primary category of "knowledge." Race, then, is always operational, although generally not acknowledged or even seen to be operational by whites among whites AND often denied to be operational in interracial relations unless the topic of discussion is race (and sometimes not even then).

Although certainly heterosexuality operates normatively, I think there are some crucial differences in consciousness between performing whiteness and performing heterosexuality. Lack of daily consciousness about heterosexuality as an institution is an important element of straightliness, but a high degree of awareness of the borders of heterosexuality—the better to police them—is also a component of straightliness. We sometimes hear sexuality dismissed as "what people do in the privacy of their own bedrooms"—often said by well-meaning, liberal people—but this dismissal ignores the ways in which sexuality is always operational, although seldom acknowledged to be operational by heterosexuals among heterosexuals of the same sex or in non-erotic relationships between heterosexuals of different sexes. In contrast, homosexuality is generally perceived by heterosexuals to be constantly operational both among gays AND in all same-sex gay/heterosexual encounters. While erotic sexuality is perceived as just ONE element of the complex identity of heterosexuals by heterosexuals, erotic sexuality is frequently seen as the significant determinant of identity of gays and lesbians by heterosexuals. Think, for example, of the numerous depictions in popular culture of hypersexual gays on the prowl; this is less true of the social image of lesbians, although lesbians also are depicted as sexual predators in some popular fiction. There is one intriguing exception to this general rule: self-consciously anti-homophobic television, fiction, and film aimed at mass audiences—few and far between as these are—usually entirely de-eroticize gay and lesbian relationships (think, for example, of Tom Hanks and Antonio Banderas in *Philadelphia*).

One place to begin making whiteness visible is to ask: What does whiteness look like to those who are not themselves white? Well, it depends, I think, on a myriad of factors; sometimes whiteness may seem omnipresent, inescapable, threatening; at other times, it may seem like a backdrop, almost as unnoticeable or at least as unremarkable as it is to whites. In "White Woman Feminist," Marilyn Frye details some of the information about whites-through-the-eyes-of-people-of-color that she garnered from books by and about people of color. Several recurring themes stand out. For example: white people believe they are intelligent; white people consider other whites to be fair and honest; white people believe in white authority and rightness. Certainly authority, which extends to race matters, is a constitutive element of whiteliness. In *Faces at the Bottom of the Well*, Derrick Bell enumerates several rules of "racial standing," identifying who has the "standing" to speak on race and racism in the U.S. His second rule goes like this: "Not only are blacks' complaints discounted, but black victims of racism are less effective witnesses than are whites, who are members of the oppressor class. This phenomenon reflects a widespread assumption that blacks, unlike whites, cannot be objective on racial issues and will favor their own no matter what" (113).

I was fascinated by a public enactment of this rule in Providence recently. At a school board meeting, the president of the Rhode Island chapter of the NAACP, Joseph Fowlkes, described the virulent racism he saw in two Providence public high schools (where, by the way, the school-age population is only 23% white but where faculty and administrators are roughly 90% white). He said that the situations in these schools were so bad that he recommended shutting the schools down and reorganizing them entirely. A few days later, the acting principal of one of the schools—a white man—was featured in a newspaper story, rebutting Fowlkes. Let me quote from the story: "As for questions of racism, either at the level of teachers or students, Vallente said he has seen none. 'I think everyone lives together very nicely—probably most of our teachers are white,' he said. 'But I think our faculty is very diverse, and I don't think race is a problem with the faculty." "Diverse"? Diverse HOW?

Reading Frye's article for the first time and reviewing her sources, I found myself thinking, "well, not ALL white people" and mentally "excusing myself," so to speak, from the category (white) under discussion. Reflecting on my own response, which I think would probably be widely shared by whites, I realized that it was a clue to one important element of whiteliness that Frye does not address. That is, whiteness is constructed as diverse, various, multiple. Hence the principal's idea that his almost all-white faculty is "very diverse." Following from that construction is the view that all whites are unique individuals, and that therefore to speak of "white people" in the aggregate is a logical absurdity; in some sense, whiteness is constructed in a way that makes it possible to think that there is no such thing as "white people." This construction of whiteness as endlessly varied stands in direct contrast to white constructions of other races as undifferentiated. It also contributes to making whiteness-as-a-social-construct invisible and—perhaps paradoxically—in that way is a component of one ritual of whiteness that I think is worth examining: white bonding. I will return to white bonding in a few moments.

Similarly, heterosexuals are considered unique individuals; however heterosexuality is not quite so endlessly diverse as is whiteness. According to historians of sex, in the nineteenth century, masturbation and homosexuality, positioned outside the reproductive economy, were constructed as avatars of the primitive. Both were figured as indicators of "racial degeneration" among whites. Nineteenth-century drawings (and even medical texts) depict supposed outward signs of male homosexuality and masturbation such as hairy hands, mental deficiency (vacant looks), and stooped posture. These images have much in common with racist images of the same period; indeed, colonized and enslaved people were seen as inherently sexually degenerate. Furthermore, colonized people—especially Africans, Jews, and Irish—were figured as "dirty," with their supposed sexual deviance an element of that "dirt." This notion of "dirt" figured largely in the vocabulary of sex, with some heterosexual sex—marital, reproductive, between whites—seen as "clean" and other heterosexual sex (along with all homosexual sex) cast as "dirty." This rather quaint notion of "clean" sex is as foundational to even contemporary constructions of heterosexuality as is the fantasy of the "purity" of whiteness to constructions of race. Constructions of white heterosexuality—leading to whiteliness and straightliness—admit only "clean" sex. And "straightly" bonding largely depends on this division of "dirty sex" and "clean sex."

Formal, legal regulation of sex follows this dirty/clean logic, codifying fantasies of white purity and "clean" heterosexual sex. Laws prohibiting interracial marriage were struck down only in 1967 with the Supreme Court's decision in *Loving v. Virginia* that such legislation is unconstitutional. Gay and lesbian couples still are not granted the protection of marriage in the United States; at best, they can register as "domestic partners" in some localities, and, for an additional fee, in San Francisco, duly registered domestic partners can have a judge preside over an entirely symbolic formalization of registration. Numerous laws regulating sexual activity remain in effect, with "clean" sex identifiable largely through examining what is not prohibited. The boundaries of "clean" sex differ for heterosexual men and heterosexual women, and are constantly in flux. For the most part, any sexual act that takes place within the confines of legal marriage is now clean de facto if not de jure. Anti-sodomy laws, for instance, remain on the books in many states but are enforced very selectively, almost always against gay men.

Just as the gender system makes sense only if we apply binary logic, with each gender defined against the Other in a more or less coherent pattern of complementary traits, so too do whiteness and heterosexuality define themselves chiefly by what they are not, over against racial or sexual Others. In the U.S., the ultimate racial Other of whiteness has historically been blackness. The slavocracy devoted considerable thought to demarcating the boundaries of whiteness, as we can see through the many legislated definitions of blackness throughout the South in the 18th and 19th centuries. One set of laws held that children followed the conditions of their mothers—regardless of their fathers' race or condition—so that children born of enslaved mothers would themselves be enslaved. Other sets of laws, such as those in Louisiana (where, by the way, they remain in force), defined degrees of blackness, with terms invented to cover each degree of Black ancestry up to 1/32 (in other words, one great-great-great-grandparent). No corresponding degrees of whiteness were defined, because the myth held that there were no "degrees" of whiteness—all white people were "pure" white. Eventually, most of these legislated definitions collapsed into the "one drop" rule, still in wide use today: a Black person is any person with one drop of Black blood—any "known" Black ancestry. I run through all this to suggest that the corresponding definition of whiteness, then, would be "any person without a single drop of Black blood AND without any known Asian, Latino, or Native American ancestry." In short, the "mixed" condition of blackness is directly acknowledged in such definitions, while the "mixed" condition of whiteness is denied. Whiteness is defined as absence, as purity. In fact, of course, virtually all of the world's people are racially "mixed," including nominally white people. Further, race has no scientific significance (or existence, actually); its entire meaning is social, so these pseudo-scientific determinations of race are absurd. The fantasy of white purity would be laughable if it did not have such powerful social consequences. In parallel fashion, heterosexuality is defined as pure, with similarly absurd but powerful social consequences.

I want to return now to the idea of "white bonding," thinking of it in conjunction with "straight bonding." Both kinds of bonding are rooted, I believe, in responses to notions of purity and superiority. Obviously, the fantasy of purity—racial or sexual—leads to anxiety about one's actual impurity being uncovered. That purity must constantly be defended, the impurity constantly suppressed, in order to maintain social superiority. I think there is a continuum of both straight and white bonding, with only one small part of that continuum usually visible. Hate crimes—the spate of murders of gay men in Texas, for example, or the New York police assault on Abner Louima—are usually group activities, analogous to gang rape, and can be seen as bonding rituals in which a group—almost always of straight white men—"proves," indeed celebrates, its shared whiteliness and straightliness on the bodies of the Other. But there are related rituals that are more subtle: laughter at stereotypical depictions of gays, lesbians, and people of color, for instance, or—far more insidiously—high comfort levels with other whitely/straightly people, in classrooms, in the workplace, in neighborhoods.

The stories with which I began illustrate disrupted whitely or straightly bonding rituals. The woman in the bank assumed that I would share her views because I am white. She never imagined, I'm sure, that my own children are black. My student articulated a usually unarticulated assumption about heterosexual people: that we wish our children also to be heterosexual, that raising children is about reproducing oneself in a manner akin to cloning. This assumption, by the way, is related to the commonly held view that people "naturally" desire children "like themselves," with "like themselves" quite narrowly defined. Further, I think this assumption is at the root of the ignorant belief that gay and lesbian parents produce gay and lesbian children. Having this article of faith challenged clearly disturbed my student, and those who supported her in class. I am not at all interested in producing children exactly like me, except in some specific political ways; I AM interested in helping my children to keep their options open. I suspect that one reason for my views is my children's race, as I have been forced to become conscious of race and, therefore, perhaps have become more aware than I might otherwise have been about other assumptions that limit people's lives.

The eighth-grade name-calling episode was also an instance of disrupted straightly bonding. Adolescents are famously insecure about everything, especially their developing sexuality; one common way to mask that insecurity, to avoid some anxiety, is to assert one's own straightliness by scapegoating a child who is perceived as insufficiently straightly. For boys, it is unsurprising that this ritual plays itself out most often with aggressive sports (which is where, by the way, my son had observed kids being called "fag" for fumbling the ball and so on). The ritual eventually moves to conquest of girls and women. My son's protest called the ritual's foundational beliefs into question; I suspect that he was empowered to speak and that he was fairly successful in his protest—he at least got the issue on the class's agenda—in part because he was not the target of the teasing, but was someone included in the straightly bonding ritual who refused to participate.

I have come to see the many episodes with my daughter and well-meaning but ill-informed strangers and acquaintances as ongoing attempts to socialize my daughter into feminine heterosexuality, more insidious than name-calling because less direct and, therefore, more difficult to disrupt. I have started mildly questioning people who remark on her future heterosexual desirability by saying things like, "That's interesting. How can you tell she'll be heterosexual?" as if I really want to know what "signs" they see that I do not.

Once we become aware of whiteliness and straightliness, we need to remain aware of them and to work constantly to deconstruct them. We need to be especially alert, as Marilyn Frye points out, in environments in which high degrees of whiteliness, and straightliness, are rewarded. The academy, at all levels, is one such location. We need to imagine and practice new ways of being. We need to disrupt white and straight bonding whenever we are implicitly invited to participate in such rituals. This is a collective process, and a long one. It begins, I think, with the recognition that whiteness and heterosexuality may be OBSTACLES to understanding the world, not aids.

Becoming aware of whiteliness and straightliness has irrevocably altered my view of my own classrooms and has prompted me to launch an ongoing experiment in disrupting bonding. The college where I teach is predominantly white. Quite often, I face a class consisting of 24 or 25 white students and only five or six students of color; sometimes the ratio is even worse. For many years—since my own college days, in fact—I have been alert to the ugly phenomenon of white students expecting the vastly outnumbered students of color to speak for their entire racial/social group. From the time I began teaching, I have deliberately disallowed that in my classes. However, it is only in the past four or five years that I have really grappled with the hidden underbelly of that overt expression of racism. That is, without my assent or even awareness, white students have in all likelihood experienced a high degree of comfort with me as a professor because I am also white. Unless I deliberately disrupt that comfort level, white students remain at an advantage in my classes. The same is true of straight students, I think, because of a presumption of my heterosexuality. Even though the content of my courses does not privilege whiteness and heterosexuality, my presence at the front of the class does, unless I correct my students' assumptions and disallow whitely/straightly bonding of the silent, subtle variety. Of the various strategies I have tried, only one has consistently worked well: directly addressing the subject by finding a way to make it part of the course content early each term. I suspect that whitely and straightly bonding are so normative that only direct confrontation can disrupt them effectively in classrooms. In talking to people about trying to keep my children's options open and helping them remain alert to oppression in order to resist limits placed on them by the outside world, I have occasionally met with the comment that this seems like a big burden to place on children. On the contrary, I see this alertness and resistance as freeing, as part of enabling my children, as much as possible, to forge their own places in the world. My children, so far, seem to feel powerful, not burdened. While preparing this talk, I told my son about the topic and mentioned that I wanted to use his experience with trying to get his class to talk about homophobia. I asked him if he had encountered similar issues thus far in high school. He looked at me in disbelief: "Every day, Mom, every day." He went on to tell me about how often at football practice his teammates say some homophobic thing and he speaks up. Was that hard? No, he said, not really, and now a few other kids were following his lead. I was amazed, and he was amazed at my amazement. He explained the pecking order: "The coach keeps saying I'm their best defensive player, and really, everyone pretty much knows that. The team lost all their games until I came back after my injury. The one person no one wants to piss off is me, plus they know if they disagree with me, I'll argue them to death and they won't have any good arguments on their side. So, it's pretty easy." Brendan has learned the fundamental political lesson that we all have some power, and that we must use whatever power we have to make change. This year, Brendan has a world history class that focuses on the ancient world. Early in the fall term, he argued with his teacher about the Sumerians, whom she had depicted as uncomplainingly accepting their priests' taking two-thirds of their agricultural products and so on. Telling us at dinner about the argument, Brendan said, "I don't care what the history books say. Someone was fighting back." A valuable perspective to keep in mind.

At about age four, my daughter began to run into people whose views differed from those she has learned at home. Interestingly, thus far she has not conformed to social expectations, but has fought back. Last year, she started having disagreements with a boy in her kindergarten class who claimed that girls don't play basketball. My husband, Doug, cut some articles and photos about the NCAA women's finals out of the paper and sent them to school with her as evidence to support her case that girls DO play basketball. A day or so later, on the way to her school, Siobhan asked me if girls can marry girls. Since by "marry" she obviously meant "love and live together" not "obtain a legal license," I said yes. "I KNEW it!" she said, "John Michael said girls HAVE to marry boys, but I knew we could marry girls! That kid is dense! I need a break!"

White bonding is not open to my children, and I don't know if straight bonding is. With any luck, they'll hang on to their freedom and resist it, taking breaks when they need them but remaining vigilant.

References

Bell, Derrick. *Faces at the Bottom of the Well: The Permanence of Racism.* New York: Basic Books, 1992.

Dyer, Richard. "White." *Screen* 29:4 (1988): 44–64.

Frye, Marilyn. "White Woman Feminist." In *Overcoming Racism and Sexism.* Ed. Linda A. Bell and Davis Blumenfeld. Lanham, MD: Rowman & Littlefield, 1995; 113–134.

Smith, Barbara. "Toward a Black Feminist Criticism." *The New Feminist Criticism.* 2nd ed. Ed. Elaine Showalter. New York: Pantheon, 1985 [1977]; 168–185.

13
Class and Race

The New Black Elite

bell hooks

Collectively, black folks in the United States have never wanted to highlight the issue of class and class exploitation, even though there have
always been diverse caste and class groups among African-Americans.
Racist biases shaped historical scholarship so that the information about
African explorers who came to the Americas before Columbus was suppressed along with elementary knowledge of the black folks who came as
explorers and immigrants who were never slaves. Indeed, until recently
most black people telling the story of our presence here in the so-called
New World would begin that narrative with slavery. They would not talk
about the Africans who came here bringing gifts of cotton seed, or the
small numbers of black immigrants who came seeking the same freedom
as their white counterparts.

While a few white Americans are willing to acknowledge that a large
majority of the European colonizers who came to these shores were indi-
gents and working-class folks seeking to improve their lot, mostly they tell
the story of their arrival on these shores by calling attention to the journeys of the privileged. Like their black counterparts, those whites who

could count themselves among the privileged were few. The vast majority of whites who entered states of indentured servitude were working class and poor. Yet the journeys of the privileged have come to constitute the norm "white" colonizer and/or immigrant experience, whereas the norm for black people continues to be slavery.

Annals of history do let us know that there was caste and class division between the small number of free blacks and the majority of the enslaved black population. More often than not racial solidarity forged a bond between black-skinned folks even if they did not share the same caste or class standing. They were bonded by the knowledge that at any moment, whether free or enslaved, they could share the same fate.

This did not mean that free blacks did not at times "lord" it over their enslaved counterparts. Nor did enslavement keep some black folks from emulating white colonizers by embracing a color caste hierarchy wherein fair-skinned individuals had higher rank than their darker counterparts. This hierarchy based on color would later be reflected in postslavery class divisions. Since racially mixed slaves often received greater material benefits from their slaveholding white relatives even when those relatives did not publicly acknowledge these blood ties, they often had more resources than their darker counterparts.

Despite segregation and legal racial apartheid, by the onset of the twentieth century distinct class divisions were emerging in segregated black communities. Still, racial solidarity became even more the norm as postslavery white exploitation and oppression intensified. The logic of racial uplift meant that black folks on the bottom of the class hierarchy were encouraged to regard with admiration and respect peers who were gaining class power. In those days, the tiny privileged black middle class was not seen as the enemy of the working poor and indigent. They were examples that it was possible for everyone to rise. It was this belief that informed W. E. B. DuBois's vision of a talented tenth that would lead efforts to uplift the race and change the collective lot of African-Americans. In 1903 he emphasized this point, insisting that it was important to develop "the Best of this race that they may guide the Mass away from the contamination and death of the Worst, in their own and other races." By 1948 he critiqued this earlier supposition, stating: "When I came out of college into the world of work, I realized that it was quite possible that my plan of training a talented tenth might put in control and power, a group of selfish, self-indulgent, well-to-do men, whose basic interest in solving the Negro Problem was personal; personal freedom and unhampered enjoyment and use of the world, without any real care, or certainly no arousing care, as to what became of the mass of American Negroes, or of the mass of any people." Growing up in the fifties, I was acutely aware of the contempt black folks with class privilege directed toward the masses.

In our segregated town, the black folks with relative class power, whom group sociologist E. Franklin Frazier would later identify as the black bourgeoisie, enjoyed their role as mediators between the black masses and the white folks who were really in charge. They openly espoused contempt for less-privileged black folks even as they needed that group to stay on the bottom so they could measure how far up they had gotten by how far down the black masses remained. At the end of the day, no matter our class, all black folks lived together in segregated neighborhoods. The surrounding white supremacist world reminded all of us through exploitation and domination that even the richest black person could be crushed by racism's heavy weight.

That sense of solidarity was altered by a class-based civil rights struggle whose ultimate goal was to acquire more freedom for those black folks who already had a degree of class privilege, however relative. By the late 1960s class-based racial integration disrupted the racial solidarity that often held black folks together despite class difference. Pressured to assimilate into mainstream white culture to increase their class power and status, privileged black individuals began to leave the underprivileged behind, moving into predominantly white neighborhoods, taking their money and their industry out of the segregated black world. Historically, white colleges and universities had not yet hired the best and the brightest of black thinkers. Anti-racist sentiment was not the reason for racial integration. Strategically, white politicians recognized the threat that a decolonized militant self-determined black population could pose to the existing status quo.

Desegregation was the way to weaken the collective radicalization of black people that had been generated by militant civil rights and black power movements. It was better to give privileged black people greater access to the existing social structure than to have a radical talented tenth that would lead the black masses to revolt and cultural revolution. Concurrently, a shift in global politics had made it apparent that white people would have to do business with people of color globally to maintain U.S. imperialist economic domination. The old colonialism could not form the basis of contemporary economic exchanges globally. It was vital that new generations of white people learn to relate in new and different ways to people of color globally if the ruling class power of the United States was to remain intact. Given these concerns racial integration was useful. It diffused politics of racial uplift and black radicalization and simultaneously produced a new class of privileged, upwardly mobile black folks who would see their interests as more allied with the existing white power structure than with any group of black people. After years of collective struggle, by the end of the sixties liberal individualism had become more the norm for black folks, particularly the black bourgeoisie, more so than the previous politics of communalism, which emphasized racial uplift and sharing resources.

In the community of my growing up it was not difficult to distinguish those black folks with class privilege who were committed to racial uplift, to sharing resources, from those who were eager to exploit the community solely for their own individual gain. The latter were fixated on making money, on flaunting their status and power. They were not respected or revered. That, however, began to change as market values wiped out core beliefs in the integrity of communalism and shared resources, replacing them with the edict that every woman and man "live for yoself, for yoself and nobody else."

Traditional black communities, like the one I grew up in, which had always included everyone, all classes, were changed by the end of the seventies. Folks with money took their money out of the community. Local black-owned business all but ceased with the exception of the undertakers. Exercising their equal rights as citizens, black folks began to live, and most importantly, to shop, everywhere, seemingly not noticing the changes in predominantly black communities. These changes happened all over the United States. By the early nineties, the black poor and underclass were fast becoming isolated, segregated communities. Big business, in the form of a booming drug trade, infiltrated these communities and let addiction and the violence it breeds and sustains chip away and ultimately erode the overall well-being of the poor, and working-class black folks left.

Militant black power advocates of the sixties (many of whom were from privileged class backgrounds) successfully working to end racism, to feed the poor, and raise the consciousness of all would no doubt be shocked to see gates walling off indigent black communities all around this nation. The black middle and upper classes in no way protest these modern-day concentration camps. Historical amnesia sets in and they conveniently forget that the fascists who engineered the Nazi holocaust did not begin with gas chambers but rather began their genocidal agenda by herding people together and depriving them of the basic necessities of life—adequate food, shelter, health care, etc. Lethal drugs like crack cocaine make gas chambers unnecessary in these modern times. Without outright naming, concentration camp–like conditions now exist in this nation in all major urban communities. Like their uncaring counterparts in other racial groups, most black privileged folks need never enter these communities, need never see the slow genocide that takes place there. They can choose to stand at a distance and blame the victims.

A thriving, corrupt "talented tenth" have not only emerged as the power brokers preaching individual liberalism and black capitalism to everyone (especially the black masses), their biggest commodity is "selling blackness." They make sure they mask their agenda so black capitalism looks like black self-determination. Whether it is movies made by black filmmakers that glamorize and celebrate black-on-black predatory violence while placing blame on the victims, or literature produced by black academics and/or writers that does the same, it is evident that the vast majority of privileged-class black folks feel they have nothing in common with the black poor. Whenever well-to-do black persons justly complain about the ways racism operates to keep them from reaching the highest pinnacle of career success or the way everyday racism makes it hard for them to get a taxi or does not exempt them from being treated unjustly by the police, if these complaints are not linked to an acknowledgment of how their class power mediates racial injustice in a way that it does not for the poor and underprivileged, they collude in the nation's refusal to acknowledge the solace and protection that class privilege affords them.

Prior to civil rights and militant black power struggle, class privilege did little to help upwardly mobile black folks if white folks wanted to exploit and oppress them with impunity. This is no longer the case. This does not mean that racism does not daily assault black people with class privilege; it does. The pain of the privileged is linked to the pain of the indigent who also daily suffer racial assault, just as anti-racist struggle to end

that suffering promises liberation to all classes. However, as the gap between privileged blacks and the black poor widens, all who are truly committed to justice and an end to racial domination must break through the
denial that allows the haves to disavow the myriad ways class privilege mediates the pain of racial assault. The black working class, poor, and underclass cannot use class status and privilege to escape racial assault or to
pacify wounds when they are inflicted.

In large and small ways, middle-class, upper-class, and wealthy black
people can create lifestyles that enable them to minimize contact with
harsh racism. Numerous privileged black folks hire white underlings to interface between them and a racist white world. Assimilation is yet another
strategy they deploy to deflect harsh racism away from them and onto
"other" blacks. Ellis Cose's book *The Rage of the Black Middle Class* reminded everyone that class privilege does not mean that well-off blacks
will not suffer racial assault, and it enrages them. Yet he did not link their
rage with a rage against the conditions imposed upon the black poor and
indigent by white supremacist exploitation and oppression. While all our
rage at racism is justifiable, it undermines anti-racist struggle and the call
for social justice when well-off black folks attempt to create a social context where they will be exempt from racist assault even as the underprivileged remain daily victimized.

Nowadays, practically every public representation of blackness is created by black folks who are materially privileged. More often than not,
they speak about the black poor and working class but not with them, or
on their behalf. The presence of a small number of privileged black folks
who continue to work for justice, who work to change this culture so that
all black people can live fully and well, is often obscured by the dominant
white culture's focus on those who are fundamentally opportunistic
and/or corrupt. These conservative black elites, chosen and appointed to
positions of authority by the mainstream, not only take charge of interrupting and shaping public policy that will affect the lives of underprivileged black folks, they police black folks who do not agree with them or
support their agendas. That policing may take the form of preventing folks
from getting jobs or getting heard if they speak and/or write publicly, or
deploying various forms of psychological terrorism.

When possible they use their class power to censor and silence, deploying
their greater access to white mainstream media, and all other avenues of
power, in ways that discredit dissenting black voices. They censor and isolate

these voices to diffuse the power of those lone individuals who care for justice enough to link word and deed, theory and practice. Ideologically, they
perpetuate the false assumption that everyone is really corrupt, that all privileged-class blacks by virtue of their achievements and status betray those
without privilege. As this thinking gains widespread acceptance they need
not worry about critique or exposure. They take advantage of the fact that
the poor and underclass masses know nothing about their lives and have no
power to expose their contradictions or their betrayals. They isolate and ignore dissenting voices whether they come from progressive visionary underprivileged sources or their more radical privileged-class counterparts.

More individual black folks than ever before are entering the ranks of
the rich and upper class. Allegiance to their class interests usually super-
sedes racial solidarity. They are not only leaving the underprivileged black
masses behind, they collude in the systems of domination that ensure the
continued exploitation and oppression of the poor. Unlike many of their
middle-class peers who may be bonded with lower-class and poor people,
who are compelled by kinship ties to share resources, they refuse identification with the black poor, unless it serves their interests to act concerned.
Michael Jordan, one of the richest men in the world, epitomizes this perspective. His commitment to capitalist profit at any cost has characterized
his economic success. For mainstream culture he is the global example
that colonized mind can strengthen one's class power. There are many
wealthy and upper-class black people who "think like Mike" but they are
not in the public eye, or if they are visible they do not openly reveal their
identification with the values of a ruling class elite.

When Harvard academic Henry Louis Gates, Jr., deemed by mainstream white culture to be one of the most powerful black spokespersons
in this society, did a program for public television where he candidly challenged the notion that black people across class share common perspectives, he was subject to forms of critique that had not previously
characterized black folks' response to his success. Even so, he and many
folks like him live in and conduct business in a world where black people's
response, whether positive or negative, is not perceived as influential or
important. Black people do not have the power to invite the black elite to
the White House and do not reward them with unprecedented fame, status, and financial remuneration.

The miseducation of all underprivileged black groups strengthens the
class power of the nonprogressive black elite. Without anti-racist reparations,

a central one being affirmative action programs, which once offered financial aid to the poor and working class, these groups are not allowed entry
into the ranks of the talented tenth. Since they are the individuals who are
best situated to experientially understand the dynamics of class among
black folks, who may retain allegiance to their class of origins and breed
dissent in the world of the privileged, denying them access to higher education is a strategic act of repression. Without quality education, which
broadens the mind and strengthens one's capacity to think critically, they
are less likely to threaten the status quo. Increasingly, there are few black
folks from poor and working-class backgrounds being educated in elite
settings. They simply do not have the means. Those select few who receive
aid are far more likely to share the conservative perspectives of their well-
to-do counterparts.

Unlike my generation (poor and working-class children of the late sixties and seventies), who were able to receive college educations because of
financial aid but were not seduced by the fantasy of becoming rich or entering the ranks of the mainstream black elite, as that elite was not yet in
place, the underprivileged today are more tempted by the goodies offered
by the status quo. Since they have no organized visionary radical movement for social justice to make them more conscious and to sustain them
should they rebel, they fear dissent. They are more likely than not to claim
that racism has ended or that if it exists it does not affect them. They are
more likely to believe that the economic plight of the black masses is
caused by a lack of skills, will, and know-how and not by systemic exploitation and oppression. They have learned to think this way from the
lessons mainstream culture teaches them about what they must do to succeed. They stand ready to ascend to the heights of class privilege by any
means necessary. And now more than ever, there is a corrupt talented
tenth in place to guide them along the way.

Significantly, even though a growing majority of privileged-class black
folks condemn and betray the black poor and underclass, they avoid critique and confrontation themselves by not focusing on their class power.
In the nineties they prefer to talk about race and ignore class. All black
people know that no matter your class you will suffer wounds inflicted by
racism, however relative. Fewer black people know intimately the concrete
everyday ways class power and privilege mediate this pain, allowing some
black folks to live luxuriously despite racism. Sadly, to escape this pain or

to shield themselves from the genocide that is assaulting black masses, they surrender all transformative forms of racial solidarity in anti-racist struggle to protect their class interests. They betray their people even as they maintain their status and public image by pretending that they know best and are best positioned to protect the collective public good of all black people irrespective of class.

The black masses are encouraged by an empowered privileged few to believe that any critique they or anyone makes of the class power of black elites is merely sour grapes. Or they are made to feel they are interfering with racial uplift and racial solidarity if they want to talk about class. They live the reality of class divisions among black people. Unlike the black elite, they are not ashamed or afraid to talk about class; they simply have few or no public venues in which to air their views. Radical black voices, especially those with some degree of class privilege, must have the courage to talk about class. Racial solidarity in anti-racist struggle can, sometimes does, and must coexist with a recognition of the importance of ending class elitism.

Vigilant critique of the politics of class in diverse black communities is and should be a dynamic dimension of all progressive struggles for black self-determination. Being upwardly mobile need not mean that one betrays the people on the bottom. Yet we need to know more about the concrete ways we can have a degree of class privilege without abandoning allegiance to those who are underprivileged or accountability for their fate. Progressive black folks who have class privilege must intervene when our more conservative and liberal counterparts seek to deny the reality of black-on-black class cruelty and exploitation.

We must courageously challenge the privileged who aggressively seek to deny the disadvantaged a chance to change their lot. Privileged people are the individuals who create representations of blackness where education is deemed valueless, where violence is glamorous, where the poor are dehumanized. These images are not just produced by white folks. Understanding that many black people seeking success in the existing white supremacist capitalist patriarchy embrace white supremacist thought and action, we need sophisticated strategies to challenge and resist their exploitation and oppression of the masses. Saying that they are not "black" or that they are "Uncle Toms" is a shallow critique that does not address in any meaningful way the reality that any viable anti-racist movement for social justice must have a program aimed at decolonizing and converting those black folks who act in collusion with the status quo. Conversion empowers; judgmental assaults alienate.

Until visionary black thinkers, from all walks of life, can create strategies and lifestyles that embrace the idea of empowerment without domination for all classes, all efforts toward black self-determination will fail. Were the black poor and underclass able to create constructive class solidarity, there would be hope that their needs would be articulated and addressed. Progressive black "elites" must humanely confront and challenge conservative peers. It is our task to forge a vision of solidarity in ending domination, which includes anti-racist struggle that realistically confronts class difference and constructively intervenes on the growing class antagonism between black folks with class privilege and the black masses who are daily being stripped of class power. While we need not return to the notion of leadership by a talented tenth, we do need to draw on the legacy of constant radical commitment to social justice for all, which undergirds the dream of liberatory black self-determination that was at the heart of DuBois's vision.

14

How Gay Stays White and What Kind of White It Stays

Allan Bérubé

The Stereotype

When I teach college courses on queer history or queer working-class studies, I encourage students to explore the many ways that homosexuality is shaped by race, class, and gender. I know that racialized phantom figures hover over our classroom and inhabit our consciousness. I try to name these figures out loud to bring them down to earth so we can begin to resist their stranglehold on our intelligence. One by one, I recite the social categories that students have already used in our discussions—immigrant, worker, corporate executive, welfare recipient, student on financial aid, lesbian mother—and ask students first to imagine the stereotypical figure associated with the category and then to call out the figure's race, gender, class, and sexuality. As we watch each other conjure up and name these phantoms, we are stunned at how well each of us has learned by heart the same fearful chorus.

Whenever I get to the social category "gay man," the students' response is always the same: "white and well-to-do." In the United States today, the dominant image of the typical gay man is a white man who is financially better off than most everyone else. *-Differs in the city*

My White Desires

Since the day I came out to my best friend in 1968, I have inhabited the social category "gay white man." As a historian, writer, and activist, I've examined the gay and the male parts of that identity, and more recently I've explored my working-class background and the Franco-American ethnicity that is so intertwined with it. But only recently have I identified with or seriously examined my gay male whiteness.[1]

Several years ago I made the decision to put race and class at the center of my gay writing and activism. I was frustrated at how my own gay social and activist circles reproduced larger patterns of racial separation by remaining almost entirely white. And I felt abandoned as the vision of the national gay movement and media narrowed from fighting for liberation, freedom, and social justice to expressing personal pride, achieving visibility, and lobbying for individual equality within existing institutions. What emerged was too often an exclusively gay rights agenda isolated from supposedly nongay issues, such as homelessness, unemployment, welfare, universal health care, union organizing, affirmative action, and abortion rights. To gain recognition and credibility, some gay organizations and media began to aggressively promote the so-called positive image of a generic gay community that is an upscale, mostly male, and mostly white consumer market with mainstream, even traditional, values. Such a strategy derives its power from an unexamined investment in whiteness and middle-class identification. As a result, its practitioners seemed not to take seriously or even notice how their gay visibility successes at times exploited and reinforced a racialized class divide that continues to tear our nation apart, including our lesbian and gay communities.

Client does not relate

My decision to put race and class at the center of my gay work led me as a historian to pursue the history of a multiracial maritime union that in the 1930s and 1940s fought for racial equality and the dignity of openly gay workers.[2] And my decision opened doors that enabled me as an activist to join multiracial lesbian, gay, bisexual, and transgender groups whose members have been doing antiracist work for a long time and in which gay white men are not the majority—groups that included the Lesbian, Gay, Bisexual, and Transgender Advisory Committee to the San

Francisco Human Rights Commission and the editorial board of the now-defunct national lesbian and gay quarterly journal *Out/Look*.

But doing this work also created new and ongoing conflicts in my relationships with other white men. I want to figure out how to handle these conflicts as I extend my antiracist work into those areas of my life where I still find myself among gay white men—especially when we form new activist and intellectual groups that once again turn out to be white. To do this I need "to clarify something for myself," as James Baldwin put it, when he gave his reason for writing his homosexual novel *Giovanni's Room* in the 1950s.[3]

I wanted to know how gay gets white, how it stays that way, and how whiteness is used both to win and attack gay rights campaigns.

I want to learn how to see my own whiteness when I am with gay white men and to understand what happens among us when one of us calls attention to our whiteness.

I want to know why I and other gay white men would want to challenge the racist structures of whiteness, what happens to us when we try, what makes me keep running away from the task, sometimes in silent despair, and what makes me want to go back to take up the task again.

I want to pursue these questions by drawing on a gay ability, developed over decades of figuring out how to "come out of the closet," to bring our hidden lives out into the open. But I want to do this without encouraging anyone to assign a greater degree of racism to gay white men, thus exposed, than to other white men more protected from exposure, and without inviting white men who are not gay to more safely see gay men's white racism rather than their own.

I want to know these things because gay white men have been among the men I have loved and will continue to love. I need them in my life and at my side as I try to make fighting racism a more central part of my work. And when students call out "white" to describe the typical gay man, and they see me standing right there in front of them, I want to figure out how, from where I am standing, I can intelligently fight the racist hierarchies that I and my students differently inhabit.

Gay Whitening Practices

Despite the stereotype, the gay male population is not as white as it appears to be in the images of gay men projected by the mainstream and gay media, or among the "out" men (including myself) who move into the public spotlight as representative gay activists, writers, commentators, and spokesmen. Gay men of color, working against the stereotype, have engaged in long, difficult struggles to gain some public recognition of their cultural heritages, political activism, and everyday existence. To educate gay white men, they've had to get our attention by interrupting our business as usual, then convince us that we don't speak for them or represent them or know enough about either their realities or our own racial assumptions and privileges. And when I and other gay white men don't educate ourselves, gay men of color have done the face-to-face work of educating us about their cultures, histories, oppression, and particular needs—the kind of personal work that tires us out when heterosexuals ask us to explain to them what it's like to be gay. Also working against their ability to put "gay" and "men of color" together in the broader white imagination are a great many other powerful *whitening practices* that daily construct, maintain, and fortify the idea that gay male means white.

How does the category "gay man" become white? What are the whitening practices that perpetuate this stereotype, often without awareness or comment by gay white men? How do these practices operate, and what racial work do they perform?

I begin by mining my own experience for clues.[4] I know that if I go where I'm surrounded by other gay white men, or if I'm having sex with a white man, it's unlikely that our race will come up in conversation. Such racially comfortable, racially familiar situations can make us mistakenly believe that there are such things as gay issues, spaces, culture, and relationships that are not "lived through" race, and that white gay life, so long as it is not named as such, is not about race.[5] These lived assumptions, and the privileges on which they are based, form a powerful camouflage woven from a web of unquestioned beliefs—that gay whiteness is unmarked and unremarkable, universal and representative, powerful and protective, a cohesive bond. The markings of this camouflage are pale—a characteristic that the wearer sees neither as entirely invisible nor as a racial "color," a shade that allows the wearer to blend into the seemingly neutral background of white worlds. When we wear this everyday camouflage into a gay political arena that white men already dominate, our activism comes wrapped in a *pale protective coloring* that we may not notice but which is clearly visible to those who don't enjoy its protection.

I start to remember specific situations in which I caught glimpses of how other gay whitening practices work.

One night, arriving at my favorite gay disco bar in San Francisco, I discovered outside a picket line of people protesting the triple-carding (requiring three photo IDs) of gay men of color at the door. This practice was a form of racial *exclusion*—policing the borders of white gay institutions to prevent people of color from entering. The management was using this discriminatory practice to keep the bar from "turning," as it's called—a process by which a "generically gay" bar (meaning a predominantly white bar) changes into a bar that loses status and income (meaning gay white men with money won't go there) because it has been "taken over" by black, Latino, or Asian gay men. For many white owners, managers, and patrons of gay bars, only a white gay bar can be *just* gay; a bar where men of color go is seen as racialized. As I joined the picket line, I felt the fears of a white man who has the privilege to choose on which side of a color line he will stand. I wanted to support my gay brothers of color who were being harassed at the door, yet I was afraid that the doorman might recognize me as a regular and refuse to let me back in. That night, I saw a gay bar's doorway become a racialized border, where a battle to preserve or challenge the whiteness of the clientele inside was fought among dozens of gay men who were either standing guard at the door, allowed to walk through it, or shouting and marching outside. (The protests eventually made the bar stop the triple-carding.)

I remember seeing how another gay whitening practice works when I watched, with other members of a sexual politics study group, an antigay video, "Gay Rights, Special Rights," produced in 1993 by The Report, a religious right organization. This practice was the *selling* of gay whiteness— the marketing of gays as white and wealthy to make money and increase political capital, either to raise funds for campaigns (in both progay and antigay benefits, advertising, and direct-mail appeals) or to gain economic power (by promoting or appealing to a gay consumer market). The antigay video we watched used racialized class to undermine alliances between a gay rights movement portrayed as white and movements of people of color portrayed as heterosexual. It showed charts comparing mutually exclusive categories of "homosexuals" and "African Americans," telling us that homosexuals are wealthy, college-educated white men who vacation more than anyone else and who demand even more "special rights and privileges" by taking civil rights away from low-income African Americans.[6] In this zero-sum, racialized world of the religious right, gay men are white; gay, lesbian, and bisexual people of color, along with poor or working-class white gay men, bisexuals, and lesbians, simply do not exist. The recently vigorous gay media promotion of the high-income, brand-loyal gay consumer market—which is typically portrayed as a population of white, well-to-do, college-educated young men—only widens the racialized class divisions that the religious right so eagerly exploits.

During the 1993 Senate hearings on gays in the military, I saw how these and other whitening practices were used in concentrated form by another gay institution, the Campaign for Military Service (CMS).

The Campaign for Military Service was an ad hoc organization formed in Washington, D.C., by a group composed primarily of well-to-do, well-connected, professional men, including billionaires David Geffen and Barry Diller, corporate consultant and former antiwar activist David Mixner (a personal friend of Bill Clinton's, and several gay and lesbian civil rights attorneys. Their mission was to work with the Clinton White House and sympathetic senators by coordinating the gay response to hearings held by the Senate Armed Services Committee, chaired by Sam Nunn. Their power was derived from their legal expertise, their access to wealthy donors, and their contacts with high-level personnel inside the White House, Senate, and Pentagon. The challenge they faced was to make strategic, pragmatic decisions in the heat of a rapidly changing national battle over what President Clinton called "our nation's policy toward homosexuals in the military."[7]

The world in and around the CMS that David Mixner describes in his memoir, *Stranger Among Friends,* is a network of professionals passionately dedicated to gay rights who communicated with Washington insiders via telephone calls, memos, and meetings in the White House, the Pentagon, and private homes. Wearing the protective coloring of this predominantly white gay world, these professionals entered the similarly white and male but heterosexual world of the U.S. Senate, where their shared whiteness became a common ground on which the battle to lift the military's ban on homosexuals was fought—and lost.

The CMS used a set of arguments they called the *race analogy* to persuade senators and military officials to lift the military's antigay ban. The strategy was to get these powerful men to take antigay discrimination as seriously as they supposedly took racial discrimination, so they would lift the military ban on homosexuals as they had eliminated official policies requiring racial segregation. During the Senate hearings, the race analogy projected a set of comparisons that led to heated disputes over whether sexual orientation was analogous to race, whether sexual desire and conduct were like "skin color," or, most specifically, whether being homosexual was like being African American. (Rarely was "race" explicitly discussed as anything other than African American.) On their side, the CMS argued for a qualified analogy—what they called "haunting parallels" between "the words, rationale and rhetoric invoked in favor of racial discrimination in the past" and those used to "exclude gays in the military now." "The parallel is inexact," they cautioned, because "a person's skin color is not the same as a person's sexual identity; race is self-evident to many whereas sexual orientation is not. Moreover, the history of African Americans is not equivalent to the history of lesbian, gay and bisexual people in this country." Yet, despite these qualifications, the CMS held firm to the analogy. "The bigotry expressed is the same; the discrimination is the same."[8]

The military responded with an attack on the race analogy as self-serving, racist, and offensive. They were aided by Senator Nunn, who skillfully managed the hearings in ways that exploited the whiteness of the CMS and their witnesses to advance the military's antigay agenda. Working in their favor was the fact that, unlike the CMS, the military had high-ranking officials who were African American. The chairman of the Joint Chiefs of Staff, Gen. Colin L. Powell, who opposed lifting the ban, responded to the CMS with the argument that the antigay policy was not analogous to racial segregation because "skin color" was a "benign characteristic" while homosexuality constituted conduct that was neither benign nor condoned by most Americans.[9] Another African American Army officer, Lt. Gen. Calvin Waller, Gen. Norman Schwarzkopf's deputy commander and the highest-ranking African American officer in Operation Desert Storm, attacked the race analogy with these words: "I had no choice regarding my race when I was delivered from my mother's womb. To compare my service in America's armed forces with the integration of avowed homosexuals is personally offensive to me."[10] Antigay white senators mimicked his outrage.

During the race analogy debates, the fact that only white witnesses made the analogy, drawing connections between antigay and racial discrimination without including people of color, reduced the power of their argument and the credibility it might have gained had it been made by advocates who had experienced the racial discrimination side of the analogy.[11] But without hearing these voices, everyone in the debate could imagine homosexuals as either people who do not experience racism (the military assumption) or as people who experience discrimination only as homosexuals (the progay assumption)—two different routes that ultimately led to the same destination: the place where gay stays white, the place where the CMS chose to make its stand.

According to Mixner's memoir, the Senate Armed Services Committee "had asked CMS to suggest witnesses."[12] As gay gatekeepers to the hearings, the CMS utilized another whitening practice—*mirroring*. This is a political strategy that reflects back the whiteness of the men who run powerful institutions to persuade them to take "us" seriously, accept "us," and let "us" in because "we are just like you." From the witnesses they selected, it appears that the CMS tried to project an idealized image of the openly gay service member that mirrored the senators' racial makeup and their publicly espoused social values and sexual mores—the image of the highly competent, patriotic, sexually abstinent, young, male officer who had earned the right to serve with a proud record and therefore deserved equality. The CMS selected for the gay panel a group of articulate and courageous veterans—all white men, except for one white woman.[13] Cleverly, Senator Nunn's staff selected a panel of African American ministers opposed to lifting the ban to precede the gay white panel, so that both sides constructed and participated in a racialized dramatic conflict that reinforced the twin myths that gay is white and African Americans are antigay.

Missing was the testimony of service members whose lives bridged the hearings' false divide between black and gay—veterans who were both African American and lesbian, gay, or bisexual. In this context, a significant whitening practice at the hearings was the exclusion of Sgt. Perry Watkins as a witness. Watkins was an openly gay, African American veteran considered by many to be a military hero. Kicked out of the army as a homosexual shortly before his retirement, he successfully appealed his discharge to the Supreme Court, becoming what one attorney called "the first out gay soldier to retire from the Army with full honors."[14]

To my knowledge, there is no public record of how or why the CMS did not invite Watkins to testify.[15] (This is another privilege that comes with whiteness—the ability to make decisions that seriously affect people of color and then protect that decision-making process from public scrutiny or accountability.) Sabrina Sojourner, who recalls that she was the only African American at the CMS among the nonsupport staff, told me that she "got moved further and further from the decision-making process" because she "brought up race," including the problem of the racial dynamic set up by presenting only white witnesses to testify.[16]

There was a moment when I was personally involved with this process. As the author of *Coming Out under Fire: The History of Gay Men and Women in World War Two,* I was asked by the CMS to prepare to fly from California to Washington to testify, but my appearance was not approved by the Senate staff, who allowed no open homosexuals to testify as expert witnesses.[17] During a phone conversation with a white CMS staff member, I remember getting up the courage to ask him why Watkins wasn't a witness and was told that "Perry is a difficult personality." I didn't push my question any further, getting the message that I shouldn't ask for complicated explanations during the heat of battle and deferring to their inside-the-beltway tactical decisions, thus forfeiting an important opportunity to seriously challenge Watkins's exclusion. More instances of this painful struggle over Watkins's participation in and around the hearings must have been going on behind the scenes.[18] Watkins believed he was shut out because he was a "queeny" African American.[19]

It seems that the CMS considered Watkins to be the opposite of their ideal witness. His military story was indeed more complicated than the generic coming-out story. During his 1968 induction physical exam in Tacoma, Washington, he had openly declared his homosexuality, checking "Yes" to the written question "Do you have homosexual tendencies?" and freely describing his sexual experiences to the induction psychiatrist. But the army drafted him nevertheless because it needed him to fight in Vietnam, along with other mostly working-class African American men, who accounted for 20 percent of U.S. combat deaths in that war by 1966, when African Americans made up 11 percent of the U.S. population and 12.6 percent of U.S. troops in Vietnam. Journalist Randy Shilts, who later interviewed Watkins, reported that Watkins believed "the doctor probably figured Watkins would . . . go to Vietnam, get killed, and nobody would ever hear about it again."[20] So Watkins's story was not a white narrative. "If I had not been black," he told Mary Ann Humphrey in an oral history interview, "my situation would not have happened as it did. . . . Every *white* person I knew from Tacoma who was gay and had checked that box 'Yes' did not have to go into the service."[21] Watkins's story resonated more with how men of color experience antigay racism in the military than with the story so many white servicemen tell. That white narrative begins with how a gay serviceman never experienced discrimination until he discovered his homosexuality in the service and ends with his fighting an antigay discharge, without referring to how he lived this experience through his whiteness. But Watkins explicitly talked about how he lived his gay military experience through race. "People ask me," he explained, "'How have you managed to tolerate all that discrimination you have had to deal with in the military?' My immediate answer to them was, 'Hell, I grew up black. Give me a break.'"[22] Watkins had also, while in the military, danced and sang on U.S. Army bases as the flamboyant "Simone," his drag persona; as a veteran he was HIV-positive; and in some gay venues he wore body-piercings in public.[23]

Nevertheless, Watkins's testimony at the hearings could have struck familiar chords among many Americans, including working-class and African American communities, as the experience of someone who was *real* rather than an *ideal*. His story was so compelling, in fact, that after the hearings he was the subject of two films and a segment of the television news magazine "20/20."[24] But the story of his military career—which he so openly lived through race (as an African American), sexuality (had a sex life), and gender (performed in drag)—seems to have been considered by the CMS as too contaminated for congressional testimony and too distracting for the personal media stories that were supposed to focus only on the gay right to serve.

Watkins's absence was a lost opportunity to see and hear in nationally televised Senate hearings a gay African American legal hero talk about his victory over antigay discrimination in the military and expose the racist hypocrisy of how the antigay ban was in practice suspended for African Americans during wartime. The lack of testimony from any other lesbian, gay, or bisexual veteran of color was a lost opportunity to build alliances with communities of color and to do something about the "(largely accurate) perception of the gay activist leadership in Washington as overwhelmingly white."[25] Their collective absence reinforced another powerful myth that, even in a military population that is disproportionately African

American and Latino, the representative gay soldier is a white officer, and the most presentable gay face of military competence is a white face.

As the hearings progressed, some CMS activists, speaking in public forums outside the hearings, took the race analogy a step further by promoting the idea that the gay rights movement was *like* the civil rights movement. During the hearings, those who argued the race analogy had drawn parallels between racist and antigay bigotry and discrimination. But those who extended the race analogy to the civil rights movement analogy had to take several more steps. First, they had to reconceptualize the civil rights movement. They took a multiracial movement for human equality and human rights, which included many lesbian, gay, and bisexual activists, and changed it into a nongay, black movement for African American racial equality. Next, they had to imagine the gay movement as a white movement for homosexual rights rather than as a multiracial movement that grew out of and continued the work of the civil rights movement. Then they could make the analogy between these two now-separated movements—one just about race, the other just about homosexuality. The last step was to symbolically recast gay white men in the roles of African American civil rights leaders. These moves tried to correct a problem inherent in such whitening practices as excluding people of color and the wearing, mirroring, and selling of gay whiteness. Because such practices draw directly on the privileges of whiteness, they do not on their own carry much moral weight. The extended race analogy compensates for this weightlessness by first invoking the moral authority of the civil rights movement (while erasing its actual history), and then transferring that unearned moral authority to a white gay movement, without giving anything back. At its worst, the race analogy can become a form of historical erasure, political cheating, and, ultimately, a theft of cultural capital and symbolic value.

David Mixner's memoir reveals how the extended race analogy was used in and around the Campaign for Military Service. When President Clinton, at a press conference, revealed that he wouldn't rule out separating homosexuals from heterosexuals within the military, Mixner first interpreted Clinton's comments as condoning gay segregation, then began equating it with racial segregation. Mixner's account of what happened next does not include attempts to seek advice from or build alliances with people whose histories include long struggles against legal segregation.

This despite solid support for lifting the ban from civil rights veterans including Coretta Scott King and Roger Wilkins, the Black Lesbian and Gay Leadership Forum, the Congressional Black Caucus (including Ron Dellums, chairman of the House Armed Services Committee and a former marine who eventually held House hearings to counter Nunn's Senate hearings), and, in public opinion polls, a majority of African Americans (in contrast to a minority of white Americans).[26] Mixner instead describes a series of decisions and actions in which he invokes scenes from the history of racial segregation and the civil rights movement and appears to be reenacting those scenes as if he were a gay (white) version of a black civil rights leader.

A telling moment was when Mixner asked his friend Troy Perry, a gay white minister who founded and heads the gay Metropolitan Community Church, to let him use the Sunday pulpit at the MCC Cathedral in Dallas as a "platform from which to speak." Covered by network television, Mixner delivered a sermon to the nation about the gay "road to freedom." In his sermon he referred to the military's antigay policy as "ancient apartheid laws" and charged that "Sam Nunn is our George Wallace" and that "[b]igotry that wears a uniform is nothing more than a uniform with a hood." He angrily warned President Clinton, cast as antigay segregationist, that "with or without you we will be free . . . we will prevail!"[27] Shortly after the sermon, Tracy Thorne, a gay white Navy veteran who had courageously faced verbal abuse at the Senate hearings and who flew to Dallas to support Mixner, said out loud what had been implied by Mixner's words and actions. David Mixner "could be our Martin Luther King, no questions asked," Thorne told a reporter from a gay newspaper.[28]

Such dramatic race-analogy scenarios performed by white activists beg some serious questions. Are actual, rather than "virtual," people of color present as major actors in these scenarios, and if not, why not? What are they saying or how are they being silenced? How is their actual leadership being supported or not supported by the white people who are reenacting this racialized history? And who is the "we" in this rhetoric? Mixner's "we," for example, did not account for those Americans—including lesbian, gay, bisexual, and transgender activists from many racial backgrounds—who did not finally have or indeed need "our own George Wallace" or "our own Martin Luther King." "Martin Luther King is the Martin Luther King of the gay community," Dr. Marjorie Hill, board president of Unity Fellowship Church and former director of the New York City Mayor's Office for Lesbian and Gay Issues, has pointedly replied in response to those who were looking for King's gay equivalent. "His lesson of equality and truth and non-violence was for everyone."[29] If the gay rights movement is already part of the ongoing struggle for the dignity of all people exemplified in the activism of Dr. Martin Luther King Jr., then there is no need for gay equivalents of Dr. King, racial segregation, or the civil rights movement. If the gay rights movement is not already part of the civil rights movement, then what is it? Answering this question from a white position with the race analogy—saying that white gay leaders and martyrs are "our" versions of African American civil rights leaders and martyrs—can't fix the problem and ultimately undermines the moral authority that is its aim. This use of the race analogy ends up reinforcing the whiteness of gay political campaigns rather than doing the work and holding onto the dream that would continue the legacy of Dr. King's leadership and activism.[30]

What would the gay movement look like if gay white men who use the race analogy took it more seriously? What work would we have to do to close the perceived moral authority gap between our gay activism and the race analogy, to directly establish the kind of moral authority we seek by analogy? What if we aspired to achieve the great vision, leadership qualities, grass-roots organizing skills, and union-solidarity of Dr. Martin Luther King Jr., together with his opposition to war and his dedication to fighting with the poor and disenfranchised against the deepening race and class divisions in America and the world? How could we fight, in the words of U.S. Supreme Court Justice Harry A. Blackmun, for the "fundamental interest all individuals have in controlling the nature of their intimate associations with others," in ways that build a broad civil rights movement rather than being "like" it, in ways that enable the gay movement to grow into one of many powerful and direct ways to achieve race, gender, and class justice?[31]

These, then, are only some of the many whitening practices that structure everyday life and politics in what is often called the "gay community" and the "gay movement"—making *race analogies; mirroring* the whiteness of men who run powerful institutions as a strategy for winning credibility, acceptance, and integration; *excluding* people of color from gay institutions; *selling* gay as white to raise money, make a profit, and gain economic power; and daily wearing the *pale protective coloring* that camouflages the unquestioned assumptions and unearned privileges of gay whiteness. These practices do serious damage to real people whenever they mobilize the power and privileges of whiteness to protect and strengthen gayness— including the privileges of gay whiteness—without using that power to fight racism—including gay white racism.

Most of the time, the hard work of identifying such practices, fighting racial discrimination and exclusion, critiquing the assumptions of white-ness, and racially integrating white gay worlds has been taken up by les-bian, gay, bisexual, and transgender people of color. Freed from this enforced daily recognition of race and confrontation with racism, some prominent white men in the gay movement have been able to advance a gay rights politics that, like the right to serve in the military, they imagine to be just gay, not about race. The gay rights movement can't afford to "dissipate our energies," Andrew Sullivan, former editor of the *New Re-public,* warned on the Charlie Rose television program, by getting involved in disagreements over nongay issues such as "how one deals with race . . . how we might help the underclass . . . how we might deal with sexism."[32]

But a gay rights politics that is supposedly color-blind (and sex-neutral and classless) is in fact a politics of race (and gender and class). It assumes, without ever having to say it, that gay must equal white (and male and economically secure); that is, it assumes white (and male and middle-class) as the default categories that remain once one discounts those who as gay people must continually and primarily deal with racism (and sex-ism and class oppression), especially within gay communities. It is the pol-itics that remains once one makes the strategic decision, as a gay activist, to stand outside the social justice movements for race, gender, or class equality, or to not stand with disenfranchised communities, among whom are lesbian, bisexual, gay, or transgender people who depend on these movements for dignity and survival.

For those few who act like, look like, and identify with the white men who still run our nation's major institutions, for those few who can meet with them, talk to them, and be heard by them as peers, the ability to draw on the enormous power of a shared but unacknowledged whiteness, the ability never to have to bring up race, must feel like a potentially sturdy shield against antigay discrimination. I can see how bringing up explicit critiques of white privilege during high-level gay rights conversations (such as the Senate debates over gays in the military), or making it possible for people of color to set the agenda of the gay rights movement, might weaken that white shield (which relies on racial division to protect)— might even, for some white activists, threaten to "turn" the gay movement into something less gay, as gay bars "turn" when they're no longer predominantly white.

The threat of losing the white shield that protects my own gay rights raises even more difficult questions that I need to "clarify . . . for myself": What would *I* say and do about racism if someday my own whiteness helped me gain such direct access to men in the centers of power, as it almost did during the Senate hearings, when all I did was ask why Perry Watkins wasn't testifying and accept the answer I was given? What privileges would I risk losing if I persistently tried to take activists of color with me into that high-level conversation? How, and with whom, could I begin planning for that day?

Gay white men who are committed to doing antiracist activism *as* gay men have to work within and against these and other powerful whitening practices. What can we do, and how can we support each other, when we once again find ourselves involved in gay social and political worlds that are white and male?

Gay, White, Male, and HIV-Negative

A few years ago, in San Francisco, a friend invited me to be part of a new political discussion group of HIV-negative gay men. Arriving at a neighbor's apartment for the group's first meeting, I once again felt the relief and pleasure of being among men like me. All of us were involved in AIDS activism. We had supported lovers, friends, and strangers with HIV and were grieving the loss of too many lives. We didn't want to take time, attention, and scarce resources away from people with AIDS, including many people of color. But we did want to find a collective, progressive voice as HIV-negative men. We wanted to find public ways to say to gay men just coming out, "We are HIV-negative men, and we want you to stay negative, have hot sex, and live long lives. We don't want you to get sick or die." We were trying to work out a politics in which HIV-negative men, who are relatively privileged as not being the primary targets of crackdowns on people who are HIV-positive, could address other HIV-negative men without trying to establish our legitimacy by positioning ourselves as victims.

When I looked around the room, I saw only white men. I knew that many of them had for years been incorporating antiracist work into their gay and AIDS activism, so this seemed like a safe space to bring up the whiteness I saw. I really didn't want to hijack the purpose of the group by changing its focus from HIV to race, but this was important because I believed that not talking about our whiteness was going to hurt our work. Instead of speaking up, however, I hesitated.

Right there. That's the moment I want to look at—that moment of silence, when a flood of memories, doubts, and fears rushed into my head. What made me want to say something about our whiteness, and what was keeping me silent?

My memory took me back to 1990, when I spoke on a panel of gay historians at the first Out/Write conference of lesbian and gay writers, held in San Francisco. I was happy to be presenting with two other community-based historians working outside the academy. But I was also aware—and concerned—that we were all men. When the question period began, an African American writer in the audience, a man whose name I later learned was Fundi, stood up and asked us (as I recall) how it could happen, at this late date, that a gay history panel could have only white men on it. Awkward silence. I don't trust how I remember his question or what happened next—unreliable memory and bad thinking must be characteristics of inhabiting whiteness while it's being publicly challenged. As the other panelists responded, I remember wanting to distance myself from their whiteness while my own mind went blank, and I remember feeling terrified that Fundi would address me directly and ask me to respond personally. I kept thinking, "I don't know what to say, I can't think, I want to be invisible, I want this to be over, now!"

After the panel was over I spoke privately to Fundi. Later, I resolved never to be in that situation again—never to agree to be on an all-white panel without asking ahead of time why it was white, if its whiteness was crucial to what we were presenting, and, if not, how its composition might be changed. But in addition to wanting to protect myself from public embarrassment and to do the right thing, that writer's direct challenge made me understand something more clearly: that only by seeing and naming the whiteness I'm inhabiting, and taking responsibility for it, can I begin to change it and even do something constructive with it. At that panel, I learned how motivating, though terrifying, it can be as a white person to be placed in such a state of heightened racial discomfort—to be challenged to see the whiteness we've created, figure out how we created it, and then think critically about how it works.[33]

In the moment of silent hesitation I experienced in my HIV-negative group, I found myself imagining for the first time, years after it happened, what it must have been like for Fundi to stand up in a predominantly white audience and ask an all-white panel of gay men about our whiteness. My friend and colleague Lisa Kahaleole Hall, who is a brilliant thinker, writer, and teacher, says that privilege is "the ability not to have to take other people's existence seriously," the "ability not to have to pay attention."[34] Until that moment I had mistakenly thought that Fundi's anger (and I am not certain that he in fact expressed any anger toward us) was only about me, about us, as white men, rather than also about him—the history, desires, and support that enabled him to speak up, and the fears he faced and risks he took by doing it. Caught up in my own fear, I had not paid close attention to the specific question he had asked us. "The problem of conventional white men," Fundi later wrote in his own account of why he had decided to take the risk of speaking up, "somehow not being able, or not knowing how, to find and extend themselves to women and people of color had to be talked through.... My question to the panel was this: 'What direct skills might you share with particularly the whites in the audience to help them move on their fears and better extend themselves to cultural diversity?'"[35] I'm indebted to Fundi for writing that question down, and for starting a chain of events with his question that has led to my writing this essay.

I tried to remember who else I had seen bring up whiteness. The first images that came to mind were all white lesbians and people of color. White lesbian feminists have as a movement dealt with racism in a more collective way than have gay white men. In lesbian and gay activist spaces I and other gay white men have come to rely on white lesbians and people of color to raise the issue of whiteness and challenge racism, so that this difficult task has become both gendered as lesbian work and racialized as "colored" work. These images held me back from saying anything to my HIV-negative group. "Just who am I to bring this up?" I wondered. "It's not my place to do this." Or, more painfully, "Who will these men think I think I am? Will they think I'm trying to pretend I'm not a white man?"

Then another image flashed in my mind that also held me back. It was the caricature of the white moralist—another racialized phantom figure hovering in the room—who blames and condemns white people for our racism, guilt-trips us from either a position of deeper guilt or holier-than-thou innocence, claims to be more aware of racism than we are, and is prepared to catalog our offenses. I see on my mental screen this self-righteous caricature impersonating a person of color in an all-white group or, when people of color are present, casting them again in the role of spectators to a white performance, pushed to the sidelines from where they must angrily or patiently interrupt a white conversation to be heard at all. I understand that there is some truth to this caricature—that part of a destructive racial dynamic among white people is trying to determine who is more or less responsible for racism, more or less innocent and pure, more or less white. But I also see how the fear of becoming this caricature has been used by white people to keep each other from naming the whiteness of all-white groups we are in. During my moment of hesitation in the HIV-negative group, the fear of becoming this caricature was successfully silencing me.

I didn't want to pretend to be a white lesbian or a person of color, or to act like the self-righteous white caricature. "How do I ask that we examine our whiteness," I wondered, "without implying that I'm separating us into the good guys and bad guys and positioning myself as the really cool white guy who 'gets it' about racism?" I needed a way to speak intelligently from where I was standing without falling into any of these traps.

I decided to take a chance and say something.

"It appears to me," I began, my voice a little shaky, "that everyone here is white. If this is true, I'd like us to find some way to talk about how our whiteness may be connected to being HIV-negative, because I suspect there are some political similarities between being in each of these positions of relative privilege."

There was an awkward pause. "Are you saying," someone asked, "that we should close the group to men of color?"

"No," I said, "but if we're going to be a white group I'd like us to talk about our relationship to whiteness here."

"Should we do outreach to men of color?" someone else asked.

"No, I'm not saying that, either. It's a little late to do outreach, after the fact, inviting men of color to integrate our already white group."

The other men agreed and the discussion went on to other things. I, too, didn't really know where to take this conversation about our whiteness. By bringing it up, I was implicitly asking for their help in figuring this out. I hoped I wouldn't be the only one to bring up the subject again.

At the next month's meeting there were new members, and they all appeared to be white men. When someone reviewed for them what we had done at the last meeting, he reported that I'd suggested we not include men of color in the group. "That's not right," I corrected him. "I said that if we're going to be a white group, I'd like us to talk about our whiteness and its relation to our HIV-negative status."

I was beginning to feel a little disoriented, like I was doing something wrong. Why was I being so consistently misunderstood as divisive, as if I were saying that I didn't want men of color in the group? Had I reacted similarly when, caught up in my own fear of having to publicly justify our panel's whiteness, I had misunderstood Fundi's specific question—about how we could share our skills with other white people to help each other move beyond our fear of cultural diversity—as an accusation that we had deliberately excluded women and men of color? Was something structural going on here about how white groups respond to questions that point to our whiteness and ask what we can do with it?

Walking home from the meeting I asked a friend who'd been there if what I said had made sense. "Oh yes," he said, "it's just that it all goes without saying." Well, there it is. That *is* how it goes, how it stays white. "Without saying."

Like much of the rest of my gay life, this HIV-negative group turned out to be unintentionally white, although intentionally gay and intentionally male. It's important for me to understand exactly how that racial *unintentionality* gets *constructed,* how it's not just a coincidence. It seems that so long as white people never consciously decide to be a white group, a white organization, a white department, so long as we each individually believe that people of color are always welcome, *even though they are not there,* then we do not have to examine our whiteness because we can believe it is unintentional, it's not our *reason* for being there. That may be why I had been misunderstood to be asking for the exclusion of men of color. By naming our group as white, I had unknowingly raised the question of *racial intent*—implying that we had intended to create an all-white group by deliberately excluding men of color. If we could believe that our whiteness was purely accidental, then we could also believe that there was nothing to say about it because creating an all-white group, which is exactly what we had done, had never been anyone's intent, and therefore had no inherent meaning or purpose. By interrupting the process by which "it just goes without saying," by asking us to recognize and "talk through" our whiteness, I appeared to be saying that we already had and should continue to exclude men of color from our now very self-consciously white group.

The reality is that in our HIV-negative group, as in the panel of the Out/Write conference and in many other all-white groupings, we each did make a chain of choices, not usually conscious, to invite or accept an invitation from another white person. We made more decisions whether or not to name our whiteness when we once again found ourselves in a white group. What would it mean to make such decisions consciously and out loud, to understand why we made them, and to take responsibility for them? What if we intentionally held our identities as white men and gay men in creative tension, naming ourselves as gay *and* white, then publicly explored the possibilities for activism this tension might open up? Could investigating our whiteness offer us opportunities for reclaiming our humanity against the ways that racial hierarchies dehumanize us and disconnect us from ourselves, from each other, and from people of color? If we took on these difficult tasks, how might our gay political reality and purpose be different?[36]

When I told this story about our HIV-negative group to Barbara Smith, a colleague who is an African American lesbian writer and activist, she asked me a question that pointed to a different ending: "So why didn't you bring up the group's whiteness again?" The easy answer was that I left the group because I moved to New York City. But the more difficult answer was that I was afraid to lose the trust of these gay men whom I cared about and needed so much, afraid I would distance myself from them and be distanced by them, pushed outside the familiar circle, no longer welcomed as white and not belonging among people of color, not really gay and not anything else, either. The big fear is that if I pursue this need to examine whiteness too far, I risk losing my place among gay white men, forever—and then where would I be?

Pale, Male—and Antiracist

What would happen if we deliberately put together a white gay male group whose sole purpose was to examine our whiteness and use it to strengthen our antiracist gay activism?

In November 1995, gay historian John D'Emilio and I tried to do just that. We organized a workshop at the annual Creating Change conference of activists put on that year in Detroit by the National Gay and Lesbian Task Force. We called the workshop "Pale, Male—and Anti-Racist." At a conference of over 1,000 people (mostly white but with a large number of people of color), about thirty-five gay white men attended.[37]

We structured the workshop around three key questions: (1) How have you successfully used your whiteness to fight racism? (2) What difficulties have you faced in doing antiracist activism as a gay white man? And (3) what kind of support did you get or need or wish you had received from other gay white men?

Before we could start talking about our successes, warning lights began to flash. You could sense a high level of mistrust in the room, as if we were looking at each other and wondering, "Which kind of white guy are *you*?" One man wanted to make sure we weren't going to waste time congratulating ourselves for sharing our white privilege with people who don't have access to it or start whining about how hard it is to work with communities of color. Someone else wanted to make sure we weren't going to guilt-trip each other. Another said, "I'm so much more aware of my failures in this area, I can't even see the accomplishments."

But slowly, once all the cautions were out in the open, the success stories came out. About fighting an anti–affirmative action initiative. About starting a racism study group. About getting a university department to study why it had no teaching assistants who were students of color. About persuading a gay organization in Georgia to condemn the state's Confederate flag. "What keeps me from remembering," I wondered, "that gay white men publicly do this antiracist work? Why can't I keep their images in my mind?"

One possible answer to my question appeared in the next success story, which midway made a sharp turn away from our successes toward how gay white men can discipline each other for standing on the "wrong" side of the color line. A man from Texas, Dennis Poplin, told us about what happened to him as the only white man on the board of the San Antonio Lesbian and Gay Assembly (SALGA), a progressive, multiracial lesbian and gay alliance. When SALGA mobilized support that successfully canceled a so-called gay community conference whose planning committee was all-white—this in a city that was 65 percent Latina/Latino—a "community scandal" exploded, as he put it, "about political correctness, quotas, [and] reverse racism." A local newspaper, which was run by gay white men, started attacking SALGA. When a white reporter asked a man of color from SALGA why the group's board had no white men on it, and he replied that Dennis was on the board, the reporter said, "He's not white."[38]

Right away the men in the workshop started talking about the difficulties they'd had with other gay white men. "I find myself like not even knowing who it's safe to bring it up with," one man said. When he tries to talk about race, another said, "I'm just met with that smug, flippant, 'I'm tired of hearing about [all that].'" Others talked about fears of being attacked as too "PC."

At the "risk of opening a whole can of worms," as he put it, another man moved the discussion away from us to our relationships with white lesbians and people of color. Some men talked about how tired they were of being called "gay white men," feeling labeled then attacked for who they were and for what they tried to do or for not doing enough; about having to deal with their racism while they didn't see communities of color dealing with homophobia; and about how, after years of struggling, they felt like giving up. Yet here they all were at this workshop. I began to realize that all our frustrations were signs of a dilemma that comes with the privileges of whiteness: having the ability to decide whether to keep dealing with the accusations, resentments, racial categorizations, and other destructive effects of racism that divide people who are trying to take away its power; or, because the struggle is so hard, to walk away from it and do something else, using the slack our whiteness gives us to take a break from racism's direct consequences.

Bringing this dilemma into the open enabled us to confront our expectations about how the antiracist work we do should be appreciated, should be satisfying, and should bring results. One man admitted that he didn't make antiracist work a higher priority because "I [would have to face] a level of discomfort, irritation, boredom, frustration, [and] enter a lot of [areas where] I feel inept, and don't have confidence. It would require a lot of humility. All these are things that I steer away from."

Over and over the men at the workshop expressed similar feelings of frustration, using such phrases as "We tried, but . . . ," "No matter what you do, you can't seem to do anything right," and "You just can't win." These seemed to reflect a set of expectations that grew out of the advantages we have because we are American men and white and middle-class or even working-class—expectations that we *can* win, that we should know how to do it right, that if we try we will succeed.

What do we—what do I—expect to get out of doing antiracist work, anyway? If it's because we expect to be able to fix the problem, then we're not going to be very satisfied. When I talk with my friend Lisa Kahaleole Hall about these frustrations, she tells me, "Sweet pea, if racism were that easy to fix, we would have fixed it already." The challenge for me in relation to other gay white men—and in writing this essay—is to figure out how we can support each other in going exactly into those areas of whiteness where we feel we have no competence yet, no expertise, no ability to fix it, where we haven't even come up with the words we need to describe what we're trying to do. For me, it's an act of faith in the paradox that if we, together with our friends and allies, can figure out how our own whiteness works, we can use that knowledge to fight the racism that gives our whiteness such unearned power.

And whenever this struggle gets too difficult, many of us, as white men, have the option to give up in frustration and retreat into a more narrowly defined gay rights activism. That project's goal, according to gay author Bruce Bawer, one of its advocates, is "to achieve acceptance, equal rights, and full integration into the present social and political structure."[39] It's a goal that best serves the needs of men who can live our gayness through our whiteness and whose only or most important experience with discrimination is as homosexuals. James Baldwin, who wrote extensively about whiteness in America, noticed long ago the sense of entitlement embedded in a gay whiteness that experiences no other form of systematic discrimination. "[Y]ou are penalized, as it were, unjustly," he said in an interview. "I think white gay people feel cheated because they were born, in principle, into a society in which they were supposed to be safe. The anomaly of their sexuality puts them in danger unexpectedly."[40]

The gay rights project that grows out of the shocking experience of being cheated unexpectedly by society because one is gay defines the gay political problem in its narrowest form. One solution is to get back the respect one has learned to expect as a white man. Some prominent, well-connected activists do this by educating the men who run our nation's powerful institutions, using reasoned arguments to combat their homophobia and expose discrimination as irrational—a strategy that sometimes does open doors but mostly to those who look and behave like the men in power. I have heard some of these activists express a belief that less privileged members of the "gay community" will eventually benefit from these high-level successes, but this would happen apparently without the more privileged having to do the work of fighting hierarchies that enforce race, class, and gender inequality. Their belief in a kind of "trickle-down" gay activism is based on the idea that powerful men, once enlightened, will generously allow equality to flow from the top to those near the top and then automatically trickle down to those down below. An alternative belief in "bottom-up activism" is based on the idea that, with great effort, democratic power must more slowly be built from the bottom up, and out, experimenting with more equal power relations along the way by creating links of solidarity across the divides of difference. Some gay white men explicitly reject, as nongay, this broader goal of joining activists who stand and work at the intersections of the many struggles to achieve social justice and to dismantle interlocking systems of domination. In the narrow world of exclusively gay "integrationist" activism, which its advocates privilege as the site of "practical" rather than "utopian" politics,[41] college-educated gay white men have a better chance of knowing what to say and how to be heard, what to do and how to succeed within existing institutions. Because, when antigay barriers and attitudes are broken down but no other power relations are changed, we are the ones most likely to achieve "full integration into the present social and political structure." All it takes sometimes is being the white man at the white place at the white time.

When John and I asked the workshop participants our last question—"What would you need from each other to be able to continue doing antiracist work?"—the room went silent.

When push comes to shove, I wondered, holding back a sense of isolation inside my own silence, do gay white men as *white* men (including myself) have a lasting interest in fighting racism or will we sooner or later retreat to the safety of our gay white refuges? I know that gay white men as *gay* men, just to begin thinking about relying on each other's support in an ongoing struggle against racism, have to confront how we've absorbed the antigay lies that we are all wealthy, irresponsible, and sexually obsessed individuals who can't make personal commitments, as well as the reality that we are profoundly exhausted fighting for our lives and for those we love through years of devastation from the AIDS epidemic. These challenges all make it hard enough for me to trust my own long-term commitment to antiracist work, let alone that of other gay white men.

Yet at this workshop we created the opportunity for us to see that we were not alone, to risk saying and hearing what we needed from each other in fighting racism, and to assess what support we could realistically hope to get. We wanted the opportunity to complain to another gay white man, to be held and loved when we get discouraged or feel attacked, whether justifiably or not. We wanted understanding for all the frustrations we feel fighting racism, the chance just to let them out with a gay white man who knows that it's not our racism he's supporting but the desire to see it and together figure out what to do next, so we won't give up or run away. We wanted other gay white men to take us seriously enough to call us on our racist shit in ways we could actually hear without feeling attacked. And we wanted to help each other lift at least some of the work and responsibility of supporting us from the shoulders of our friends and co-workers who are white women or people of color.

As time ran out at the workshop, I asked everyone to think about another difficult question: "Who is the gay white man who has had more experience than you in supporting other gay white men who are fighting racism, and who you can look to for advice on how to do it well?" "I think the more interesting question," one man answered, "is how many of us don't have anyone like that." We looked around at each other, wondering if any of us could name someone, until somebody said, "It's us."

Staying White

By trying to figure out what is happening with race in situations I'm in, I've embarked on a journey that I now realize is not headed toward innocence or winning or becoming not white or finally getting it right. I don't know where it leads, but I have some hopes and desires.

I want to find an antidote to the ways that whiteness numbs me, makes me not see what is right in front of me, takes away my intelligence, divides me from people I care about. I hope that, by occupying the seeming contradictions between the "antiracist" and the "gay white male" parts of myself, I can generate a creative tension that will motivate me to keep fighting. I hope to help end the exclusionary practices that make gay worlds stay so white. When I find myself in a situation that is going to stay white, I want to play a role in deciding what kind of white it's going to stay. And I

want to become less invested in whiteness while staying white myself—
always remembering that I can't just decide to stand outside of whiteness
or exempt myself from its unearned privileges.[42] I want to be careful not to
avoid its responsibilities by fleeing into narratives of how I have been oppressed as a gay man. The ways that I am gay will always be shaped by the
ways that I am white.

Most of all, I want never to forget that the roots of my antiracist desires
and my gay desires are intertwined. As James Baldwin's words remind me,
acting on my gay desires is about not being afraid to love and therefore
about having to confront this white society's terror of love—a terror that
lashes out with racist and antigay violence. Following both my gay and antiracist desires is about being willing to "go the way your blood beats," as
Baldwin put it, even into the heart of that terror, which, he warned, is "a
tremendous danger, a tremendous responsibility."[43]

Notes

This is an expanded version of a personal essay I presented at the Making and Un-
making of Whiteness conference at the University of California at Berkeley in
April 1997. I want to acknowledge that my thinking has grown out of conversa-
tions with many friends and colleagues, including Nan Alamilla Boyd, Margaret
Cerullo, John D'Emilio, Arthur Dong, Marla Erlein, Jeffrey Escoffier, Charlie Fer-
nandez, Dana Frank, Wayne Hoffman, Amber Hollibaugh, Mitchell Karp,
Jonathan Ned Katz, Judith Levine, William J. Mann, David Meacham, Dennis
Poplin, Susan Raffo, Eric Rofes, Gayle Rubin, Sabrina Sojourner, Barbara Smith,
Nancy Stoller, Carole Vance, and Carmen Vasquez; the editors of this collection,
especially Matt Wray and Irene Nexica; the participants in the "Pale, Male—and
Anti-Racist" workshop at the 1995 Creating Change conference in Detroit; Lisa
Kahaleole Hall and the students I joined in her San Francisco City College class on
Lesbian and Gay Communities of Color; and the students in the courses I taught
at the University of California at Santa Cruz, Portland State University, Stanford
University, and the New School for Social Research.

1. "Caught in the Storm: AIDS and the Meaning of Natural Disaster," *Out/Look:
National Lesbian and Gay Quarterly* 1 (fall 1988), 8–19; "'Fitting In': Expanding
Queer Studies beyond the *Closet* and *Coming Out*," paper presented at Contested

Zone: Limitations and Possibilities of a Discourse on Lesbian and Gay Studies, Pitzer College, 6–7 April 1990, and at the Fourth Annual Lesbian, Bisexual, and Gay Studies Conference, Harvard University, 26–28 October 1990; "Intellectual Desire," paper presented at La Ville en rose: Le premier colloque Québécois d'études lesbiennes et gaies (First Quebec Lesbian and Gay Studies Conference), Concordia University and the University of Quebec at Montreal, 12 November 1992, published in *GLQ: A Journal of Lesbian and Gay Studies* 3, no. 1 (February 1996): 139–57, reprinted in *Queerly Classed: Gay Men and Lesbians Write about Class,* ed. Susan Raffo (Boston: South End Press, 1997), 43–66; "Class Dismissed: Queer Storytelling Across the Economic Divide," keynote address at the Constructing Queer Cultures: Lesbian, Bisexual, Gay Studies Graduate Student Conference, Cornell University, 9 February 1995, and at the Seventeenth Gender Studies Symposium, Lewis and Clark College, 12 March 1998; "I Coulda Been a Whiny White Guy," *Gay Community News* 20 (spring 1995): 6–7, 28–30; and "Sunset Trailer Park," in *White Trash: Race and Class in America,* ed. Matt Wray and Annalee Newitz (New York: Routledge, 1997), 15–39.

2. *Dream Ships Sail Away* (forthcoming, Houghton Mifflin).

3. "'Go the Way Your Blood Beats': An Interview with James Baldwin (1984)," Richard Goldstein, in *James Baldwin: The Legacy,* ed. Quincy Troupe (New York: Simon and Schuster/Touchstone, 1989), 176.

4. Personal essays, often assembled in published collections, have become an important written form for investigating how whiteness works, especially in individual lives. Personal essays by lesbian, gay, and bisexual authors that have influenced my own thinking and writing about whiteness have been collected in James Baldwin, *The Price of the Ticket: Collected Nonfiction, 1948–1985* (New York: St. Martin's, 1985); Cherríe Moraga and Gloria Anzaldúa, eds., *This Bridge Called My Back: Writings by Radical Women of Color* (Watertown, Mass.: Persephone Press, 1981); Cherríe Moraga, *Loving in the War Years* (Boston: South End Press, 1983); Audre Lorde, *Sister Outsider* (Freedom, Calif.: Crossing Press, 1984); Elly Bulkin, Minnie Bruce Pratt, and Barbara Smith, *Yours in Struggle: Three Feminist Perspectives on Anti-Semitism and Racism* (Brooklyn: Long Haul Press, 1984); Essex Hemphill, ed., *Brother to Brother: New Writings by Black Gay Men* (Boston: Alyson, 1991); Mab Segrest, *Memoir of a Race Traitor* (Boston: South End Press, 1994); Dorothy Allison, *Skin: Talking about Sex, Class and Literature* (Ithaca, N.Y.: Firebrand, 1994); and Becky Thompson and Sangeeta Tyagi, eds., *Names We Call Home: Autobiography on Racial Identity* (New York: Routledge, 1996).

5. For discussion of how sexual identities are "lived through race and class," see Robin D. G. Kelley, *Yo' Mama's Dysfunktional!* (Boston: Beacon, 1997), 114.

6. Whiteness can grant economic advantages to gay as well as straight men, and gay male couples can sometimes earn more on two men's incomes than can straight couples or lesbian couples. But being gay can restrict a man to lower-paying jobs, and most gay white men are not wealthy; like the larger male population, they are lower-middle-class, working-class, or poor. For discussions of the difficulties of developing an accurate economic profile of the "gay community," and of how both the religious right and gay marketers promote the idea that gay men are wealthy, see Amy Gluckman and Betsy Reed, eds., *Homo Economics: Capitalism, Community, and Lesbian and Gay Life* (New York: Routledge, 1997).

7. David Mixner, *Stranger among Friends* (New York: Bantam, 1996), 291. For accounts of how the Campaign for Military Service was formed, see Mixner's memoir and Urvashi Vaid, *Virtual Equality: The Mainstreaming of Lesbian and Gay Equality* (New York: Anchor, 1995). Preceding the ad hoc formation of the Campaign for Military Service in January 1993 was the Military Freedom Project, formed in early 1989 by a group composed primarily of white feminist lesbians. Overshadowed during the Senate hearings by the predominantly male Campaign for Military Service, these activists had raised issues relating the military's antigay policy to gender, race, and class; specifically, that lesbians are discharged at a higher rate than are gay men; that lesbian-baiting is a form of sexual harassment against women; and that African American and Latino citizens, including those who are gay, bisexual, or lesbian, are disproportionately represented in the military, which offers poor and working-class youth access to a job, education, and health care that are often unavailable to them elsewhere. Vaid, *Virtual Equality*, 153–59.

8. "The Race Analogy: Fact Sheet Comparing the Military's Policy of Racial Segregation in the 1940s to the Current Ban on Lesbians, Gay Men and Bisexuals," in *Briefing Book*, prepared by the Legal/Policy Department of the Campaign for Military Service, Washington, D.C. (1993).

9. Quoted from the *Legal Times*, 8 February 1993, in Mixner, *Stranger among Friends*, 286. Professor of history and civil rights veteran Roger Wilkins, responding to Powell's statement, argued that "lots of white people don't think that being black is benign even in 1993." Mixner, *Stranger among Friends*, 286.

10. Henry Louis Gates Jr., "Blacklash?" *New Yorker*, 17 May 1993.

11. For brief discussions of how the whiteness of those making the race analogy reduced the power of their arguments, see Gates, "Blacklash?" and David Rayside,

On the Fringe: Gays and Lesbians in Politics (Ithaca, N.Y.: Cornell University Press, 1998), 243.

12. Mixner, *Stranger among Friends,* 319.

13. The gay service members on this panel were former Staff Sgt. Thomas Pannicia, Sgt. Justin Elzie, and Col. Margarethe Cammermeyer. Margarethe Cammermeyer, with Chris Fisher, *Serving in Silence* (New York: Penguin, 1994), 299. Other former gay service members who testified at the hearings were Sgt. Tracy Thorne and PO Keith Meinhold. Active-duty lesbian, gay, or bisexual service members could not testify without being discharged from the military as homosexuals, a situation that still exists under the current "don't ask, don't tell" military policy.

14. Mary Dunlap, "Reminiscences: Honoring Our Legal Hero, Gay Sgt. Perry Watkins 1949–1996," *Gay Community News* (winter 1996): 21.

15. In his memoir, *Stranger among Friends,* Mixner makes no mention of Watkins.

16. Author's personal conversation with Sabrina Sojourner, 19 October 1998.

17. An expert witness who was white, male, and not a gay historian was allowed to introduce a brief written synopsis of historical evidence from my book. I was one of the white men working with the CMS behind the scenes and from afar. Early in the hearings, Senator Edward Kennedy's staff asked me to compile a list of questions for him to ask during the hearings. In July, after the hearings were over and the "don't ask, don't tell" policy had been adopted, I submitted to the House Armed Services Committee written testimony, titled "Historical Overview of the Origins of the Military's Ban on Homosexuals," that critiqued the new policy and identified heterosexual masculinity, rather than the competence or behavior of homosexual service members, as the military problem requiring investigation. And I sent the CMS a copy of a paper I had given in April, "Stripping Down: Undressing the Military's Anti-Gay Policy," that used historical documents and feminist analysis to argue for investigating the military's crisis in heterosexual masculinity. In all these writings, I was trying, unsuccessfully, to get the CMS and the Senate to adopt a gender and sexuality analysis of the military policy; I used race and class analysis only to argue that the antigay policies disproportionately affected service members who were people of color and/or working-class.

18. After Watkins's death in 1996 from complications due to HIV, Mary Dunlap, a white civil rights attorney who for years had followed his appeal case, in a tribute addressed to him, called him a "generous, tireless leader" who expressed "open and emphatic criticism and unabashed indictment of the racism of those among

us who so blatantly and hurtfully excluded your voice and face and words from the publicity surrounding the gaylesbitrans community's challenge to 'Don't Ask, Don't Tell' in the early 90s." Dunlap, "Reminiscences," 21.

19. Shamara Riley, "Perry Watkins, 1948–1996: A Military Trailblazer," *Outlines*, 8 May 1996.

20. Randy Shilts, *Conduct Unbecoming: Gays and Lesbians in the U.S. Military* (New York: St. Martin's, 1993), 60, 65; Mary Ann Humphrey, *My Country, My Right to Serve* (New York: HarperCollins, 1990), 248–57. Statistics are from D. Michael Shafer, "The Vietnam-Era Draft: Who Went, Who Didn't, and Why It Matters," in *The Legacy: The Vietnam War in the American Imagination*, ed. D. Michael Shafer (Boston: Beacon Press, 1990), 69.

21. Humphrey, *My Country*, 255–56.

22. Ibid.

23. Dunlap, "Reminiscences"; Shilts, *Conduct Unbecoming*, 155–56; Humphrey, *My Country*, 253–54.

24. A 1996 documentary film, "Sis: The Perry Watkins Story," was coproduced by Chiqui Cartagena and Suzanne Newman. On the "20/20" segment and a feature film on Watkins that was in preproduction, see Jim Knippenberg, "Gay Soldier Story to Be Filmed," *Cincinnati Enquirer*, 23 December 1997.

25. Rayside, *On the Fringe*, 243.

26. Keith Boykin, *One More River to Cross: Black and Gay In America* (New York: Anchor, 1996), 186–92.

27. Mixner, *Stranger among Friends*, 301–2, 308–10.

28. Garland Tillery, "Interview with Top Gun Pilot Tracy Thorne," *Our Own*, 18 May 1993.

29. Quoted from the documentary film "All God's Children," produced by Dee Mosbacher, Frances Reid, and Sylvia Rhue (Women Vision, 1996). I wish to thank Lisa Kahaleole Hall, Stephanie Smith, and Linda Alban for directing me to this quotation.

30. One way to measure how much moral authority the race analogy tries to take from the civil rights movement and transfuse it into a predominantly white gay movement is to see what moral authority remains when the race analogy is removed. David Mixner would be the David Mixner of the gay movement, the military's antigay policy would be a form of antigay bigotry, and Sam Nunn would be "our" Sam Nunn. Or, to reverse the terms, other movements for social change would try to gain moral authority by using a "gay analogy," declaring that their

movement was "like" the gay movement. These moves do not seem to carry the moral weight of the race analogy.

31. Quoted from Justice Blackmun's dissenting opinion in the U.S. Supreme Court's 1986 *Bowers v. Hardwick* decision. "Blackmun's Opinions Reflect His Evolution of the 24 Court Years," *New York Times,* 5 March 1999. I wish to thank Lisa Kahaleole Hall for the conversation we had on 24 October 1998, out of which emerged the ideas in this essay about how the civil rights movement analogy works and is used as a strategy for gaining unearned moral authority, although I am responsible for how they are presented here.

32. "Stonewall 25," *The Charlie Rose Show,* Public Broadcasting System, 24 June 1994. I wish to thank Barbara Smith for lending me her videotape copy of this program.

33. For Fundi's reports on this panel and the entire conference, see "Out/Write '90 Report, Part I: Writers Urged to Examine Their Roles, Save Their Lives," *San Diego GLN,* 16 March 1990, 7; "Out/Write Report, Part II: Ringing Voices," *San Diego GLN,* 23 March 1990, 7, 9; and "Out/Write Report, Part III: Arenas of Interaction," *San Diego GLN,* 30 March 1990, 7, 9.

34. Lisa Kahaleole Chang Hall, "Bitches in Solitude: Identity Politics and Lesbian Community," in *Sisters, Sexperts, Queers: Beyond the Lesbian Nation,* ed. Arlene Stein (New York: Plume 1993), 223, and in personal conversation.

35. Fundi, "Out/Write Report, Part III," 7, 9.

36. I wish to thank Mitchell Karp for the long dinner conversation we had in 1996 in New York City during which we jointly forged the ideas and questions in this paragraph.

37. I have transcribed the quotations that follow from an audio tape of the workshop discussion.

38. I wish to thank Dennis Poplin for allowing me to use his name and tell his story.

39. Bruce Bawer, "Utopian Erotics," *Lambda Book Report* 7 (October 1998): 19–20.

40. Goldstein, "Go the Way," 180.

41. Bawer, "Utopian Erotics," 19–20.

42. I wish to thank Amber Hollibaugh for introducing me to this idea of "staying white" during a conversation about how a white person can be tempted to distance oneself from whiteness and escape the guilt of its privileges by identifying as a person of color. I was introduced to the idea that white privilege is unearned and

difficult to escape at a workshop called White Privilege conducted by Jona Olssen at the 1995 Black Nations/Queer Nations Conference, sponsored by the Center for Lesbian and Gay Studies at the City University of New York. See also Peggy McIntosh, "White Privilege: Unpacking the Invisible Knapsack," *Peace and Freedom* (July/August 1989): 10–12.

43. Goldstein, "Go the Way," 177.

PART FOUR

Moving Forward

15

Subverting Racism from Within

Linking White Identity to Activism

Becky Thompson

Introduction

I recently returned from South Africa, where, among other gifts, I was graced with experiencing myself as a White person in a way I have not in the United States. For the first time in my life, I perceived being White as a flexible identity that was neither suspect nor dismissed, considered primary or essential. It was not that people were attempting to uphold the color-blind ideology—pretending that color did not matter or, worse, that White racism does not exist. Rather, I felt a level of relaxation about being a White woman I have never felt in the United States—that I was not seen or treated as if there was one monolithic White identity. Since I have been home, I have spoken at length with a White antiracist South African who recently visited her home country after many years living in the United States. She, too, experienced some of that relaxation and flexibility while she was there.

Some of this experience could have been because wherever I traveled, the Black South Africans I was staying with introduced me—I wasn't seen as an anonymous tourist. Second, even though apartheid has been officially abolished, it is still rare for White people to be in Soweto and outlying townships. When a White person who is not in a uniform does visit, warmth and respect are automatically offered. Third, and most important, while there is a long history of White people who helped to mastermind and uphold apartheid, there is also history of White people who have stood up against, and sometimes lost their lives resisting, racial injustice. The stories of Ruth First, Joe Slovo, Helen Susman, and others are part of the public iconography in South Africa. In other words, there is a known history of White antiracist activism—a history that, I believe, is at the core of why being White for me felt so different in South Africa than in the United States. Here, public imagery around whiteness might lead one to believe there are only two types of White people: those who have moved to or already live in Montana and those who would like to but are too apathetic to do so. As White people spearheaded the referendum to eliminate affirmative action throughout California, and as Pat Buchanan won the 1996 Republican primary in New Hampshire on a platform that pivoted on White supremacy, we do not need to look far to see why it is hard to claim "whiteness" when it is so often associated with bigotry and domination. Yet, there is contemporary psychological, autobiographical, and historical writing that shows links between White identity and activism. Ultimately my interest is in a radical race-conscious political agenda that would fundamentally change the cultural representations of what it means to be White.

As Whiteness Gains New Saliency

As a teacher of African American studies, American studies, and sociology during the last decade, I have seen (and lived through) many scenes that illustrate difficulties in claiming a subversive White identity. Some of the most recent are as follows:

- A light, coffee colored Jewish student comes to my office to talk about a course, "Social Movements in the Americas," that she is taking with me and her ambivalence about racial identity. In a soft and shaky voice, she confides that a big reason she took the course was its focus on Latino politics and identity. She has often been mistaken as Hispanic and has felt both complimented by this association and ashamed that she does not speak up that she is a Sephardic Jew, not Hispanic. As she talked, she revealed how taboo it felt for her to be admitting her reactions and I was struck by her deep sense of wanting to belong. The pressures of assimilation aimed at Jews historically and her ambivalence about being a Jew made it hard to see Jewish identity as a source of belonging or resistance. For her, feeling a part of a culture of resistance required being seen as Latina. She knew nothing of White resistance to racism—including the history of Jewish activism—in the United States.

- During an early meeting with a group of White antiracist activists I belong to in Boston, we went around the room as each woman talked about the history of antiracism to which she considered herself connected. A few of us named the Grimke sisters, Lillian Smith, Mab Segrest, and Jessie Daniel Ames. Three of the Jewish women in the group had more of a sense of a legacy (e.g., Bulkin, 1984; Kaye/Kantrowitz, 1996). Most of us said that our role models had been women around us whose stories have never been written about. We all felt that our hold on a history of White antiracist activism was tentative at best. We all were troubled by why we knew so little. What taboos must we face down to chronicle a history that does not valorize, romanticize, or inflate White activism, but that allows us to take stock of the work that has been and still needs to be done? The scene also underscored how much of the day-to-day work of antiracism will not reach the written page. This goes for progressive activism in general and is a perennial reason why a history of subversive political work in the United States remains scant.

- A radio reporter contacted me about speaking on one of her programs. She was aware of my writing on multicultural education and she wanted to talk about the volume on racial identity I recently co-edited with Sangeeta Tyagi (Thompson & Tyagi, 1996). As we were talking, I made some reference to being White, and she stopped the conversation to say she had been assuming all along that I am

African American. This is not the first time this has happened. In reviews of *A Hunger So Wide and So Deep,* a multiracial study of eating problems and recovery, I have alternately been referred to as a Black psychologist, an African American writer, or sometimes, an African Americanist (with my race left ambiguous). My reactions to this misnaming are contradictory and complicated. I think to myself that these assumptions must mean the work is good. If people think I am African American, then that suggests that they think I wrote about Black theory and Black women's lives well. So, I feel proud. At the same time, I feel like a fraud. Then, it dawns on me that most of the people who have mistaken my identity are White. What does that say about White people's faith in ourselves, our faith in each other? What does it say about the state of race-conscious feminist theory if multiracial work by a White woman is not even considered as a possibility?

These scenes highlight multiple vexing issues about White identity in the 1990s: the guilt and confusion many people feel about being White; a largely unwritten history of antiracist White activism; and a sense of rootlessness many White people are experiencing as the generational separation between them and their ethnic European roots increases (Alba, 1990). The scenes underscore the complexities of dealing with White identity in the 1990s, at a point in U.S. history when, as Howard Winant (1994) has explained, whiteness has gained a new saliency. The fact that White people are no longer a majority in many contexts makes it increasingly difficult for them to see themselves as raceless. The emergence of whiteness as a color, rather than a transparency, has made more obvious the ambivalence, fear, avoidance, and dismissal so often associated with what being White means in the post–civil rights period.

I come to these issues as someone who has been struggling for the past fifteen plus years to understand whiteness and my complicity in racism, and as someone who has been going through a process of racial identity development which has been neither neat nor pretty. Over time, I have come to characterize my development in four phases (Thompson, 1996). In my initial way of proceeding—in the "I am not a racist stage"—I exhibited various intensities of denial, guilt, shame, and defensiveness. As a student in a 1977 college course titled "The Black Experience," I routinely chirped in with naive abandon that "I am not racist because my mother taught in integrated schools," and "I don't understand why we can't all get along. Slavery is in the past." While outwardly resisting an examination of my own racism, internally I felt that, as a White person, I did not deserve to be in that class and that I was morally inferior to the Black students. Looking back on my behavior, chances are several students—as well as the teacher—might have liked to show me the door during the first week of class.

Through my continued exposure to community activism and scholarship of people of color in the early 1980s, I eventually made a transition to a period when I felt I needed to do everything I could to overcome racism—mine and everyone else's. During this period—my "I don't want to be White stage"—I had great difficulty accepting myself as a White woman as I shifted from denying the realities of racism to wanting to dissociate from White people entirely. At this point, close connections with other White people felt threatening. I felt as if I had had more than enough of White culture and that I needed to spend all my energy catching up—learning from and being with people of color. I felt unworthy of being friends with people of color—afraid that at any moment I would reveal my racist self and alienate them forever. Yet I thought that if I could not break through this fear, my intentions to stand up against racism would be fraudulent. I felt extremely self-conscious about being in all-White crowds and proud if I was one of the only White people at an event primarily attended by people of color. I believed I needed to take my direction from them and distrust most everything White people said. In my attempts to break away from living a segregated life, I was still measuring my credentials as an antiracist White woman through my association with people of color. Looking back on these scenes, I see the distortions in my thinking glaring back at me and it still feels risky to admit them. When I congratulated myself as one of the only White people in a social or political context, I was still seeing antiracism as some sort of competition—with only a few spaces at the table for antiracist White people.

The next stage of my identity—what I would not label the "grappling for a steady position"—I think that I and many other White women were fumbling to find ways to proceed given the complexities of identity politics. By the late 1970s and early 1980s, identity politics emerged to shape feminist political organizing in significant ways. In 1979, the now classic position paper on identity politics written by the Boston-based feminist group Combahee River Collective was first published. The promise of this politic was the assertion that those who had been subjugated historically need to be in charge of creating strategies for change. One consequence of this foundational politic—and perhaps an inevitable one—was an increased jockeying for authority based on one's belonging to a subordinated group. In this distorted arithmetic, a White straight woman was "outflanked" by a woman of color, or a White lesbian had more "credentials" than a White straight woman. With this scenario, identity politics had been twisted into an essentialism that assumed that those from subordinated communities had "biological" or "natural" access to knowledge or ideas that people from dominant groups could never have. This essentialism fed what Elly Bulkin calls "oppression privilege" which assumes that certain criticisms can only be made by those who share a given identity. Within this construct, it is unacceptable, for instance, for a non-Jewish woman to criticize a Jewish woman or for a White woman to take issue with a woman of color (Bulkin, 1984).

A subsequent stage in my racial identity evolved as I began to understand the distinctions between identity politics and an informed consciousness—a stance based on one's political affiliations and relation to subordinated communities regardless of biology (Thompson & Tyagi, 1993). Some of this came about as I became more comfortable confronting racism, regardless of whether or not it was confirmed by a person of color. In this stage, those whom I could consider authorities and role models for understanding race and racism also broadened to include White people. My earlier competitive approach had been replaced by understanding that I did not have to recreate the wheel in my own life. I began to actively seek scholarship by White people who have historically stood up against racism—Elly Bulkin, Lillian Smith, Sara Evans, Angelina Grimke, Ruth Frankenberg, Helen Joseph, Melanie Kaye/Kantrowitz, Tillie Olsen, Minnie Bruce Pratt, Ruth Seid, Joe Slovo, Mab Segrest, David Wellman, and others. I also realized I needed antiracist White people in my daily life with whom I could share stories, talk about complex "racialized" interactions (in the classroom, for example), and brainstorm about strategies. Most importantly, I needed White friends whom I could trust to give me honest feedback.

If I were to describe what my life feels and looks like now, in terms of race and racism—a task that is much more difficult to do in relation to the present than retrospectively—I would say that antiracism and multiculturalism have become the centerpiece of my life. That reality plays itself out in all areas of my life: at home, in the neighborhood, in my writing, and in my teaching. One of the most obvious ways that I deal with my whiteness is as a teacher of African American studies. People's varied receptions to my disciplinary affiliation with African American studies is but one example of these dynamics.[1] By and large, people of color and White people judge my work by the quality of my labor—my writing and teaching. But, there are some people who, in racialized ways, question me. For students of color at predominantly White schools, it makes sense that they would scrutinize me and/or express disappointment that I am White. They have lived through a long history of having to look primarily to White faculty as their role models and authorities. It is one thing to have to do that in government or biology classes. It is another to have White faculty in African American studies as well. As a White teacher, I try to be receptive to their varied reactions and to help put their understandable responses in a historical context.

The most scrutiny I have received about teaching African American studies, however, has come from White faculty, whose responses have ranged from genuine interest to outright hostility. For those who are interested, I have tried to share the formative influences that led me to see African American studies as a vibrant and comprehensive way of understanding people's longings, struggles, and cultures in the United States. As an interdisciplinary field of study with activist roots, African American studies offers unparalleled and innovative methodologies, sophisticated ethical standpoints, and rich philosophical traditions that have served to document, celebrate, and scrutinize Black culture and politics. Through the prism of African American life, I have also learned much about myself and White culture. I have found African American studies to be a way to unearth much of what has been blocked at the level of the individual and body politic. As William Pinar (1993, p. 66) explains, "The repression of memory and history is accompanied by vigorous distortions of various kinds—political, social, racial and psychological. These distortions undermine intelligence in its various modes, including technical, psychosocial and aesthetic intelligences." Studying and teaching African American studies has been an antidote to these multiple distortions.

My interpretation of White people whose inquiries have been hostile has been different, however, largely because their responses reflect an academic form of racism. In effect, their hostility reveals a patronizing attempt to maintain an academic border patrol—in the form of monitoring disciplinary boundaries—as White people continue to decide who should and should not have rights to whole bodies of knowledge (Wellman, 1996). Typically, they muse about how difficult African Americans must make it for me to do my writing and teaching. It is on these occasions that I reinforce the tremendous support I have received over the years from African American scholars—as colleagues, comrades, and friends. At a point when I want to dismiss the critics' comments or become hostile myself, it becomes important to remind myself when, in my life, I have fallen into the same traps—of considering African American studies off limits, of seeing anger and discomfort in others that is really my own, of projecting a racial politic onto others that I myself have upheld. When I am successful at not making resistant White people somehow "other" than me, I then have an opportunity to speak my mind without losing a chance to shift the conversational frame of reference.

Complicating the Framework

What I have learned from my own experience and that of other White antiracist activists has led me to see consciousness about whiteness and unearned privileges as a core process in psychic development. For this reason, I have appreciated the emerging psychological research on White identity development. During the past fifteen years, a number of models have been developed that trace White identity as a developmental process (e.g., Hardiman, 1982; Helms, 1990). While there is some variation across models, in general, the stages are described sequentially as accep-tance of White supremacy and stereotypes of people of color; dissonance or conflict with dominant cultural norms about racial hierarchies; immersion with people of color and resistance to racism; and the development of an integrated and positive White identity. This psychological research has helped interpret complicated racial dynamics in the classroom, in organizations, and in counseling (Tatum, 1992; Sue & Sue, 1990).

One trouble with the psychological models of racial identity development, however, is that they tend to outline stages that are ahistorical. Ahistoricity leaves little room for understanding how social movements and political activism shape racial identity. This limitation is particularly unfortunate since Black identity models—which were the precursors to White identity theories—initially evolved as a means of explaining the influence of the civil rights movement on racial identity development. The psychological models also tend to see racial identity as somehow separate from gender, sexuality, and class.[2] With such compartmentalization, there has been little room to consider, for example, how the feminist movement has pushed some White lesbians to deal with race in ways not often afforded to White gay men. A third limitation of most White identity models is their focus on whiteness as an identity constructed in opposition to Black people. This duality has its limits in a multiracial society, where many White people form their identities in relation to Asian Americans, Latinos, and Native Americans as well as African Americans (Rowe, Bennett & Atkinson; 1994).

While psychological models help account for individual motivations and psychic transformations, I see racial identity in sociological terms: as intimately tied to history, as informed by multiple identities, as overlapping and often consequential. For me, the interesting question about racial identity is how individual development and social movements interface: What engenders what psychologists might identify as the final stage of White identity development and how that process can be mass produced? While we do not yet have sufficient sociological or psychological data to develop a theory that links whiteness to contemporary activism, autobiographical narratives written in the last fifteen years by White antiracist activists provide an initial window into understanding this link. Fueled by the civil rights, Black Power, gay and lesbian and feminist movements, this writing has begun to tease out the turning points in people's lives that allow them to question and oppose the dominant racial order. It is this literature that I turned to for help in developing a conceptual framework that I have subsequently been using for a current book project on White antiracist activism from the 1950s to the present.

David Wellman (1996), a White man who grew up working class in Detroit in the 1950s and who is now a scholar on race and racism, never went through a period in his life when his whiteness was unmarked. He never took his whiteness for granted or experienced it as normal, invisible. Raised by parents who were Communists, Wellman grew up being treated as red, not White, and found his support—politically and culturally—from Black people in his neighborhood. Blackness was never a devalued identity in his house, nor did he see White society as a place of comfort or acceptance (his father was imprisoned for his political beliefs and his mother faced the threat of deportation). It was not until Wellman was in graduate school that whiteness was the norm—a reality that was quite uncomfortable for him, since he shared little with his White classmates in terms of politics, class background or language. Wellman's story underscores how class, family politics, geography, and historical time period shape identity development. His life also shows why it is impossible to talk about racial identity development as a singular or linear process.

Wellman's (1996) story departs dramatically from that of Mab Segrest, who, in *My Mama's Dead Squirrel* and *Memoir of a Race Traitor,* chronicles how, as the granddaughter of a Klansman, she came to be the director of Carolinians Against the Klan (Segrest, 1984; 1994). Segrest's experience is a particularly southern story. She writes about "lying on [her stomach] beneath some bushes across from the public high school" as 200 Alabama highway patrol troopers escorted twelve Black children to their first day of "integrated" school. She knew from then on that "everything people have told her was right needed to be reexamined" (Segrest, 1984, p. 20). From the title of her first book, *My Mama's Dead Squirrel,* she tells a hilarious story about how her less than fastidious housekeeper mother, upon preparing for a card party at her house, had forgotten to remove a dead squirrel that was lying next to the card table. As her guests' eyes at the party trained on the dead animal, Segrest's mother had to decide how to proceed. She deftly grabbed the squirrel by its tail and swung it around as she proclaimed, "Ain't he pretty" (p. 57). Segrest uses this as a metaphor about how racism is smack in the middle of social relations in this country—under the carpet or not, everyone knows it is there. It is from this vantage point that Segrest traces her coming to race consciousness: how being a lesbian facilitated her willingness to question racial domination, how her mother's contradictory relations with Black women taught her that knowing Black women was not itself a form of antiracism, and why she came to organize against the Klan.

Narratives by antiracist activists also underscore how social movements (and the music, art, political meetings, friendships, and alliances that frequently develop) can catapult people into whole new levels of consciousness. Involvement in social movements often forever change people's political priorities, work choices, and even who they call family. This is beautifully portrayed in Joan Nestle's (1987) essay "This Huge Light of

Yours," in which she describes traveling to Selma, Alabama, in 1965 to participate in freedom marches, boycotts, and voter registration drives. It was there that she learned for the first time that "fear had a taste, that terror could make you clench your ass muscles, to keep from soiling yourself" (p. 57). It was there that she saw and felt the "sunlight and hope and courage, and the dryness of brutality."

Along with class and sexuality, religion and ethnicity also inform how people see themselves racially. Writings by Elly Bulkin, Melanie Kaye/Kantrowitz, and Adrienne Rich, among others, explore the relationship between being Jewish and opposing racism (Bulkin, 1984; Rich, 1979). These writings demonstrate why it is impossible for these women to see themselves as White outside of being Jewish. Their commitment to racial justice is so informed by the legacy of Jewish justice work and their understanding of oppression is so shaped by their experience of anti-Semitism, that attempting to identify themselves as White in a way that is separate from being Jewish makes little sense. At the same time, as Ashkenazi Jews who are light skinned, all three believe that it is crucial to recognize White privilege in order to be effective allies with people of color.

Chronicling links between people's activism and their racial identities can help us avoid reinventing some political wheels. Creating a critical mass of activists requires that people recognize each other, network, and consider these ties crucial for further political work. Identity development is, in fact, a profoundly communal affair. It will take collective recognition and organizing for White people to break out of the racial scripts we have gotten stuck in. In her important article, Susan Stanford Friedman (1995) explains three of these scripts. The first and most well known is the "I am not racist" script of denial. The second script is one of accusation: "You are a racist," followed by "You are not like me." The third script is one of confession, "I am a racist, please forgive me." Friedman cautions against these three scripts, saying that they hinder the development of a multi-issue, antiracist feminist agenda. My interest is in how White people can work together to create new scripts in the future.

The Work Ahead: Organizing in a Campus Context

The work ahead for White people organizing against racism on college campuses is substantial. Of course, that is not the only—nor even the main—location for antiracist organizing, but I focus on it here since I am most familiar with that context. One challenge currently facing White people is the need to develop collective identities that are not rooted in denial and avoidance—that say as much about what we are against as what we are for. This requires grappling with a number of complicated questions. What does a White identity and politic look like that is based on undermining itself? Once domination, exploitation, and unearned privileges are accounted for, is there anything left to whiteness? What, outside of someone's class, ethnicity, sexuality, or religion, constitutes whiteness? Does standing against the racial order for White people require self-annihilation? If whiteness is nothing outside of an invented system of domination, then where does the power come to undermine it from the inside?

Based on my reading of recent writing on whiteness, there are at least two distinct perspectives on these issues. For some theorists, well represented in the work of legal theorist Barbara Flagg (1993), for example, becoming antiracist depends upon developing what she calls a "positive white identity." She does not mean "positive" in any kind of glorified or romanticized way. She does assert, however, that dealing with race in this country requires that all people understand that they are raced—including White people. For Flagg, race is not, itself, the problem. Racism is. So the task is to develop a White identity that is not based on subjugating others.

Ian Haney López (1996), a critical race theorist, disagrees with Flagg, positing that any attempt to find goodness or acceptance of whiteness in this country is problematic. He writes, "Given the inextricable relationships of meaning binding White and Black, it is impossible to separate an assertion of White goodness from the implication of Black badness. . . . For Whites even to mention their racial identity puts notions of racial supremacy into play, even when they merely attempt to foreground their Whiteness" (p. 173). For this reason, López asserts that the only acceptable White identity in the United States is one bent on destroying whiteness, on becoming what has increasingly been called a "race traitor." For López, an example of this approach is seen in the Boston-based periodical *Race Traitor: A Journal of the New Abolitionism,* published with the slogan "Treason to Whiteness is Loyalty to Humanity" (Ignatiev & Garvey, 1996). The basic ethic of this periodical is that a race traitor is someone who "is nominally classified as White, but who defies the rules of whiteness so flagrantly as to jeopardize his or her ability to draw upon the privileges of white skin"

(Haney López, 1996, p. 189). The editors of this journal, Noel Ignatiev and John Garvey, explain the logic behind this approach through analogy. They ask this question: How many counterfeit bills does it take to ruin the money system? Just as the presence of only a few counterfeit bills can undermine the integrity of the money system, White people who refuse to act and be White can undermine the integrity of whiteness as a whole. López sees race traitors as "potentially racially revolutionary." López reasons, "If enough seemingly white people were to reject such differentiation by claiming to be among the "them," the "us" at the base of white identity would collapse" (p. 189).

I first heard the term "race traitor" through antiracist activist Mab Segrest (1994) in her book *Memoir of a Race Traitor*. I have to admit that my first thought was one of relief. I finally found a term that described what I was trying to do. Likewise, López's analysis of the need to overturn White identity as it now stands makes sense to me. I also like the term "race traitor" because it captures how my life often feels. Like Wellman (1996), I often feel like a spy, listening in on conversations I plan on undermining in whatever ways I can. I am drawn to the radical connotations of the term "traitor." I see racism as something so large and all encompassing that nothing short of a national revolution will suffice.

On the other hand, I still find myself wary about this notion that whiteness has to be annihilated, in part because it took me so many years to stop denying my whiteness. I had to work through shame, doubt, and guilt to describe myself as White without feeling like I was choking. During the ten years that I have been teaching, I have watched many White students struggle through a process of identifying themselves as White without feeling the need to apologize. Flagg's (1993) understanding of gaining a positive White identity might be part of a process people go through on their way to becoming a "race traitor." But I worry about the ways in which the idea of becoming a race traitor can be a stand-in for continuing to hate ourselves, for continuing to look to people of color for cues, and for continuing to distrust our abilities to identify and stand against racism. None of the White activists I know of (or have read about) have come to their activism without accepting themselves as White people. The two go hand in hand. In other words, it may not be possible to do antiracist work as White people in this country and not see oneself as White. This reality requires getting past—or at least trying to confront—the denial, avoidance and fear that many people experience about being identified as White. White people's abilities to talk with each other about racism and activism depends upon dealing with the daily realities of our lives, the formative influences in our understanding of race, as well as the trials and tribulations that most of us have been taught never to share with each other.

My final concern about the writing on "race traitors" is the tendency to conflate race and racism, as if the two were one and the same. In the introduction to *Race Traitor,* the editors write, "Our intention . . . is to focus on whiteness and the struggle to abolish the white race from within" (Ignatiev & Garvey, 1996, p. 2). I agree with their first goal—to focus on whiteness—particularly as a means of countering the academic history of diverting attention away from White supremacy by focusing on Black "pathology." But I would amend the second part of the editors' assertion. To me, the task is not to eliminate the White race from within but rather to eliminate racism from within. Although the analogy is imprecise, I would argue in a parallel way that eliminating patriarchy need not mean destroying men. I am intent upon recognizing the fluidity between genders (and that there may well be more than two genders) and resisting sexism. I do not want boy children to grow up thinking it is wrong to be a man, nor am I willing to reject all forms of masculinity as oppressive.

Ultimately, I agree with Winant (1994) that race, as a central organizing principle in the world, is here to stay. He convincingly argues against the dominant notion that the significance of race is on the decline. He sees attempts to get rid of race as unrealistic and a way of feeding the debilitating ideology of color blindness. His proposal is not to eliminate racial categorizing, but rather to democratize it. As a way of organizing the world, race is not inherently oppressive. The problem is the ranking of racial categories as a means to uphold inequality.

Unfortunately, I think the continuing vacillation about labels and the search for names that effectively describe White antiracists are not simply issues of semantics. Rather, the lack of terminology that is precise and subversive speaks to the reality that White people who challenge racism have not yet created the critical mass needed to name ourselves collectively. History has shown repeatedly that names that capture the essence of a political movement come out of struggle and collectivity. Such slogans as

"Black is beautiful," and "the personal is political" and such terms as "African American," and "womanist" come out of organized political struggle. So will terms that accurately describe what it means to be a White person who both acknowledges whiteness and rejects the ideology of supremacy it sustains.

Doing Work Together as White People

To facilitate this naming, White people need to find ways to open conceptual doors for each other. Rarely, however, in academic contexts, do I hear about White antiracist organizing as a method of political activism. Yet, without these political spaces, we are not afforded the chance to ask each other some of the hard questions about antiracist work. For example, why do White antiracist people often have such a hard time seeing each other eye to eye? A few years ago, a White friend of mine noted that when she and her partner, who is South Asian, attend an event that includes only a few other South Asians, the South Asian women make an effort to acknowledge each other—if not by talking, then at least through eye contact. But, my White friend noticed that no such comradery typically exists between White people when there tends to be just a few White people in a multiracial context. The contrast I am making may be a bit reductionist because what my White friend perceives as comradery from the outside may well not feel like that between South-Asian women, given differences in class, religion, nationality and political relations to one's country of origin (Women, 1993). But my White friend's perceptions do trigger questions about why White antiracists often maintain physical and emotional distance between each other.

My guess is that a complicated combination of fear of competition and fear of intimacy keep us away from each other. White people who are attempting to confront racism are often so hard on each other. When I have been honest, I have seen myself apply standards of conduct and communication for other White people that leave little room for a process of growing. Sometimes, my anger at other White people has really been anger at myself that I have deflected elsewhere. Subconsciously I have been quick to point fingers at other White people as a way to deflect possible critique aimed in my direction. White people need to somehow learn how to give each other and ourselves a break. Demonizing White people is a frequent trap many of us fall into that only backfires. If I think I am better than other people, there is no way I can work with them as equals. The task for me, then, is to try to see every White person as a potential ally—even when they act in ways that do not even vaguely approximate such a politic. Ultimately, the biggest trouble I have with the concept "race traitor" is, as Lisa Hall has said, "its implied refusal to see other white people as kin."[3] Being "kin" does not mean that we have to like, never mind love, each other. But it does mean we are in this thing together—this way of organizing life based on the invention of racism—and we need to collectively refuse to participate in it in small and big ways throughout our lives.

Such alliance building requires understanding that lessons about race often take years to integrate. We need to take race and racism seriously enough to not believe that it is something that students, teachers, and administrators can understand through a crash course. In analyzing a specific essay she once wrote, Audre Lorde explained,

> The piece I wrote . . . was useful, but limited, because I didn't ask some essential question. And not having asked myself that question, not having realized that it was a question, I was deflecting a lot of energy in that piece. . . . It was a question of how much I could bear and of not realizing I could bear more than I thought I could at the time. It was also a question of how I could use that perception other than just in rage or destruction. (1984, p. 106)

This quote has tremendous relevance for racial identity development. In my own life, there have been many questions that I have not known how to ask about race that only years later I found the resources or courage to raise. For example, for the longest time, I was hesitant to explore how my lover and friendship relationships with women of color have influenced my activism. Looking back, I unconsciously dodged that question out of fear that I would be accused of having these relationships solely to facilitate my activism. I feared that teasing out connections between my personal life and public commitments might expose me as a wanna-be. It was only through working with other White antiracist activists, many of whom are in primary relationships with people of color, that I began to explore possible connections with less judgment, with more affection, with a possibility for insight I never allowed myself before.

Finding ways to look each other in the eye will help us to identify what motivates people to question and oppose racism. Many White people see the exclusions they faced growing up—on the basis of sexuality, class, and religion—as the springboards that spurred them to question racial exclusions. We need to identify what those springboards are and figure out ways to work with them. My own experience suggests that dealing with childhood trauma may be a necessary part of racial reorientation for many White people. Surviving abuse is no guarantee of political consciousness. All that abuse promises is scars. The rest is left up to fate, resources, and the healing that may come from collectively naming and organizing to stop abuse. A radicalizing force in my life did come from understanding the origins of my own "outsider's lens" and beginning to see how that lens enabled me to question other injustices.

It is tricky, however, for White people to explore the initial reasons for an outsider's vision if they then make simple equations between being an "outsider" and understanding racism. As Sally Lee, a self-identified African American, Norwegian, and German student in one of my courses recently wrote, "Anything which puts a distance between white people and privilege is a dissociation of whiteness."[4] This dissociation can lead to an unwillingness to recognize unearned privileges. The challenge is to recognize what has motivated us to question authority without using it as a way to imply that the injustices we have faced are worse or more long-standing than racism. In the process, White people need to acknowledge what we have been through without appropriating the writing and art by people of color to express it. There has been such vivid and creative work by people of color about processes of exclusion and their psychological effects that it makes sense why White people might want to latch onto their artistic creations. But we have to find our own language and our own imagery to describe our lives and struggles.

White students, faculty, and administrators also need to intervene when we try to out-Black, out-Latina, or out-Asian people. As Lee explains, this can be seen among White students when they attempt to adopt non-White symbols—rap, styles of dance, dress, talk—as ways of showing they are "free," or "loose," or "cool." This appropriation can severely hinder cross-cultural communication. It treats culture as some kind of commodity rather than a way of life. As Lorde has written, "You don't have to be me in order for us to fight along side of each other. I do not have to be you to recognize that our wars are the same" (1984, p. 142). Cherokee critic Geary Hobson coined the term "white shamanism" to describe a historical pattern whereby non-Indian people "appropriate indigenous cultures and distort them for their own purposes" (Rose, 1992, p. 404). White shamanism occurs when non-Indian poets "assume the persona of the shaman, usually in the guise of an American Indian medicine man" (p. 403). The critique of White shamanism in relation to non-Indian appropriation of Indian culture can be generalized to include White appropriation of Black culture. White hair that is not combed for years on end is not the same as dreadlocks. How bad White uncombed straight hair looks is symbolic for how foolish it is to try to out-Black or out-Latina someone.

This pattern is what antiracist educator Patti DeRosa (1996) calls "racism as tourism"—stopping along the road of life to learn bits and pieces of other cultures but not understanding the political implications of misappropriation, cultural intrusion, and seeing the "other" as "exotic." "Racism as tourism" occurs among White faculty when we assume that it is possible to incorporate one or two Black or Latino authors into a course syllabus without examining the course framework to begin with. "Racism as tourism" occurs when faculty assume that African American studies should be "mainstreamed" into a discipline without affording it an autonomous and stable base of its own. "Racism as tourism" flourishes when White faculty allow students of color to be their teachers because that is less threatening than developing peer relationships with faculty of color. I give these examples not as a means of castigating others, since many come from mistakes I have made myself, but rather to flesh out daily ways that racial tourism gets played out and supported within the academy.

The fact that White people have been racialized in the post–civil rights era will inevitably spur more work on the meaning of whiteness. My hope is that this work will usher in more attention to the links between White identity development and activism. Faculty need to find ways to reach out to White students—as racialized beings—and talk with them about our own processes of racial development. People from my generation can learn much from what students are now negotiating. Recently, I spent a few hours with a group of White students as they talked about what whiteness means to them and why they have become antiracist activists. They offered a level of sophisticated analysis I never could have mustered as an undergraduate. This sharp contrast gives me hope.

Notes

I want to thank Elly Bulkin for her substantial contributions to this article, and Lisa Hall, who pushed me to put my ideas down on paper. Thanks as well to the Virginia Women's Studies Association for supporting this work.

1. Other racialized dynamics involve classroom politics, curriculum decisions, and negotiations among faculty. Unfortunately, space limits my ability to analyze these issues in this chapter.

2. For important essays that do consider multiple identities see Connie S. Chan, "Issues of Identity Development among Asian American Lesbians and Gay Men," *Journal of Counseling and Development* 68 (September/October 1989): 16–20; Darryl K. Loiacano, "Gay Identity Issues among Black Americans: Racism, Homophobia and the Need for Validation," *Journal of Counseling and Development* 68 (September/October 1989): 21–25.

3. Personal conversation, April 1996.

4. Paper written for "National, Transnational and Diasporic Feminist Theories," at Wesleyan University, Spring 1996. Quoted with permission.

References

Alba, R. D. 1990. *The Invention of the White Race*. London: Verso Press.

Bulkin, Elly. 1984. "Hard Ground: Jewish Identity, Racism and Anti-Semitism." In E. Bulkin, M. B. Pratt, and B. Smith (eds.), *Yours in Struggle: Three Perspectives on Racism and Anti-Semitism*. Brooklyn, NY: Long Haul Press, pp. 76–92.

Chan, C. S. 1989. "Issues of Identity Development among Asian-American Lesbians and Gay Men." *Journal of Counseling and Development* 68(5):16–20.

DeRosa, P. 1996. "Learning about Racism: Lessons from Oneonta and Beyond." Unpublished speech.

Flagg, B. 1993. "'Was Blind but Now I See': White Race Consciousness and the Requirement of Discriminatory Intent." *Michigan Law Review* 91(3):953–1017.

Friedman, S. S. 1995. "Beyond White and Other: Relationality and Narratives of Race in Feminist Discourse." *Signs* 21(1):25–37.

Haney López, I. 1996. *White by Law: The Legal Construction of Race*. New York: New York University Press.

Hardiman, R. 1982. "White Identity Development: A Process Model for Describing the Racial Consciousness of White Americans." *Dissertation Abstracts International 432*, 104A University Microfilms No. 82–10330.

Helms, J. E. (ed.). 1990. *Black and White Racial Identity: Theory, Research and Practice.* Westport, CT: Greenwood.

Ignatiev, N., and Garvey, J. (eds.) 1996. *Race Traitor.* New York: Routledge.

Kaye-Kantrowitz. M. 1996. "Jews in the U.S.: The Rising Costs of Whiteness." In B. Thompson and S. Tyagi (eds.), *Names We Call Home: Autobiography on Racial Identity.* New York: Routledge, pp. 221–243.

Lorde, A. 1984. *Sister Outsider.* New York: Crossing Press.

Nestle. J. 1987. *A Restricted Country.* Ithaca, NY: Firebrand.

Pinar, W. F. 1993. "Notes on Understanding Curriculum as a Racial Text." In C. McCarthy and W. Crichlow (eds.), *Race, Identity and Representation in Education.* New York: Routledge, pp. 117–134.

Rich, A. 1979. "'Disloyal to Civilization': Feminism, Racism Gynephobia." In A. Rich (ed.), *On Lies, Secrets and Silences.* New York: Norton, pp. 13–29.

Rose, W. 1992. "The Great Pretenders: Further Reflections on White Shamanism." In M. A. Jaimes (ed.), *The State of Native America: Genocide, Colonization, and Resistance.* Boston: South End Press, pp. 117–138.

Rowe, W., Bennett, S. K., and Atkinson, D. R. 1994. "White Racial Identity Models: A Critique and Alternative Proposal." *The Counseling Psychologist* 22(1):129–146.

Segrest, M. 1984. *My Mama's Dead Squirrel: Lesbian Essays on Southern Culture.* Ithaca, NY: Firebrand.

Segrest. M. 1994. *Memoir of a Race Traitor.* Boston: South End Press.

Sue, D. W., and Sue D. 1990. *Counseling the Culturally Different: Theory and Practice.* New York: John Wiley.

Tatum, B. D. 1992. "Talking About Race, Learning About Racism: The Application of Racial Identity Development Theory in the Classroom." *Harvard Educational Review* 62(1): 1–24.

Thompson, B., and S. Tyagi (eds.). 1993. *Beyond a Dream Deferred: Multicultural Education and the Politics of Excellence.* Minneapolis: University of Minnesota.

Thompson, B., and S. Tyagi (eds.). 1996. *Names We Call Home: Autobiography on Racial Identity.* Minneapolis: University of Minnesota.

Thompson, B. 1996. "Time Traveling and Border Crossing: Reflections on White Identity." In B. Thompson and S. Tyagi (eds.), *Names We Call Home: Autobiography on Racial Identity.* Minneapolis: University of Minnesota Press.

Wellman, D. 1996. "Red and Black in America." In B. Thompson and S. Tyagi (eds.), *Names We Call Home: Autobiography on Racial Identity.* New York: Routledge, pp. 13–29.

Winant, H. 1994. *Racial Conditions.* Minneapolis: University of Minnesota Press.

Women of the South Asian Diaspora. 1993. *Our Feet Walk the Sky.* San Francisco: Aunt Lute.

16
Toward a New Vision

Race, Class, and Gender as
Categories of Analysis and Connection

Patricia Hill Collins

The true focus of revolutionary change is never merely the oppressive
situations which we seek to escape, but that piece of the oppressor which
is planted deep within each of us.

Audre Lorde, *Sister Outsider*

Audre Lorde's statement raises a troublesome issue for scholars and activists working for social change. While many of us have little difficulty assessing our own victimization within some major system of
oppression, whether it be by race, social class, religion, sexual orientation,
ethnicity, age, or gender, we typically fail to see how our thoughts and actions uphold someone else's subordination. Thus, White feminists routinely point with confidence to their oppression as women but resist
seeing how much their white skin privileges them. African-Americans
who possess eloquent analyses of racism often persist in viewing poor

White women as symbols of white power. The radical left fares little better. "If only people of color and women could see their true class interests," they argue, "class solidarity would eliminate racism and sexism." In essence, each group identifies the type of oppression with which it feels most comfortable as being fundamental and classifies all other types as being of lesser importance.

Oppression is full of such contradictions. Errors in political judgment that we make concerning how we teach our courses, what we tell our children, and which organizations are worthy of our time, talents, and financial support flow smoothly from errors in theoretical analysis about the nature of oppression and activism. Once we realize that there are few pure victims or oppressors, and that each one of us derives varying amounts of penalty and privilege from the multiple systems of oppression that frame our lives, then we will be in a position to see the need for new ways of thought and action.

To get at that "piece of the oppressor which is planted deep within each of us," we need at least two things. First, we need new visions of what oppression is, new categories of analysis that are inclusive of race, class, and gender as distinctive yet interlocking structures of oppression. Adhering to a stance of comparing and ranking oppressions—the proverbial, "I'm more oppressed than you"—locks us all into a dangerous dance of competing for attention, resources, and theoretical supremacy. Instead, I suggest that we examine our different experiences within the more fundamental relationship of domination and subordination. To focus on the particular arrangements that race, class, and gender take in our time and place without seeing these structures as sometimes parallel and sometimes interlocking dimensions of the more fundamental relationship of domination and subordination may temporarily ease our consciences. But while such thinking may lead to short-term social reforms, it is simply inadequate for the task of bringing about long-term social transformation.

While race, class, and gender as categories of analysis are essential in helping us understand the structural bases of domination and subordination, new ways of thinking that are not accompanied by new ways of acting offer incomplete prospects for change. To get at that "piece of the oppressor which is planted deep within each of us," we also need to change our daily behavior. Currently, we are all enmeshed in a complex web of problematic relationships that grant our mirror images full human subjectivity while stereotyping and objectifying those most different from us. We often assume that the people we work with, teach, send our children to school with, and sit next to . . . will act and feel in prescribed ways because they belong to given race, social class, or gender categories. These judgments by category must be replaced with fully human relationships that transcend the legitimate differences created by race, class, and gender as categories of analysis. We require new categories of connection, new visions of what our relationships with one another can be. [. . .]

[This discussion] addresses this need for new patterns of thought and action. I focus on two basic questions. First, how can we reconceptualize race, class, and gender as categories of analysis? Second, how can we transcend the barriers created by our experiences with race, class, and gender oppression in order to build the types of coalitions essential for social exchange? To address these questions I contend that we must acquire both new theories of how race, class, and gender have shaped the experiences not just of women of color, but of all groups. Moreover, we must see the connections between the categories of analysis and the personal issues in our everyday lives, particularly our scholarship, our teaching, and our relationships with our colleagues and students. As Audre Lorde points out, change starts with self, and relationships that we have with those around us must always be the primary site for social change.

How Can We Reconceptualize Race, Class, and Gender as Categories of Analysis?

To me, we must shift our discourse away from additive analyses of oppression (Spelman, 1982; Collins, 1989). Such approaches are typically based on two key premises. First, they depend on either/or, dichotomous thinking. Persons, things and ideas are conceptualized in terms of their opposites. For example, Black/White, man/woman, thought/feeling, and fact/opinion are defined in oppositional terms. Thought and feeling are not seen as two different and interconnected ways of approaching truth that can coexist in scholarship and teaching. Instead, feeling is defined as antithetical to reason, as its opposite. In spite of the fact that we all have "both/and" identities (I am both a college professor and a mother—I don't stop being a mother when I drop my child off at school, or forget everything I learned while scrubbing the toilet), we persist in trying to classify each other in either/or categories. I live each day as an African-American

woman—a race/gender specific experience. And I am not alone. Everyone
has a race/gender/class specific identity. Either/or, dichotomous thinking
is especially troublesome when applied to theories of oppression because
every individual must be classified as being either oppressed or not oppressed. The both/and position of simultaneously being oppressed and
oppressor becomes conceptually impossible.

A second premise of additive analyses of oppression is that these dichotomous differences must be ranked. One side of the dichotomy is typically labeled dominant and the other subordinate. Thus, Whites rule
Blacks, men are deemed superior to women, and reason is seen as being
preferable to emotion. Applying this premise to discussions of oppression
leads to the assumption that oppression can be quantified, and that some
groups are oppressed more than others. I am frequently asked, "Which has
been most oppressive to you, your status as a Black person or your status
as a woman?" What I am really being asked to do is divide myself into little
boxes and rank my various statuses. If I experience oppression as a
both/and phenomenon, why should I analyze it any differently?

Additive analyses of oppression rest squarely on the twin pillars of
either/or thinking and the necessity to quantify and rank all relationships
in order to know where one stands. Such approaches typically see African-
American women as being more oppressed than everyone else because the
majority of Black women experience the negative effects of race, class, and
gender oppression simultaneously. In essence, if you add together separate
oppressions, you are left with a grand oppression greater than the sum of
its parts.

I am not denying that specific groups experience oppression more
harshly than others—lynching is certainly objectively worse than being
held up as a sex object. But we must be careful not to confuse this issue of
the saliency of one type of oppression in people's lives with a theoretical
stance positing the interlocking nature of oppression. Race, class, and gender may all structure a situation but may not be equally visible and/or important in people's self-definitions. In certain contexts, such as the
antebellum American South and contemporary South America, racial oppression is more visibly salient, while in other contexts, such as Haiti, El
Salvador, and Nicaragua, social class oppression may be more apparent. For
middle-class White women, gender may assume experiential primacy unavailable to poor Hispanic women struggling with the ongoing issues of

low-paying jobs and the frustrations of the welfare bureaucracy. This recognition that one category may have salience over another for a given time and place does not minimize the theoretical importance of assuming that race, class, and gender as categories of analysis structure all relationships.

In order to move toward new visions of what oppression is, I think that we need to ask new questions. How are relationships of domination and subordination structured and maintained in the American political economy? How do race, class, and gender function as parallel and interlocking systems that shape this basic relationship of domination and subordination? Questions such as these promise to move us away from futile theoretical struggles concerned with ranking oppressions and toward analyses that assume race, class, and gender are all present in any given setting, even if one appears more visible and salient than the others. Our task becomes redefined as one of reconceptualizing oppression by uncovering the connections among race, class, and gender as categories of analysis.

1. INSTITUTIONAL DIMENSION OF OPPRESSION

Sandra Harding's contention that gender oppression is structured along three main dimensions—the institutional, the symbolic, and the individual—offers a useful model for a more comprehensive analysis encompassing race, class, and gender oppression (Harding 1989). Systemic relationships of domination and subordination structured through social institutions such as schools, businesses, hospitals, the work place, and government agencies represent the institutional dimension of oppression. Racism, sexism, and elitism all have concrete institutional locations. Even though the workings of the institutional dimension of oppression are often obscured with ideologies claiming equality of opportunity, in actuality, race, class, and gender place Asian-American women, Native American men, White men, African-American women, and other groups in distinct institutional niches with varying degrees of penalty and privilege.

Even though I realize that many . . . would not share this assumption, let us assume that the institutions of American society discriminate, whether by design or by accident. While many of us are familiar with how race, gender, and class operate separately to structure inequality, I want to focus on how these three systems interlock in structuring the institutional dimension of oppression. To get at the interlocking nature of race, class, and gender, I want you to think about the antebellum plantation as a guiding metaphor for a variety of American social institutions. Even though slavery is typically analyzed as a racist institution, and occasionally as a class institution, I suggest that slavery was a race-, class-, and gender-specific institution. Removing any one piece from our analysis diminishes our understanding of the true nature of relations of domination and subordination under slavery.

Slavery was a profoundly patriarchal institution. It rested on the dual tenets of White male authority and White male property, a joining of the political and the economic within the institution of family. Heterosexism was assumed and all Whites were expected to marry. Control over affluent White women's sexuality remained key to slavery's survival because property was to be passed on to the legitimate heirs of the slave owner. Ensuring affluent White women's virginity and chastity was deeply intertwined with maintenance of property relations.

Under slavery, we see varying levels of institutional protection given to affluent White women, working-class and poor White women, and enslaved African women. Poor White women enjoyed few of the protections held out to their upper-class sisters. Moreover, the devalued status of Black women was key in keeping all White women in their assigned places. Controlling Black women's fertility was also key to the continuation of slavery, for children born to slave mothers themselves were slaves.

African-American women shared the devalued status of chattel with their husbands, fathers, and sons. Racism stripped Blacks as a group of legal rights, education, and control over their own persons. African-Americans could be whipped, branded, sold, or killed, not because they were poor, or because they were women, but because they were Black. Racism ensured that Blacks would continue to serve Whites and suffer economic exploitation at the hands of all Whites.

So we have a very interesting chain of command on the plantation—the affluent White master as the reigning patriarch; his White wife helpmate to serve him, help him manage his property, and bring up his heirs; his faithful servants, whose production and reproduction were tied to the requirements of the capitalist political economy; and largely propertyless, working-class White men and women watching from afar. In essence, the foundations for the contemporary roles of elite White women, poor Black women, working-class White men, and a series of other groups can be seen in stark relief in this fundamental American social institution. While Blacks experienced the most harsh treatment under slavery, and thus made slavery clearly visible as a racist institution, race, class, and gender interlocked in structuring slavery's systemic organization of domination and subordination.

Even today, the plantation remains a compelling metaphor for institutional oppression. Certainly the actual conditions of oppression are not as severe now as they were then. To argue, as some do, that things have not changed all that much denigrates the achievements of those who struggled for social change before us. But the basic relationships among Black men, Black women, elite White women, elite White men, working-class White men, and working-class White women as groups remain essentially intact.

A brief analysis of key American social institutions most controlled by elite White men should convince us of the interlocking nature of race, class, and gender in structuring the institutional dimension of oppression. For example, if you are from an American college or university, is your campus a modern plantation? Who controls your university's political economy? Are elite White men overrepresented among the upper administrators and trustees controlling your university's finances and policies? Are elite White men being joined by growing numbers of elite White women helpmates? What kinds of people are in your classrooms grooming the next generation who will occupy these and other decision-making positions? Who are the support staff that produce the mass mailings, order the supplies, fix the leaky pipes? Do African-Americans, Hispanics, or other people of color form the majority of the invisible workers who feed you, wash your dishes, and clean up your offices and libraries after everyone else has gone home?

If your college is anything like mine, you know the answers to these questions. You may be affiliated with an institution that has Hispanic women as vice-presidents for finance, or substantial numbers of Black men among the faculty. If so, you are fortunate. Much more typical are colleges where a modified version of the plantation as a metaphor for the institutional dimension of oppression survives.

2. THE SYMBOLIC DIMENSION OF OPPRESSION

Widespread, societally sanctioned ideologies used to justify relations of domination and subordination comprise the symbolic dimension of oppression. Central to this process is the use of stereotypical or controlling images of diverse race, class, and gender groups. In order to assess the power of this dimension of oppression, I want you to make a list, either on paper or in your head, of "masculine" and "feminine" characteristics. If your list is anything like that compiled by most people, it reflects some variation of the following:

Masculine	Feminine
aggressive	passive
leader	follower
rational	emotional
strong	weak
intellectual	physical

Not only does this list reflect either/or dichotomous thinking and the need to rank both sides of the dichotomy, but ask yourself exactly which men and women you had in mind when compiling these characteristics. This list applies almost exclusively to middle-class White men and women. The allegedly "masculine" qualities that you probably listed are only acceptable when exhibited by elite White men, or when used by Black and Hispanic men against each other or against women of color. Aggressive Black and Hispanic men are seen as dangerous, not powerful, and are often penalized when they exhibit any of the allegedly "masculine" characteristics. Working-class and poor White men fare slightly better and are also denied the allegedly "masculine" symbols of leadership, intellectual competence, and human rationality. Women of color and working-class and poor White women are also not represented on this list, for they have never had the luxury of being "ladies." What appear to be universal categories representing all men and women instead are unmasked as being applicable to only a small group.

It is important to see how the symbolic images applied to different race, class, and gender groups interact in maintaining systems of domination and subordination. If I were to ask you to repeat the same assignment, only this time, by making separate lists for Black men, Black women, Hispanic women, and Hispanic men, I suspect that your gender symbolism would be quite different. In comparing all of the lists, you might begin to see the interdependence of symbols applied to all groups. For example, the elevated images of White womanhood need devalued images of Black womanhood in order to maintain credibility.

While the above exercise reveals the interlocking nature of race, class, and gender in structuring the symbolic dimension of oppression, part of its importance lies in demonstrating how race, class, and gender pervade a wide range of what appears to be universal language. Attending to diversity in our scholarship, in our teaching, and in our daily lives provides a new angle of vision on interpretations of reality thought to be natural, normal, and "true." Moreover, viewing images of masculinity and femininity as universal gender symbolism, rather than as symbolic images that are race, class, and gender specific, renders the experiences of people of color and of non-privileged White women and men invisible. One way to dehumanize an individual or a group is to deny the reality of their experiences. So when we refuse to deal with race or class because they do not appear to be directly relevant to gender, we are actually becoming part of someone else's problem.

Assuming that everyone is affected differently by the same interlocking set of symbolic images allows us to move forward toward new analyses. Women of color and White women have different relationships to White male authority, and this difference explains the distinct gender symbolism applied to both groups. Black women encounter controlling images such as the mammy, the matriarch, the mule, and the whore, that encourage others to reject us as fully human people. Ironically, the negative nature of these images simultaneously encourages us to reject them. In contrast, White women are offered seductive images, those that promise to reward them for supporting the status quo. And yet seductive images can be equally controlling. Consider, for example, the views of Nancy White, a 73-year-old Black woman, concerning images of rejection and seduction:

> My mother used to say that the black woman is the white man's mule and the white woman is his dog. Now, she said that to say this: we do the heavy work and get beat whether we do it well or not. But the white woman is closer to the master and he pats them on the head and lets them sleep in the house, but he ain't gon' treat neither one like he was dealing with a person. (Gwaltney, 1980, p. 148)

Both sets of images stimulate particular political stances. By broadening the analysis beyond the confines of race, we can see the varying levels of rejection and seduction available to each of us due to our race, class, and gender identity. Each of us lives with an allotted portion of institutional privilege and penalty, and with varying levels of rejection and seduction inherent in the symbolic images applied to us. This is the context in which we make our choices. Taken together, the institutional and symbolic dimensions of oppression create a structural backdrop against which all of us live our lives.

3. THE INDIVIDUAL DIMENSION OF OPPRESSION

Whether we benefit or not, we all live within institutions that reproduce race, class, and gender oppression. Even if we never have any contact with members of other race, class, and gender groups, we all encounter images of these groups and are exposed to the symbolic meanings attached to those images. On this dimension of oppression, our individual biographies vary tremendously. As a result of our institutional and symbolic statuses, all of our choices become political acts.

Each of us must come to terms with the multiple ways in which race, class, and gender as categories of analysis frame our individual biographies. I have lived my entire life as an African-American woman from a working-class family, and this basic fact has had a profound impact on my personal biography. Imagine how different your life might be if you had been born Black, or White, or poor, or of a different race/class/gender group than the one with which you are most familiar. The institutional treatment you would have received and the symbolic meanings attached to your very existence might differ dramatically from what you now consider to be natural, normal and part of everyday life. You might be the same, but your personal biography might have been quite different.

I believe that each of us carries around the cumulative effect of our lives within multiple structures of oppression. If you want to see how much you have been affected by this whole thing, I ask you one simple question—who are your close friends? Who are the people with whom you can share your hopes, dreams, vulnerabilities, fears, and victories? Do they look like you? If they are all the same, circumstance may be the cause. For the first seven years of my life I saw only low-income Black people. My friends from those years reflected the composition of my community. But now that I am an adult, can the defense of circumstance explain the patterns of people that I trust as my friends and colleagues? When given other alternatives, if my friends and colleagues reflect the homogeneity of one race, class, and gender group, then these categories of analysis have indeed become barriers to connection.

I am not suggesting that people are doomed to follow the paths laid out for them by race, class, and gender as categories of analysis. While these three structures certainly frame my opportunity structure, I as an individual always have the choice of accepting things as they are, or trying to change them. As Nikki Giovanni points out, "we've got to live in the real world. If we don't like the world we're living in, change it. And if we can't change it, we change ourselves. We can do something" (Tate 1983, 68). While a piece of the oppressor may be planted deep within each of us, we each have the choice of accepting that piece or challenging it as part of the "true focus of revolutionary change."

How Can We Transcend the Barriers Created by Our Experiences With Race, Class, and Gender Oppression in Order to Build the Types of Coalitions Essential for Social Change?

Reconceptualizing oppression and seeing the barriers created by race, class, and gender as interlocking categories of analysis is a vital first step. But we must transcend these barriers by moving toward race, class, and gender as categories of connection, by building relationships and coalitions that will bring about social change. What are some of the issues involved in doing this?

1. DIFFERENCES IN POWER AND PRIVILEGE

First, we must recognize that our differing experiences with oppression create problems in the relationships among us. Each of us lives within a system that vests us with varying levels of power and privilege. These differences in power, whether structured along axes of race, class, gender, age, or sexual orientation, frame our relationships. African-American writer June Jordan describes her discomfort on a Caribbean vacation with Olive, the Black woman who cleaned her room:

> . . . even though both "Olive" and "I" live inside a conflict neither one of us created, and even though both of us therefore hurt inside that conflict, I may be one of the monsters she needs to eliminate from her universe and, in a sense, she may be one of the monsters in mine (1985, 47).

Differences in power constrain our ability to connect with one another even when we think we are engaged in dialogue across differences. Let me give you an example. One year, the students in my course "Sociology of the Black Community" got into a heated discussion about the reasons for the upsurge of racial incidents on college campuses. Black students complained vehemently about the apathy and resistance they felt most White students expressed about examining their own racism. Mark, a White male student, found their comments particularly unsettling. After claiming that all the Black people he had ever known had expressed no such beliefs to him, he questioned how representative the viewpoints of his fellow students actually were. When pushed further, Mark revealed that he had participated in conversations over the years with the Black domestic worker employed by his family. Since she had never expressed such strong feelings about White racism, Mark was genuinely shocked by class discussions. Ask yourselves whether that domestic worker was in a position to speak freely. Would it have been wise for her to do so in a situation where the power between the two parties was so unequal?

In extreme cases, members of privileged groups can erase the very presence of the less privileged. When I first moved to Cincinnati, my family and I went on a picnic at a local park. Picnicking next to us was a family of White Appalachians. When I went to push my daughter on the swings, several of the children came over. They had missing, yellowed, and broken teeth, they wore old clothing, and their poverty was evident. I was shocked. Growing up in a large eastern city, I had never seen such awful poverty among Whites. The segregated neighborhoods in which I grew up made White poverty all but invisible. More importantly, the privileges attached to my newly acquired social class position allowed me to ignore and minimize the poverty among Whites that I did encounter. My reactions to those children made me realize how confining phrases such as "well, at least they're not Black," had become for me. In learning to grant human subjectivity to the Black victims of poverty, I had simultaneously learned to demand White victims of poverty. By applying categories of race to the objective conditions confronting me, I was quantifying and ranking oppressions and missing the very real suffering which, in fact, is the real issue.

One common pattern of relationships across differences in power is one that I label "voyeurism." From the perspective of the privileged, the lives of people of color, of the poor, and of women are interesting for their entertainment value. The privileged become voyeurs, passive onlookers who do not relate to the less powerful, but who are interested in seeing how the "different" live. Over the years, I have heard numerous African-American students complain about professors who never call on them except when a so-called Black issue is being discussed. The students' interest in discussing race or qualifications for doing so appear unimportant to the professor's efforts to use Black students' experiences as stories to make the material come alive for the White student audience. Asking Black students to perform on cue and provide a Black experience for their White classmates can be seen as voyeurism at its worst.

Members of subordinate groups do not willingly participate in such exchanges but often do so because members of dominant groups control the institutional and symbolic apparatuses of oppression. Racial/ethnic groups, women, and the poor have never had the luxury of being voyeurs of the lives of the privileged. Our ability to survive in hostile settings has hinged on our ability to learn intricate details about the behavior and world view of the powerful and adjust our behavior accordingly. I need only point to the difference in perception of those men and women in abusive relationships. Where men can view their girlfriends and wives as sex objects, helpmates, and a collection of stereotyped categories of voyeurism—women must be attuned to every nuance of their partners' behavior. Are women "naturally" better in relating to people with more power than themselves, or have circumstances mandated that men and women develop different skills? [. . .]

Coming from a tradition where most relationships across difference are squarely rooted in relations of domination and subordination, we have much less experience relating to people as different but equal. The classroom is potentially one powerful and safe space where dialogues among individuals of unequal power relationships can occur. The relationship between Mark, the student in my class, and the domestic worker is typical of a whole series of relationships that people have when they relate across differences in power and privilege. The relationship among Mark and his classmates represents the power of the classroom to minimize those differences so that people of different levels of power can use race, class, and gender as categories of analysis in order to generate meaningful dialogues. In this case, the classroom equalized racial difference so that Black students who normally felt silenced spoke out. White students like Mark, generally unaware of how they had been privileged by their whiteness, lost that privilege in the classroom and thus became open to genuine dialogue. [. . .]

2. COALITIONS AROUND COMMON CAUSES

A second issue in building relationships and coalitions essential for social change concerns knowing the real reasons for coalition. Just what brings people together? One powerful catalyst fostering group solidarity is the presence of a common enemy. African-American, Hispanic, Asian-American, and women's studies all share the common intellectual heritage of challenging what passes for certified knowledge in the academy. But politically expedient relationships and coalitions like these are fragile because, as June Jordan points out:

> It occurs to me that much organizational grief could be avoided if people understood that partnership in misery does not necessarily provide for partnership for change. When we get the monsters off our backs all of us may want to run in very different directions (1985, 47).

Sharing a common cause assists individuals and groups in maintaining relationships that transcend their differences. Building effective coalitions involves struggling to hear one another and developing empathy for each other's points of view. The coalitions that I have been involved in that lasted and that worked have been those where commitment to a specific issue mandated collaboration as the best strategy for addressing the issue at hand.

Several years ago, master's degree in hand, I chose to teach in an inner-city parochial school in danger of closing. The money was awful, the conditions were poor, but the need was great. In my job, I had to work with a range of individuals who, on the surface, had very little in common. We had White nuns, Black middle-class graduate students, Blacks from the "community," some of whom had been incarcerated and/or were affiliated with a range of federal anti-poverty programs. Parents formed another part of this community, Harvard faculty another, and a few well-meaning White liberals from Colorado were sprinkled in for good measure.

As you might imagine, tension was high. Initially, our differences seemed insurmountable. But as time passed, we found a common bond that we each brought to the school. In spite of profound differences in our personal biographies, differences that in other settings would have hampered our ability to relate to one another, we found that we were all deeply committed to the education of Black children. By learning to value each other's commitment and by recognizing that we each had different skills that were essential to actualizing that commitment, we built an effective coalition around a common cause. Our school was successful, and the children we taught benefited from the diversity we offered them.

[. . .] None of us alone has a comprehensive vision of how race, class, and gender operate as categories of analysis or how they might be used as categories of connection. Our personal biographies offer us partial views. Few of us can manage to study race, class, and gender simultaneously. Instead, we each know more about some dimensions of this larger story and less about others. [. . .] Just as the members of the school had special skills to offer to the task of building the school, we have areas of specialization and expertise, whether scholarly, theoretical, pedagogical, or within areas of race, class, or gender. We do not all have to do the same thing in the same way. Instead, we must support each other's efforts, realizing that they are all part of the larger enterprise of bringing about social change.

3. BUILDING EMPATHY

A third issue involved in building the types of relationships and coalitions essential for social change concerns the issue of individual accountability. race, class, and gender oppression form the structural backdrop against which we frame our relationship—these are the forces that encourage us to substitute voyeurism . . . for fully human relationships. But while we may not have created this situation, we are each responsible for making individual, personal choices concerning which elements of race, class, and gender oppression we will accept and which we will work to change.

One essential component of this accountability involves developing empathy for the experiences of individuals and groups different from us. Empathy begins with taking an interest in the facts of other people's lives, both as individuals and as groups. If you care about me, you should want to know not only the details of my personal biography but a sense of how race, class, and gender as categories of analysis created the institutional and symbolic backdrop for my personal biography. How can you hope to assess my character without knowing the details of the circumstances I face?

Moreover, by taking a theoretical stance that we have all been affected by race, class, and gender as categories of analysis that have structured our treatment, we open up possibilities for using those same constructs as categories of connection in building empathy. For example, I have a good White woman friend with whom I share common interests and beliefs. But we know that our racial differences have provided us with different experiences. So we talk about them. We do not assume that because I am Black, race has only affected me and not her or that because I am a Black woman, race neutralizes the effect of gender in my life while accenting it in hers. We take those same categories of analysis that have created cleavages in our lives, in this case, categories of race and gender, and use them as categories of connection in building empathy for each other's experiences.

Finding common causes and building empathy is difficult, no matter which side of privilege we inhabit. Building empathy from the dominant side of privilege is difficult, simply because individuals from privileged backgrounds are not encouraged to do so. For example, in order for those of you who are White to develop empathy for the experiences of people of color, you must grapple with how your white skin has privileged you. This is difficult to do, because it not only entails the intellectual process of seeing how whiteness is elevated in institutions and symbols, but it also involves the often painful process of seeing how your whiteness has shaped your personal biography. Intellectual stances against the institutional and symbolic dimensions of racism are generally easier to maintain than sustained self-reflection about how racism has shaped all of our individual biographies. Were and are your fathers, uncles, and grandfathers really more capable than mine, or can their accomplishments be explained in part by the racism members of my family experienced? Did your mothers stand silently by and watch all this happen? More importantly, how have they passed on the benefits of their whiteness to you?

These are difficult questions, and I have tremendous respect for my colleagues and students who are trying to answer them. Since there is no compelling reason to examine the source and meaning of one's own privilege, I know that those who do so have freely chosen this stance. They are making conscious efforts to root out the piece of the oppressor planted within them. To me, they are entitled to the support of people of color in their efforts. Men who declare themselves feminists, members of the middle class who ally themselves with anti-poverty struggles, heterosexuals who support gays and lesbians, are all trying to grow, and their efforts place them far ahead of the majority who never think of engaging in such important struggles.

Building empathy from the subordinate side of privilege is also difficult, but for different reasons. Members of subordinate groups are understandably reluctant to abandon a basic mistrust of members of powerful groups because this basic mistrust has traditionally been central to their survival. As a Black woman, it would be foolish for me to assume that White women, or Black men, or White men or any other group with a history of exploiting African-American women have my best interests at heart. These groups enjoy varying amounts of privilege over me and therefore I must carefully watch them and be prepared for a relation of domination and subordination.

Like the privileged, members of subordinate groups must also work toward replacing judgments by category with new ways of thinking and acting. Refusing to do so stifles prospects for effective coalition and social change. Let me use another example from my own experiences. When I was an undergraduate, I had little time or patience for the theorizing of the privileged. My initial years at a private, elite institution were difficult, not because the coursework was challenging (it was, but that wasn't what distracted me) or because I had to work while my classmates lived on family allowances (I was used to work). The adjustment was difficult because I was surrounded by so many people who took their privilege for granted. Most of them felt entitled to their wealth. That astounded me.

I remember one incident of watching a White woman down the hall in my dormitory try to pick out which sweater to wear. The sweaters were piled up on her bed in all the colors of the rainbow, sweater after sweater. She asked my advice in a way that let me know that choosing a sweater was one of the most important decisions she had to make on a daily basis. Standing knee-deep in her sweaters, I realized how different our lives were. She did not have to worry about maintaining a solid academic average so that she could receive financial aid. Because she was in the majority, she was not treated as a representative of her race. She did not have to consider how her classroom comments or basic existence on campus contributed to the treatment her group would receive. Her allowance protected her from having to work, so she was free to spend her time studying, partying, or in her case, worrying about which sweater to wear. The degree of inequality in our lives and her unquestioned sense of entitlement concerning that inequality offended me. For a while, I categorized all affluent White women as being superficial, arrogant, overly concerned with material possessions, and part of my problem. But had I continued to classify people in this way, I would have missed out on making some very good friends whose discomfort with their inherited or acquired social class privileges pushed them to examine their position.

Since I opened with the words of Audre Lorde, it seems appropriate to close with another of her ideas. [. . .]

> Each of us is called upon to take a stand. So in these days ahead, as we examine ourselves and each other, our works, our fears, our differences, our sisterhood and survivals, I urge you to tackle what is most difficult for us all, self-scrutiny of our complacencies, the idea that since each of us believes she is on the side of right, she need not examine her position (1985).

I urge you to examine your position.

References

Butler, Johnella. 1989. "Difficult Dialogues." *The Women's Review of Books* 6, no. 5.

Collins, Patricia Hill. 1989. "The Social Construction of Black Feminist Thought." *Signs.* Summer.

Gwaltney, John Langston. 1980. *Drylongso: A Self-Portrait of Black America.* New York: Vintage.

Harding, Sandra. 1986. *The Science Question in Feminism.* Ithaca, New York: Cornell University Press.

Jordan, June. 1985. *On Call: Political Essays.* Boston: South End Press.

Lorde, Audre. 1984. *Sister Outsider.* Trumansburg, New York: The Crossing Press.

_____. 1985. "Sisterhood and Survival." Keynote address, conference on the Black Woman Writer and the Diaspora, Michigan State University.

Spelman, Elizabeth. 1982. "Theories of Race and Gender: The Erasure of Black Women." *Quest* 5: 36–32.

Tate, Claudia, ed. 1983. *Black Women Writers at Work.* New York: Continuum.

17

Dismantling Privilege and Becoming an Activist

Abby L. Ferber

Traditional diversity or multicultural approaches tend to focus on marginalized groups and on one dimension of inequality at a time (race *or* gender *or* class, etc.). These approaches are limited in many ways. They frequently focus on celebrating differences, understanding diversity, and teaching tolerance. These lead to stereotyping, essentializing, and overgeneralizing. In addition, they tend to fragment people, leading to us-versus-them divisions—the isolation of various parts of our identity from other parts—and can lead to individualistic conceptions of power. Over the years, through my work as director of the Matrix Center for the Advancement of Social Equity and Inclusion, I have cofacilitated The Knapsack Institute: Transforming the Curriculum and worked with the planning team of the White Privilege Conference. Synthesizing the accumulated insights and research of many scholars and activists, I have sought to bring them together into a model for understanding oppression and privilege from an intersectional perspective. I have worked to distill the outlines of a basic framework to inform classroom practice and to use it as a tool in explaining these concepts to others. This framework is informed by a sociological perspective, and draws upon the notion of a "matrix of domination" developed by Patricia Hill Collins (1990). Key features of this framework are outlined below.

The Matrix Framework

1. Recognize the Importance of Examining Both Privilege and Oppression: Privilege and oppression are two sides of the same coin; you cannot have one without the other.

2. Intersectional: Emphasizes that forms of privilege and oppression interact and intersect, so it makes visible diversity within groups. For example, no one has just a racial identity. This approach emphasizes that African Americans are not a homogenous group; the experiences of African Americans vary, depending upon other important social classifications, such as gender, class, and sexual orientation.

3. Social Constructionist: Categories of race, gender, class, sexuality, nation, and so forth are social classifications and are historically and culturally variable. These classifications are largely the result of inequality—created and perpetuated to support specific configurations of power. This framework focuses on inequality instead of differences.

4. Inclusive: Everyone experiences privilege (whether race, gender, ethnic, sexual orientation, class, ability), thus it is one experience we all share. We all have a racial identity, a gender identity, and so on, and no group is assumed to be the cultural norm. White people have a race, men have a gender, and these affect their life experiences and opportunities. Racism, sexism, homophobia, and other forms of oppression and privilege are about everyone. We all experience some form of privilege; thus we are all a part of the problem and need to be a part of the solution.

5. Inequality Is Institutional: This approach does not blame individuals. Privilege and oppression are seen not as characteristics of people but of society. According to Allan Johnson, "Oppression and dominance name social realities that we can participate in without being oppressive or dominating people" (13). This framework focuses on outcomes and impact, which may result independently of one's intention. We receive privileges whether we want to or not. We may not be consciously heterosexist, however, heterosexuals receive privileges in our society that LGBTQ people do not.

6. Recognizes Inequality as Harmful to All: This perspective emphasizes that narrow group identities can be harmful to everyone, even those who are privileged.

7. Encourages Ongoing Self-Examination: Because we are all implicated in the dynamics of privilege and oppression, we all need to do the difficult personal and emotional work required of us.

8. Proactive Focus on Social Change: We are all a part of the problem and need to be part of the solution. Racism is not a people-of-color problem. This can be empowering—we can all make a difference. We all must take ownership of these issues, and we should all be involved in trying to create change. It is helpful to see role models from privileged groups fighting to end inequality, and to see examples of movements of diverse people working together as allies. This is, at its roots, a social justice approach.

Become an Activist

Many authors have written about the importance of being an ally. Anyone who experiences privilege has the potential to be an ally to those who are oppressed. Based on the assumptions outlined above, in order to be a strong ally, we must be an ally to *all* oppressed groups. We know that systems of oppression and privilege are interacting and mutually constitutive and reinforcing. Therefore, we cannot oppose only one system of inequality and meet with any success. We must work to undermine all forms of inequality simultaneously. Further, these guidelines are relevant for all of us, because we all experience some form of privilege. Even those of us who experience oppression likely experience privilege in other areas. (Consider race, gender, sexuality, class, nation, age, ability, religion, etc.). Starting with the Matrix framework as a foundation, I offer the following guidelines. (Many points have been adapted from Wijeyesinghe, Griffin, and Love; Gorski; and Kivel.) They differ from previous lists in a couple of ways. First, they assume an intersectional framework, and thus they speak to everyone. They are not addressed only to white people, or only to men.

Second, rather than advocating becoming an ally, they ask that we each become activists. If these struggles directly involve each one of us, is it really appropriate to call ourselves allies? The term *ally* implies supporting and uniting with others for a cause, rather than seeing it as *our own* cause. From an intersectional, privilege/oppression framework, *activist* is a more appropriate term. The term *activist* implies intentional action.

- Take responsibility for learning about how oppression and privilege works, and teach others. Do not expect others to teach you.

- Assume that inequality and oppression are everywhere, all the time, even when not visible to you.
- Work continuously to be aware of your own privilege and the way privilege operates. Notice who is the center of attention and who has access to power.
- Notice the ways in which oppression and privilege are denied, ignored, minimized, or justified.
- Learn from history: from the history of specific forms of inequality as well as from social movements that have worked for change and social justice.
- Understand the connections between the various forms of oppression and privilege, and pay attention to how they intersect and support each other.
- Speak out! Take a stand against injustice. Take risks and be willing to act in spite of your own fear and the resistance you face from others.
- Recognize that learning to see oppression and privilege is an ongoing, lifelong process.
- Recognize that you will make mistakes, and approach them as learning opportunities. Be willing to be confronted about your own behavior and attitudes. It is okay to be uncomfortable; it is a sign that you are learning!
- Pick your battles, taking action against social injustice in your own sphere of influence.
- Pay attention to mundane, daily interactions and media messages. Privilege is normalized in very subtle ways and is so pervasive that we often do not recognize it.
- Listen to, respect, and support the leadership, perspectives, and experiences of members of oppressed groups.
- Protect yourself from burnout, and find support among other individuals, groups, and organizations. Take advantage of opportunities to reenergize and recommit yourself to this difficult work (for example, attend the White Privilege Conference). Strive to cultivate a community of activists.

I think it is particularly important to emphasize that privilege is manifested all the time. Working to dismantle privilege is not just a question of confronting major cases of injustice or embracing specific social movements or organizations. No matter what we do in our life, no matter where we are, we encounter experiences of privilege and oppression being normalized and institutionalized on a daily basis. Every one of these experiences presents an occasion for educating ourselves and others and working for change. Let me provide one very simple example. My daughter used to love playing the game of "Life" when she was younger. If you have ever played this game, you will recall that you select a pink or blue character to represent yourself and drive around the board in a little plastic car, going through the events of life (education, career, buying a home, purchasing insurance, etc; notice immediately the class privilege assumed here). Most of the time players automatically select a different gender spouse when landing on the spot that commands marriage. When I started playing this game as an adult with my own daughter and her friends, I started selecting a same-gender spouse. The game presented a convenient, easy opportunity to refrain from normalizing heterosexual marriage. Very simple actions like these can be taken every day as the occasions present themselves. It is our choice whether we continue to uncritically normalize privilege or commit to challenging it when and where we can.

References and Recommended Resources

Books

Adams, Maurianne, Lee Anne Bell, and Pat Griffin, eds. 1997. *Teaching for Diversity and Social Justice: A Sourcebook.* New York: Routledge.

Collins, Patricia Hill. 1990. *Black Feminist Thought: Knowledge, Consciousness, and the Politics of Empowerment.* New York: HarperCollins.

Ferber, A., A. O'Reilly Herrera, C. Jimenez, and D. Samuels, eds. 2008. *The Matrix Reader: Examining the Dynamics of Oppression and Privilege.* New York: McGraw-Hill.

Johnson, Allan G. 2006. *Privilege, Power, and Difference*, 2nd ed. Mountain View, CA: Mayfield.

Kimmel, Michael S., and Abby L. Ferber. 2003. *Privilege: A Reader.* Boulder, CO: Westview.

Kivel, Paul. 1996. *Uprooting Racism.* Gabriola Island, BC, Canada: New Society Publishers.

McIntosh, Peggy. 1988. "White Privilege and Male Privilege: A Personal Account of Coming to See Correspondences through Work in Women's Studies." Excerpted from Working Paper 189, Wellesley College Center for Research on Women, Wellesley, MA.

Tochluk, Shelly. 2008. *Witnessing Whiteness: First Steps toward an Antiracist Practice and Culture*. Lanham, MD: Rowman & Littlefield.

Wijeyesinghe, Charmaine L., Pat Griffin, and Barbara Love. 1997. "Racism Curriculum Design." In *Teaching for Diversity and Social Justice: A Sourcebook*. New York: Routledge.

Websites

http://www.paulgorski.efoliomn2.com

http://www.paulkivel.com

Knapsack Institute, www.uccs.edu/matrix

White Privilege Conference, www.uccs.edu/wpc

"White Privilege 101: Getting in on the Conversation," DVD from www.uccs.edu/wpc

Index